**Educational
Planning and
Decision Making**

Educational Planning and Decision Making

A View Through the Organizational Process

C. Kenneth Tanner
The University of Tennessee
Earl J. Williams
Anchorage School District

LexingtonBooks
D.C. Heath and Company
Lexington, Massachusetts
Toronto

To our wives, Jackie Tanner and
Virginia Williams,
and our children, Kip, Todd, and
Mitzie Tanner and
Jennifer Williams

Library of Congress Cataloging in Publication Data

Tanner, C Kenneth.
  Educational planning and decision making.

  Includes index.
  1. School management and organization—Decision making. 2. Universities and college—Administration—Decision making. 3. Educational planning—Decision making. I. Williams, Earl J., joint author. II. Title.
LB2806.T33   371.2'07   80-8631
ISBN 0-669-04330-3

Copyright © 1981 by D.C. Heath and Company

Published simultaneously in Canada

Printed in the United States of America

International Standard Book Number: 0-669-04330-3

Library of Congress Catalog Card Number: 80-8631

Contents

List of Figures

List of Tables

Preface and Acknowledgments

This book provides an overview of educational planning and describes how this developing concept relates to organizational processes in public education. Students interested in school and higher education administration will find the work to be candid, exposing many conflicts and compromises between theory and the real world. Our major purpose is to illustrate that planning to effect change must consider the way organizations function rather than the optimal results of our well-known systems-planning models and quantitative decision strategies. This book also supports the ideas of merger and modification of quantitative and qualitative planning procedures without diminishing the value of either school of thought.

We will illustrate how totally rational systems-planning methods have been less successful than they could have been. We emphasize the fact that if planners knew more about the organizational process, there would be a greater tolerance level for organizations' sluggishness regarding results-oriented planning activities. Similarly, there would be less failure of the systems approach to planning, not because the output of the models would be any different but because the implementation would be more in tune with organizational routine.

We contend that decision making resulting from systems-planning models has been less than optimal, thereby causing a great deal of concern in the ranks of educational planners. To illustrate how the planner may be more proactive instead of reactive, we have concentrated on three process models: management by objectives, evaluative research, and Delphi. As a point of departure, the student or the practitioner may build his or her own set of guidelines for effecting change from our views of the organizational and planning theories without contributing to the development of a chaotic situation in the organization.

Perhaps the rational systems models have been misused by overly ambitious planners, but this need not occur if planners understand that these strategies frequently have complementary planning theories that are amenable to the organizational process. The major purpose of these theories, models, and processes is to improve the educational environment. Hence we present theories, process models, organizational processes, and three case studies as examples of positive and negative results of planning. We believe that better planning will result from analyzing both good and bad planning approaches and carefully studying the situations in which planning activities are conducted.

Acknowledgments

We would like to acknowledge the contribution of Dr. James B. Phillips in the chapters on management by objectives. Special thanks are due to The University of Tennessee and the Anchorage School District for providing us with the opportunity to complete this work. Special thanks are reserved for our typist and secretary, Ms. Rebecca Bledsoe.

Part I
Introduction

1 Some Basic Elements of Planning

Introduction

Growth, change, cooperation, and conflict are abundantly present in our technologically based society with highly interdependent and complex organizations. The well-being of the individual citizen is clearly and closely linked to the quality and level of performance of these organizations. How well an organization functions depends on its ability to facilitate planning, to foresee events, to utilize current knowledge and methods to solve problems, and to control and accommodate forces within and without its boundaries. Paramount to its existence are planning and coping with change.

We believe that the primary purpose of an organization's being is to attain specific goals. However, achieving these goals is not sufficient reason alone to sustain its life. Additionally, through appropriate planning, organizations must accomplish the secondary tasks of "(1) maintaining the internal system and coordinating the 'human side of the enterprise' . . . and (2) adapting to and shaping the external environment."[1] Adapting to and shaping its environment is best achieved through a well-balanced planning process.

School systems, universities, state departments of education—all must adapt to change, follow standard operating procedures, and plan effectively in order to survive as a social system. Resources are limited, however, and must be captured in a highly competitive sociopolitical arena. Just how successful an organization is depends in large measure on its ability to plan in such a manner so as to effectively and efficiently achieve its primary goals, to manage change, to relate to and influence its external environment, and to internally remain healthy and cohesive as a contrived social system. Planning is the key factor to an organization and its operation, a process that in fact ties together the functions and the processes of its managerial subsystem—administration.

What then is planning? This is merely the beginning of a long list of equally complicated questions when considering the process of planning in educational organizations. Hence, in this book we propose to deal primarily with some major attributes of organizational process and educational planning as they affect educational environments.

If we ask ten people in education to define "educational planning," the chances are indeed great that ten different answers will result. This disagreement, perhaps resulting from misconceptions, need not continue to be a problem if we first realize that educational planning is a developing concept. We often see or hear questions such as, who are planners? For what and for whom do they plan?

By taking a brief look at the purposeful actions of the developing discipline of statistics, we will perhaps gain insight into the problem of understanding what planning really is. Since the turn of the century statistics has established itself as a process for estimating probabilities of events. For example, production levels in the agricultural world may be predicted through probability statements. Crop yields have been measured against seed varieties and levels of soil nutrients whereby, with certain assumptions about environmental conditions, production is predicted. Simultaneously, mathematical theories were sometimes developed independently of practical applications such as in agriculture, and the discipline of mathematical statistics has evolved primarily on its own as a distinct and well-recognized content area. Paralleling the development of mathematical statistics, we have witnessed the emergence of applied statistics from which business and educational statistics have evolved. But basic to all these various applications and developments is one well-known principle: the central limit theorem. It is therefore hypothesized that there must be at least one basic conceptualization, or theory, of planning as well.

For a better understanding of planning we might look for a distinct principle underlying deliberate actions in educational organizations. One of the more recent actions we have observed is planning-programming-budgeting systems (PPBS). Cost-effectiveness analysis, policy analysis, and management by objectives (MBO) are others, and there are more. While some of these have failed, others are still around but in modified forms. We may consider these action-oriented packages as results of "the rational systems approach"; yet in their pure rationalistic conceptualizations, many have failed so far in education. We perceive these failures in educational environments as being a function of rationalistic constraints and principles inherent in business, industry, and the military services (where the models were developed) more than in the potential usefulness of the models. Many rational planning approaches were quickly absorbed in educational organization complexities and permanently deformed or discredited by an unusual political system in education that just does not exist the way it does in the business and industrial environments. Perhaps if the administrative planners in charge of these "good" approaches to planning and decision making had better understood the major attributes of organizational processes, we could tell a different and positive story. Or, if beginner planners seeking simple solutions had not been allowed to cover too much territory too fast, more of these good rational models would be working better for us today.

On a more positive note, we can report, for example, that management by objectives is still around, although not in its original form, for organizational processes have modified many of its rational systems concepts, and we contend for the better. Many other developing models without clear boundaries that covered too much territory are, however, decaying or even deceased. Our fear is that educational planning may continue to cover a great expanse of territory without clear theoretical baselines. Could it be that educational planning, as we have known it up until today, will become permanently deformed or move rapidly toward extinction?

Planning, like statistics, overlaps far into the terrain of several professions. The frontiers of planning expand continuously with the historical evolution of social problems to be analyzed. Perhaps one way for us to take a critical look at planning is to identify the locus of planning activities through a classification scheme highligting comparative distinctions among current planning traditions without necessarily pinning down their outer limits.[2] Once this task is accomplished, we may then further refine the procedure through an investigation of some important characteristics of organizational processes to locate educational planning.

Among numerous planning traditions, Hudson has identified five that we believe can complement organizational processes. His classifications are described as synoptic planning, incremental planning, transactive planning, advocacy planning, and radical planning, where synoptic planning is the centerpiece or locus of planning activities.[3] Often in the literature we see the synoptic classification as "the rational systems approach" and "rational comprehensive planning." The four remaining traditions take their points of departure from the limits of synoptic planning. Thus we propose that the synoptic tradition is to planning what the central limit theorem is to statistics—not in well-defined equations, however, but in the initiation of planning thought.

The Synoptic Planning Process

Synoptic planning involves centralized control of decision making more than the other four classifications. This approach may best be characterized as feasible for translating policy implications and adapting to problems and social settings. With its major emphasis on producing plans, the synoptic approach is goal oriented, relying heavily on deterministic and probabilistic models with some acknowledgement of the judgmental process in decision making. For example, the Delphi technique and MBO have origins in the synoptic school of thought, and later in this book we shall illustrate how they may complement the planning process in organizations.

Despite its capacity for great methodolical refinement and elaboration, the real power of the synoptic approach is its basic simplicity. The fundamental issues addressed—ends, means, trade-offs, action-taking—enter into virtually any planning endeavor.[4]

The methodological limitations of the synoptic approach are challenged by the other theories, yet these counterpoint schools of thought really cannot do without synoptic planning and vice versa. Thus Hudson has stated, "Each helps define the other by its own shortcomings; each sharpens the other's discriminatory edge of intentions and accomplishments."[5]

Since the synoptic tradition is our point of departure and the central focus of planning activities, we shall view it as a process with three phases and six interdependent and overlapping areas of concentration, as shown in figure 1-1. These are:

Phase I. *Awareness*
1. *R*ecognition of the problem and its immediate environment
2. *E*stimation of the scope of the problem in its neighborhood
3. *C*lassification of the possible solution(s) in terms of goals and objectives

Phase II. *Analysis*
4. *I*nvestigation of the problem within its immediate neigborhood
5. *P*rediction of alternative futures based on formal quantitative analysis

Phase III. *Assessment*
6. *E*valuation of the progress made toward the specified solution(s) (Implementation is assumed.)

The synoptic planning process has too frequently been looked upon as a "AAA RECIPE" for action-oriented results requiring a short amount of time. While the synoptic tradition involves the progressive study of the problem in its respective neighborhood, it has sometimes overlooked the environment when affected by new ideas, physical change, alternative values, and cultural tranformations. Planning should therefore include the investigation of the nature, functions, and relationships of the problem in its neighborhood as well as the influence of the neighborhood on its organizational environment. Because organizations move through various stages that are not necessarily clearly defined, we see the need for planning in organizations to be a dynamic process as well as follow some definable pattern. Synoptic planning may be at fault regarding the awareness of organizational dynamics, yet it has attempted to provide simple solutions in a straightforward manner and also pursue unitary decisions.

At the core of the synoptic process is a rational baseline. Thus synoptic

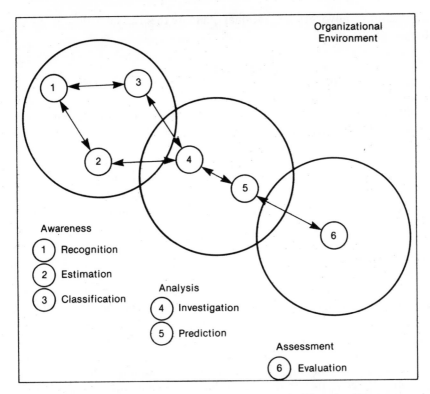

Figure 1-1. Conceptualization of the Synoptic Planning Process

thought depends frequently on observations and ample data to determine key judgmental factors. These observations facilitate problem awareness and the generation of ideal solutions and objectives with the possibility of uncovering new problems not readily seen at the start. Hence there exists a strong likelihood for the prediction of alternative futures as the formal analysis progresses. Frequently in the synoptic tradition these proposed solutions' impact on the environment is not adequately considered, and when the ajudication of the progress toward the solution(s) is accomplished we find that we have often planned for the sake of planning.

In his classic work on educational system planning, Kaufman describes a possible taxonomy of educational planning.[6] Just how this system approach to planning fits into a comprehensive organization is still of concern to the many professional planners who strive to influence change in our environment. We are not implying that the synoptic strategy is bad. What we are proposing is that a careful look be taken at the organization and complementary planning processes. Thus how do synoptic, incremental, transactional, advocacy and rational planning theories interrelate in educational organizations?

Complementary Planning Processes

In this section we shall present an overview of four concepts of planning discussed by Hudson that may add some important dimension to educational planning and decision making. First, we shall discuss briefly the concept of incremental planning. This tradition has been described by Lindblom as "partisan mutual adjustment," "the science of muddling through," or "disjointed incrementalism."[7] Incremental planning favors decentralized control, and planners are characterized as being sensitive to institutional performances and capabilities in the problem-solving process. Hence things get done through a decentralized bargaining process amenable to a democratic and political economy where there exists continuity in value systems. Under the incremental approach the organization has autonomous self-governing subunits where planning takes place through a mixture of deterministic, probabilistic, and judgmental techniques heavily flavored with experience, intuition and many consultations.[8] Policy decisions are reached through give-and-take—push-and-shove—and pull-and-tug approaches in an open environment.

Transactive planning, like incremental planning, emphasizes the decentralized concept with individuals having a representative voice in their own welfare. Friedman proposes that in transactive planning, action validates the continual evolution of ideas.[9] There is also a heavy emphasis on personal and organizational development as well as on achieving goals and objectives. Under the transactive approach we observe that planning is effected through face-to-face contact with persons affected by the resulting decisions. Emphasis is placed on interpersonal communications involving mutual discovery of knowledge and data collection. Quantitative analysis is minimized while the human dimensions of worth and dignity are highlighted.

The advocacy-planning tradition hinges on perceptions of inequity existing in the environment and has evolved primarily because of the lack of trust in the establishment. Controversial issues regarding the public interest tend to place the large against the small where legal adversaries advocate small groups as opposed to the establishment.[10] Plural plans instead of a unitary plan are called for, and the end results are aimed at more humanistic decisions. Advocacy planning then has in many ways brought decision making from behind closed doors resulting in the "sunshine laws." We also observe that collective bargaining, equal rights, and social justice are some outcomes of the advocacy school of thought.

Radical planning stresses the importance of cooperation, freedom, and personal growth, yet it is contingent upon dissatisfaction with a given situation and instability concerning traditional solutions. The radical planning process is frequently the enemy of progressive politics and deplores manipulation by anonymous forces. Although radical planning draws on historical sources,[11] it is at best an ambiguous tradition.[12] Planning through this process depends on the ability to see the root of a problem instead of challenging the system forthright. Radical planning favors the public interest with maximum participation by individuals and minimum intervention by top officials. Yet through collective actions radical planning often produces short-range and observable results. This decentralized approach is distinctly different from synoptic planning in that group decision making supercedes unitary decision strategies.

Although there are many more planning strategies, the preceding five traditions provide us with the necessary core theories to conclude that there is not just one way to plan or effect change. Hudson has summed up these five planning approaches with the acronym, SITAR, based on the first letter of each descriptor. The sitar is a five-stringed musical instrument that can be played by performing on a single string or by weaving a blend of harmony and dissonance from all five. "The same applies to SITAR as a taxonomy of planning theories; each can render a reasonable solo performance in good hands, but fuller possibilities can be created by use of each theory in conjunction with the others."[13] We therefore propose that educational planning is best performed in the same manner by planners familiar with planning theories as well as organizations.

In this text we shall concentrate on organizational processes in planning, emphasizing change and process models and how they relate to the five theories (SITAR) introduced here. To illustrate the relationship among these theories and organizational processes, we discuss evaluative research, MBO, and Delphi procedures as change processes used in a form modified from their original conceptualizations, geared to a harmonious blend according to environmental situations. (*Change* is defined as measurable intervention through the utilization of resources to reshape the total organization or some part thereof.)

Summary

Our concerns in this chapter have been with what is planning, and under which theories do educational planners plan. We have proposed that synoptic planning (the rational systems approach) is the locus of all planning activities. There are three general phases of synoptic planning that include awareness, analysis, and assessment. Six interrelated steps facilitating these phases are: recognition, estimation, classification, investigation, prediction, and evaluation. We have called the synoptic tradition the "'AAA RECIPE'' for planning activities, but there are more planning theories that we believe to be necessary for purposeful planning and decision making in organizations.

Thus, we have discussed incremental, transactive, advocacy, and radical planning as complementary processes that blend together in many situations to yield the best approach to planning in complex organizations. We believe that these five planning traditions mixed with the organizational process provide us with the core theories needed to plan for change. Chapter 2, therefore, concerns the nature of planning and change.

Notes

1. Warren G. Bennis, *Changing Organizations: Essays on the Development and Evaluation of Human Organizations* (New York: McGraw-Hill Company, 1966), p. 7. Reprinted with permission.

2. Barclay M. Hudson, "Comparison of Current Planning Theories: Counterparts and Contradictions," *Journal of the American Planning Association* (no. 4) (October 1979):389.

3. Ibid., p. 388.

4. Ibid., p. 389.

5. Ibid.

6. Roger A. Kaufman, *Educational System Planning* (Englewood Cliffs, N.J.: Prentice-Hall, 1972), pp. 142–143.

7. Charles E. Lindblom, "The Science of Muddling Through," *Public Administration Review* 19(1959):79–88; and Charles E. Lindblom, *The Intelligence of Democracy: Decision Making Through Mutual Adjustment* (New York: The Free Press, 1967), as quoted in Hudson, p. 389. "Comparison of Current Planning Theories," p. 389.

8. Branko Hovart, "Planning in Yugoslavia," in *The Crisis of Planning,* vol. 2, eds. Mike Faber and Dudley Seers. (London: Chatto and Windus for the Sussex University Press, 1972), presented by Hudson, "Comparison of Current Planning Theories," p. 389.

9. John Friedman, *Retracking America: A Theory of Transactive Planning* (Garden City, N.Y.: Doubleday, 1973).

10. Saul D. Alinsky, *Rules for Radicals* (New York: Vintage Books, 1972), outlined by Hudson, "Comparison of Current Planning Theories," p. 390.

11. Alfred Katz and Eugene Bender, *The Strength in Us* (New York: New View Points, 1976).

12. Hudson, "Comparison of Current Planning Theories," p. 390.

13. Ibid.

2 The Nature of Planning and Change

In this text we do not wish to equate planning with change. However, we cannot plan programs or solve problems effectively in an organization without some process to guide our actions. Thus we believe that the basic elements of planning presented in chapter 1 are necessary but not always sufficient to bring about planned change. Planning may be perceived as a set of purposeful actions influencing an organization or some part therein to effect change. Also planning may be defined as a methodology directed at future change of a present situation.[1] Hence, we devote this chapter to an overview of some theories and models of change that may facilitate planning and decision making in educational organizations.

Planning theories usually comprise several discrete purposes or reasons, which should not be interpreted to mean that each function can exist or operate separately: "Planning must relate to a desired and identifiable change. Change . . . must relate to and be the result of a well conceived . . . plan."[2] The essential relationship between change and planning has been presented in terms of an agent of change and a planner. For example, any agent of change may be viewed as a planner and vice versa. Thus the planner (agent of change) may be an administrator, a producer, or a politician. Hence there are many kinds of planners that perform different roles, depending on the problem or the situation with which he or she must deal. Their concern is primarily instituting change so that the future will be different from the present.[3]

We shall assume that most educational change must be effected; thus the need for better understanding of the basic planning and organizational processes becomes important. Through what theories and methodologies are planning activities best directed? How is planned change effected? What are some successful patterns of change? These are questions all planners need more information about.

Planning and Effecting Change

Agreeing that educational planning influences the organization to bring about change and limiting our boundaries to changes that are planned, we now consider three general change strategies suggested by Chin that have relevance for educational planners.[4] First, he elaborates on the word *strategy* (an excellent idea given the problem of communicating across lines of disciplines) by suggesting that "strategies of change" include but are not limited to dissemination and provisions for utilization of pertinent information regarding given aspects of proposed plans. One important preface should be added: When a writer communicates specific strategies for change, without any question, it is wise to take into consideration the magnitude of such a job. Casting complex activities aimed at change into a model is indeed a perilous task. However, we must venture some if progress is to be made beyond the surface phenomena.[5]

Chin describes the first major group of strategies as *empirical rational.* This fundamental process is based on reason and utilitarianism where the given change to be effected is demonstrated to be desirable and effective and then brought to the attention of the changee (the client system). Therefore, because the changee is a reasonable person (organization) or because he or she can gain through using this new form of action, it is adopted. His second group of strategies, founded on attitude change through direct interventions, is the *normative-reeducative* type. Supported by concisely worked-out theory of change, these interventions are applied to organizations, small groups, and individual behavior. *Power types,* the third classification, is based on power (of some form) with compliance.

In organizations as complex as those we find in education, it is rather impossible to utilize one single strategy independent of others. Thus Chin contends that certain procedures are geared for special uses since planners, researchers, and administrators at state, local, and national levels have different needs requiring different ways to bring about change.[6]

An extension of Chin's empirical-rational strategy for change has been presented as "Effecting Change Through a Diffusion Process."[7] The main concepts presented in this work deal with research as well as development where effectiveness of the research resulting from a sound plan is distributed or demonstrated. Currently the National Diffusion Network (NDN) provides an information system responsible for reporting progress of successful educational programs. Demonstrable evidence of effectiveness of an intervention is the major requirement for a program to be included in the diffusion process and tangible evidence is believed to be the primary advantage in gaining acceptance of the intervention. Thus NDN is "a significant catalyst for sharing nationally what is learned in education."[8]

By actually observing a certain positive change brought about through an intervention such as those reported through NDN, can we assume a better understanding will evolve? Will this expanded experience provide a foundation for effecting change through attitude modification? The U.S. Department of Agriculture has utilized the diffusion process successfully for several decades as a means for improving crop yields, for example. We are familiar with the "demonstration farm" where, say, a new variety of experimental seed has been shown to be more successful in yield per acre as compared to a more common variety. The result is indeed obvious since we now produce excessive quantities of wheat and corn, for example, even with imposed limitations on acreage. Thus the normative-reeducative approach to effecting change has merit in that not only the need for change is recognized but the preparation for change is realized through reeducation. Furthermore, attitudes are changed through approval and acceptance of a given intervention. Regarding the agricultural experimental-farm model for change, a group generates its own pressure for change and the more effective the intervention, the greater the likelihood that change time is minimized. Obviously, desirable change is not a function of outside forces exclusively but is a cooperative effort of showing, explaining, sharing, reshowing, and reexplaining with a considerable amount of deliberateness, and, above all, tempered with patience. This participatory procedure facilitates a favorable climate for change.

The concept of power approaches to effecting change is perhaps the oldest "change strategy" known to man. Implicit in this approach is the small size of the group in charge of decision making—in some cases only one individual. When sufficient power or excessive pressure is applied, people will react—either positively or negatively; hence change as a result of power is indeed possible. Bennis delineates this strategy as coercive change, characterized by nonmutual goal setting, an imbalanced power ratio, and one-sided deliberateness.[9]

Potential to influence another, the classic definition of "power" by Parsons,[10] has been extended by Robbins to mean the degree of influence an individual or group has in decision making.[11] Three bases of power have been outlined by Etzioni: coercive, remunerative, and normative.[12] First, if power is dependent on fear, then it is coercive—its opposite is remunerative, which is based on providing material rewards such as benefits and wages. Etzioni's third classification of power depends on one's ability to provide symbolic rewards, including prestigious rewards, mass-media manipulation, the control of rituals, and influence over acceptance and positive response. According to Robbins, the normative classification presented by Etzioni fails to specify power bases in a form that can be easily understood.[13] Hence, he suggests French and Raven's more comprehensive classification of power bases that includes reward power, coercive power, legitimate power, referent power, and expert power.[14] Reward power, coercive power, and legitimate power derive their influence primarily from the organization—that is, they are inherent—while referent power and expert power are based within the individual, relating to his or her own unique characteristics.

Professional guidance as a method of achieving or effecting change (improvement in a personality or social system) has been proposed by

Lippitt, Watson, and Westly.[15] Their methodology specifying a collaborative approach on the part of the changee and the agent of change—the planner in the context proposed in this work—is aimed at a constructive or positive change. Change that is planned may be effected through collaborative planning, transactive planning, for example, and implementing a strategy of change in an organization through utilization of knowledge. Hence the cliché that "knowledge is power" has relevant meaning if we agree that knowledge of research, of development, of politics, of technology, and of planning theories, to name a few areas, are amenable to change.

Six major components involved in the process of effecting change, according to Jones,[16] are as follows: agent of change, strategies and tactics, goals, client system, structuring of change, and evaluation. If we allow ourselves to think of these six components in terms of activities influencing an organization to bring about change, the parallel descriptor for each one in the context of educational planning might be: the *planner,* as an agent of change; *methodology*, as strategies and tactics; *goals;* the *organization* or a subpart thereof, as the client system; the *intervention,* as the structuring of change; and *evaluation.* In order to understand educational planning, at least when defined generically and given an organization where planned change is to be effected, we might consider the change process as including these six components plus *organizational theories* and *theories of planning.* Obviously these eight elements are not independent of each other, and the degree of quality found in one perhaps influences all others.

As noted in table 2-1, the nature of planning is complex involving many action forces. Knowledge of goals—organizational, individual, and group goals, for example—linked to planning theories, organizational theories, and methodology substantiate a framework for defining problems and prescribing solutions. These solutions, known as *interventions,* are introduced into an organization where positive results are observed in operation. We have deliberately used the term *positive* since it is our contention that given a sound understanding of goals, theories, and methodology for change, a greater percentage of the results will be positive. We would be quick to acknowledge, however, that there are those environmental influences that may cause negative results. But this is one of the hazards of administrative planning or perhaps life itself.

We shall assume that the planner must be knowledgeable of the components outlined in table 2-1 and that no single action force is appropriate exclusively for application to educational problems. It is the contention of the authors, however, that planners are underexposed to organizational theories and those methodologies described as normative reeducative and power types. Benveniste has discussed some of the limitations of rational or synoptic approaches when educational planning encounters organizations.[17] He sees the rational theory reorienting collective action

Table 2-1
The Nature of Planning

Action ⟵	⟶ Forces
The administrative planner or planning team, through	(Agent)
Goals, Planning theories, Organizational theories, and Methodology Develops and prescribes	(Knowledge)
Intervention(s) for an organization, whereby positive results may be evaluated	(Solution) (Client) (Change)

within organizations toward measurable outputs in the future, and professional direction more sophisticated than is recognized under the rational method. We must not overlook the fact that organizational interests and their peculiar reward structures are powerful inhibitors on the most rational of plans.[18]

An organization must coordinate the behaviors of individuals in the planning and implementation of change, and Leavitt has noted four organizational variables that may be changed: task, structure, technology, and actors.[19] He refers to "task" as a specific job within the organization to provide goods and services while the patterns of behavior of organizational members are called "structure." Any change in the technology used by the organization may result in changed patterns of structure or in tasks involved in providing goods and services; hence all variables are interdependent whereby change in one variable has a good chance of effecting change in the others. From the literature and our experiences, we agree that power is the key factor in all strategies and tactics of change.

In the preceding paragraphs, we noted the influence of power in effecting change as presented by Parsons, Robbins, and Etzioni. Jones has presented six major components involved in the process of effecting change[20] and has enlarged upon the component entitled "strategies and tactics," which includes coercive strategies, normative strategies, utilization strategies, and other change strategies.[21] The coercive strategies may employ force, threats, and pressure to effect change. Goal setting is nonmutual. Strategies emphasizing control through normative power are characterized by education, training, and group participation. Power gained through the use of material rewards is utilitarian and represents control by manipulation. Jones defines "other change techniques" as those related to the other three classifications, including marginality, research, and technical modification. Marginality implies that the client system as well as the change agent (or planner) have an intersection of their value systems.

In his writings on the process of change, Bennis has observed that all change is not planned change.[22] He has shown eight species of change as planned change, indoctrinational change, coercive change, technocratic change, interactional change, socialization change, emulative change, and natural change. Amplifying classifications presented earlier in this chapter is Bennis's notion of a power relationship with respect to goal setting. Mutual goal setting involves planned change and indoctrinational change, which are characterized by deliberate power on both sides with 50/50 and 100/0 power ratios, respectively; but mutual goal setting through interactional change and socialization change have nondeliberate power ratios of 50/50 and 100/0, respectively. Nonmutual goal setting or goals set by one side where the power ratio is deliberate on the part of one side of the relationship entails technocratic change and coercive change, which have 50/50 and 100/0 power ratios, respectively. Natural change and emulative change, possessing a 50/50 and 100/0 power ratio, in the order given, are two species of change where nonmutual goal setting, nondeliberate on the part of both sides, is effected. Bennis admits that this typology may be difficult to link to reality; yet he contends that the classification does distinguish "planned change" from other change processes.

The nature of planned change and how it is effected in organizations is of primary importance to the planner; hence he or she should have some idea of the phases through which change progresses. Lewin has conceptualized that the equilibrium of an organization remains stable when opposing forces acting on the system remain equal[23]; yet when these forces are disturbed by subtracting or adding another force, the system reacts, and a new organizational equilibrium is established at a different level. When such a change is enacted, Lewin has noted that the organization may move back to its earlier level of functioning. This action indicates that merely defining the objective of planned change in group performance as reaching a different level is not sufficient but that permanency of the performance period is essential. Lewin suggests that a successful change includes *unfreezing* the present level, *moving* to a new level, and freezing group life at the new level.

Lippitt has expanded Lewin's conceptualization of change progressing through three phases as the development of a need for change (unfreezing), establishing a change relationship, working toward change (moving), generalization and stabilization of change (freezing), and achieving a terminal relationship.[24] Lippitt has observed that change does not necessarily move through phases in sequential order but probably follows a cyclic pattern, starting over and over again as one set of problems is solved and a new set is encountered.

Patterns of Change

Planned change in organizations may be considered as an intervention whereby the planner and the client system work together mutually. We have noted that perhaps the phases of change are cyclical instead of linear. With this knowledge of how planned change works, we shall review the results of a study of organizational change conducted by Greiner, where successful programs of change appeared to have a marked effect on behavior resulting in improved organization performance.

We have extracted nine patterns of change that Greiner discovered as common to successful programs of planned change.[25]

1. The organization is under extreme pressures for improvement before an attempt to change is initiated.
2. The organization is experiencing considerable problems in dealing with these pressures.
3. A new person, experienced at methods and procedures of organization improvement, enters the organization at the top of the organization structure.
4. The first action by the new person is to clarify the kind of relationship he or she would like to establish with the organization.
5. The new person at the top of the organization takes on a direct and highly involved role in planning and implementing changes.
6. The new person involves many parts of the organization in collaborative fact finding or incremental problem diagnosis of organizational problems.
7. The new person through careful procedures recommends solutions through action-oriented methods.
8. The new person's methods and suggestions are tested for credibility on a small scale before they are introduced to the rest of the organization.
9. The change effort spreads with each success experience to other parts of the organization and over time is absorbed into the organization's way of life.

There are several important assumptions and broad generalizations for planners that can be made from the preceding patterns of successful programs of change. First, we shall assume that administrative planning is the role of the new person at the top. Being at the top as a planner has a distinct advantage, if we can assume that legitimate power has been inherited through the position. Furthermore, because this new person at the top is experienced at procedures of improvement, we must assume he or she possesses expert power, skill in technology and politics, and knowledge of planning theories and of the organization. The administrative planner in our example must have desirable personal traits, and since he or she has been elected, there is reason to believe that such a person possesses referent power. One important advantage that the administrative planner has over the nonadministrative planner is power to reward—remunerative power. Because the methods and suggestions of the new person at the top were found credible through testing, we shall assume that the change strategy entitled "empirical-rational type" was effected successfully. Furthermore, because the change effort spread with each success experience, we must agree that elements of the normative-reeducative type of change strategies were utilized.

Relative to theories of planning and the nine patterns of change, we suggest that pattern 5 involved face-to-face, contact-transactive planning since the administrative planner took on a direct and higly involved role. Furthermore, a hint of incremental planning is evident in pattern 6 through collaborative fact finding. Unquestionably the new person at the top exerted effective leadership where the force of knowledge of goals, planning theories, organizational theories, and methodology acted to prescribe methods and recommendations for solving problems.

We have discussed the more positive elements of the change process in the preceding section. The negative considerations shall be left for our discussion of management by objectives and planned intervention in this text.

An additional factor of the change process is important—that is, time. It should be pointed out that time was a variable whether the discussion focused on Lewin's model of change or others. Likert has identified time as a key variable in organizational change, and he contends that neither time nor its influence have been fully recognized or understood in the change process. Hence, he has proposed the concept that a major organizational change may take up to five years before its full impact is realized.[26] As Likert's studies imply, a change program in organization, which is destined to eventually produce profound effects on the total organization, may only show minor impact the first year. Yet many changes in the intervening variables such as morale, group cohesiveness, and motivational forces may occur during the first year. However, the full impact of a planned change program may not be felt in the end-result variables (production, attendance, academic achievement, waste) until well into the second year or even later. An important implication then is the monitoring of change. In interventions involving organizations, therefore, a knowledge of evaluation and systems theory is also essential.

One reason for this assertion is that the systems approach to planning focuses on the interrelationships among the change strategies as they influence the total organization or its subunits. Knowledge and application of systems theory provides a means for viewing an organization (over time) in terms of its general properties and specific dynamics. But, this knowledge, apart from organizational and complementary planning theories, is of little value where effective change is required.

Summary

The basic elements of planning when mixed with theories and strategies of change facilitate decision making in educational organizations. Thus we have proposed that the educational planner is an agent of change; yet we do not equate planning with change since all change is not necessarily planned. The administrative planner, through goals and knowledge of planning theories, organizational theories, and appropriate methodology develops interventions for an organization whereby positive results may be measured and evaluated.

We have shown that patterns of change are more likely to be cyclical than linear as frequently outlined in the literature on the systems approach. We contend that observable organizational changes are more frequently obtained through a good mix of synoptic, incremental, transactive, advocacy, and radical planning strategies than through a single approach. A sound understanding of the organizational process is therefore a necessary additive for successful planning. To make planners more aware of this need, we have devoted part II to an overview of the organizational process.

Notes

1. Don Adams and Robert M. Bjork, *Education in Development Areas* (New York: David McKay, 1969).

2. Edgar L. Morphet, David L. Jesser, and Arthur P. Ludka, *Planning and Providing for Excellence in Education* (Publishers Press/Monitor, 1971), p. 124.

3. Walt LeBaron, adapted from a paper prepared for the project, Improving State Leadership in Education, as quoted in Morphet, Jessen, and Ludka *Planning and Providing for Excellence,* p. 124.

4. Robert Chin, "Basic Strategies and Procedures in Effecting Change," in *Designing Education for the Future,* no. 3, eds. Edgar L. Morphet and Charles O. Ryan, (New York: Scholastic Magazines, Citation Press, 1967), pp. 39–57.

5. Ibid., p. 43.

6. Ibid., p. 53.

7. Morphet, Jesser, and Ludka, *Planning and Providing for Excellence,* pp. 127–128.

8. *NDN: A Success Story,* Far West Laboratory for Educational

Research and Development (LEA Associates, 80 South Main, Concord, N.H., June 1978), p. 2.

9. Warren G. Bennis, Kenneth D. Benne, and Robert Chin, eds., *The Planning of Change: Readings in the Applied Behavioral Sciences* (New York: Holt, Rinehart and Winston, 1961), p. 154–155.

10. Talcott Parsons, *The Social System* (New York: Free Press, 1951), p. 121.

11. Stephen P. Robbins, *The Administrative Process: Integrating Theory and Practice* (Englewood Cliffs, N.J.: Prentice-Hall, 1976), p. 86.

12. Amitai Etzioni, *A Comprehensive Analysis of Complex Organizations* (New York: Free Press, 1961).

13. Robbins, *The Administrative Process,* p. 87.

14. John R. P. French, Jr., and Bertram Raven, "The Bases of Social Power," in *Group Dynamics: Research and Theory,* eds. Darwin Cartwright and A.F. Zander, (New York: Row, Peterson and Company, 1960), pp. 607–623.

15. Ronald Lippitt, Jeane Watson, and Bruce Westly, *The Dynamics of Planned Change* (New York: Harcourt, Brace, and Co., 1958).

16. Garth N. Jones, "Change Behavior in the Planned Organizational Change Process: Application of Socioeconomic Exchange Theory," *Philippine Journal of Public Administration,* no. 13 (October 1969):4.

17. Guy Benveniste, "Consequences of Excessive Educational Planning," *Educational Planning* 1(no. 2) (October 1974):1–8.

18. Robert L. Crowson, "Educational Planning and Models of Decision-Making," *Educational Planning* 2(no. 1) (May 1975):57.

19. Harold J. Leavitt, *Managerial Psychology* (Chicago: University of Chicago Press, 1958), pp. 55–70.

20. Jones, "Change Behavior," p. 4.

21. Garth N. Jones, "Strategies and Tactics of Planned Organizational Change: Case Examples in the Modernization Process of Traditional Societies," *Human Organizations* 24(no. 3) (Fall 1965):192–200.

22. Warren G. Bennis, "A Typology of Change Processes" in Bennis, Benne, and Chin, eds., *The Planning of Change,* pp. 154–156.

23. Kurt Lewin, "Frontiers in Group Dynamics," *Human Relations* 1(June 1947):74.

24. Lippitt, Watson, and Westly, *The Dynamics of Planned Change,* p. 130.

25. Larry E. Greiner, *Organizational Change and Development: A Study of Changing Values, Behavior, and Performance in a Large Industrial Plant* (Ann Arbor, Mich.: University Microfilms, 1965), pp. 23–67.

26. Rensis Likert, *The Human Organization: Its Management and Value* (McGraw-Hill, 1967), pp. 78–100.

Part II
The Organizational Process

To the reader who has been thoroughly indoctrinated in the rational systems approach and who has experienced considerable planning from this perspective, the organizational process may appear as a waste of time. It is if one wishes to plan for the sake of planning. On the other hand, to effect change through planning strategies and theories, the organizational process cannot be ignored.

We propose that the educational organization is an open system interacting continuously with its environment, and we emphasize that those theories proven to have been effective are deeply rooted in open-systems concepts. Interaction and collaboration are chief characteristics of organizational processes. Knowledge of how individuals and groups relate to the organization is another key factor in understanding how change can be effected. We propose that planners with multiple power bases are more effective than those that plan for the joy of planning iself. We characterize the administrative planner as results oriented-positive results. In part II we elaborate on the requirements of time and patience in the organizational setting and contend that these characteristics are inherent in an organization where planned change is desired.

The decision maker who also wears the administrative-planning hat has a good chance, we believe, for reaching change that is planned. The rational systems approach to decision making and planning, although shown for its shortcomings, is not ignored in the organizational process, which we see as heavily seasoned with politics. In the organization we believe that decisions most frequently result through compromise rather than through selecting the best alternative generated through synoptic or rational planning traditions.

3 Organizational Theories and Practices

A basic knowledge of organizational processes is one of the tools that successful educational planners must have on hand. And in the context of this book, we would like to forward the notion of organizational theories and practices as implements of administrative planners. We contend that an administrative-planning position is an ideal place to maximize power to effect change and to minimize the practice of planning for the sake of planning. Hence, we shall assume that the act of administrative planning closely parallels what we have called "planned change" in chapter 2. By studying the development of organizational theories and practices over time, administrative planners will gain a perspective as well as a foundation for understanding just how prescribed interventions can be utilized to yield optimal results within a given organizational framework.

Bennis, speaking from an evolutionary frame of reference, has advanced the idea that an organizational form is developed in every age that fits the peculiar needs, characteristics, and circumstances of that period of time.[1] Organizational theories and practices during any period of time are likely to reflect the then-current underlying basic assumptions and concepts concerning the nature of man. For example, the ideological support of industrial capitalism and the resulting organizational theories and practices at the end of the nineteenth century can be attributed largely to the widely held concepts about the nature of man as espoused in the Protestant ethic, the competitive economic model of Adam Smith, and Social Darwinism. As the social ethic has changed through time in consonance with changing circumstances, organizational theories and practices too have changed. In addition to social change, technological developments have been a pervasive force on organizational practices,[2] and given the massive analysis of change, no general or comprehensive theory of change exists.[3] Although changes in organizational practices have occurred, they have not always followed social and technological changes closely enough to prevent some conflicts from developing between the organization and the large social system.

In a brief survey of the literature concerning the development of organizational theories and practices, certain landmarks are identified under three periods of time arbitrarily labeled as classical, human relations, and modern. Our major purpose of this chapter is to provide a common understanding of the history of organizational theories and practices to serve as a spring board from which to move into some examples of planning through an organizational process approach.

It should be pointed out that the periods of time used in this brief history of organizational practices were by no means as sharply separated as this schematic presentation may imply. In fact, though the periods did generally follow the pattern used in the discussion, they overlapped, and many important concepts and practices were probably neither completely absent nor completely present in any given period.

The Classical Period

Organizational theories and practices of the classical period, characterized by the "machine model," were largely developed because of a need for greater predictability, effectiveness, and efficiency in organizations.[4] Organizational management prior to this time was in large measure based on the particular personality of the individual manager as opposed to being based on any type of organizational theory. As Jenks has observed, management was an uncertain mixture of the traditional thought, perhaps an autocracy with some benevolence, and an outflow of the personality of the chief administrator.[5] Organizational practices under such conditions obviously varied from one geographic area to another and from one "type" of owner-manager to another, resulting in very unpredictable practices in an organization. Bureaucracy was developed as a reaction to the unpredictable decision-making practices, patronage, cruelty, and other subservient and demeaning treatment of workers by managers during the early period of the industrial revolution.[6] The bureaucratic "machine-model" of organization, described by Bennis, is not the single development of any one person but rather is the generic name under which the writings and practices of several individuals may be subsumed.

Taylor and his followers, in what came to be termed the "Scientific Management" movement, provided the basic rationale for the "machine model" of organization; hence the basis for the scientific-management approach was the notion of man as machine.[7] In most organizations, prior to Taylor, standard procedures for workers to follow in accomplishing a specific task were nonexistent. Consequently, two workers in the same organization, doing the same kind of task, might be using different tools and different work procedures. Therefore, a major concern of Taylor was to develop orderliness in the organization by establishing certain standards and procedures for individual workers as they engaged in a specific task.[8] These standards and procedures for performing tasks were established, based on the use of scientific observations and measurements of the individuals as they performed the specific task. The most important element in the scientific-management movement was the idea of task. This included planning the work of a person at least one day in advance, often in writing, with the instructions for completing the job at hand. Instructions included specificity as well as the time needed for doing the work.[9]

Taylor's approach was a theory of motivation as well as one of organization, in which the key to motivation was seen as being economic rewards tied to the performance of the individual worker in accomplishing a task. In this approach, time-and-motion studies, rigid work procedures, discipline, and motivation based completely on an incentive pay system were the dominant features. "Eventually Taylor came to view human and machine resources not so much as mutually adaptable; but rather man functioning as an appendate to the industrial machine."[10]

March and Simon have also commented on the restricted view of man under which Taylorism operated. They described the scientific-management group as those specifying a well-defined program of behavior for a general-purpose mechanism such as a human into a special-purpose mechanism. Hence, scientific management focused on utilizing the characteristics of the complex human organism as one might use a simple machine for completing a relatively simple task.[11]

Taylorism spread to both public and private organizations[12] with equal disregard for the individuality of the workers in the organization.[13] Griffiths has noted that Taylorism was fostered in the schools by the same social climate that gave birth to it in industry. Taylorism in schools focused on efficiency, and "school districts were viewed as mechanisms and people were considered as a given rather than a variable in the total system. This meant that motivation was narrowly conceived, or, indeed, ignored. The idea of fixed positions and interchangeable personnel has since permeated the American education system."[14] Indeed, Taylorism had profound influence on the practices in educational systems during the early 1900s when efficiency was the central concern of administration. Callahan has vividly described this period (1900–1930) in *Education and the Cult of Efficiency*. He observed that:

> perhaps the tragedy was not inherent in the borrowing from business and industry but only in the application. It is possible that if educators had sought "the finest product at the lower cost"—a dictum which is sometimes claimed to be a basic premise in American manufacturing—the results would not have been unfortunate.[15]

In addition to Taylor's influence on educational organizations, Weber's ideas have been a very important force in shaping the administration and organization of educational institutions. Weber, a major contributor to the "machine model" of organization, gave the world the first completely developed principles of bureaucracy.[16] Using the construct of an "ideal type," he developed a theory of bureaucracy that was not intended to mirror reality perfectly but to extract certain characteristics of given phenomena, accentuating them in order to facilitate the making of comparisons.[17]

Weber's thinking was influenced by the growing industrial organizations in Germany, his experience in the German army, and his concern for the low reliability of people making judgments, often in a personal and highly charged atmosphere.[18] Weber's ideal-type bureaucracy may or may not be found in the real world; however, it highlights basic tendencies of actual organizations.[19] His construct of an ideal type of organization was based on an organizational structure that emphasized depersonalization and that minimized emotional and irrational factors of the individual in the organization. Weber saw such an organization as a way to increase predictability and to minimize friction and confusion in the human element of the organization. Weber believed this form of bureaucracy was superior to any other form regarding precision, stability, the stringency of its discipline, as well as its reliability. It is therefore possible to have a particularly high degree of measurability of results for the heads of the organization and other persons acting in relation to it.[20]

Weber's rationale for his ideal type parallels Taylor's rationale for scientific management since both men were concerned with authority relationships, technical competence, rationality, predictability, and impersonality. Weber, in evaluating his ideal type, has expressed firmly and unequivocally in his writings, his judgment of its superiority to other forms of organization.[21] Pfiffner and Presthus have described Weber's ideal type with the following generalizations:

1. Hierarchy implies that offices are arranged in a hierarchical manner.
2. Bureaucracy can be applicable to public as well as private efforts.
3. Rationalized job structure means a rational division of labor where each position has the legal authority for accomplishing goals.
4. Formalization implies that rules are made and recorded in writing relative to decisions and activities.
5. Management's being separated from ownership means that there is a hired, professional administrative group.
6. Members of a bureaucracy have no permanent right to office.
7. The administrative group requires special competencies and training.
8. Members are hired on the basis of competency.
9. Weber's construct reflects the legalistic flavor, characteristic of administration in continental Europe.[22]

A third major contributor to organizational theory during the classical period was Henri Fayol. He was one of the first advocates of the general theory of management.[23] Whereas Taylor focused on the individual worker as he performed a specific task, Fayol assumed a much broader perspective of organization by directing his attention to the improvement of the organization's top executives. He believed that top executives need special administrative skills that should and could be gained first through appropriate schooling and then later in the actual work place.[24]

Fayol believed that administration was a universal function, which he defined as being composed of five primary elements: planning, organizing, commanding, coordinating, and controlling. In addition to these elements of administration, he also developed the following fourteen principles to guide administrators: (1) division of work, (2) authority, (3) discipline, (4) unity of command, (5) unity of management, (6) subordination of individual interest to the general interest, (7) remuneration, (8) centralization, (9) scalar chain, (10) order, (11) equity, (12) stability of tenure for personnel, (13) initiative, and (14) esprit de corps.[25] With some modifications, these are basic to organizations today. Again, unlike Taylor, Fayol believed that the applications of these principles had to be flexible and in consonance with the particular circumstances of the situation. Thus he saw administration as being a highly skilled art in which the effective administrator must be intelligent, experienced, sensitive, and creative as he functioned in a complex setting.[26]

Luther Gulicks' and Lyndall Urwicks' works are also important because of their contributions and influence on the practice of grouping the parts of an organization by function, task, and geographic area. For example, Urwick combined and synthesized concepts of Taylor, Fayol, Follett, and others into a unified whole.[27] An important practice was the use of the formal organizational chart to show the exact relationships of various offices, departments, and divisions in an organization. Thus, as Etzioni noted, the central principle of their theory is the division of labor.[28]

The machine model of organization did bring increased order, predictability, technical competence, rationality, and impersonality to organizations, which were needed very much during this period of time. However, its focus was on the formal aspects of the organization with little or no concern given to the sociological and psychological factors of individual actors in an organization. Motivation of the workers was conceived narrowly with economic motives occupying a central place. Thus only man's lowest order of needs[29] was given attention by the organization in motivating the workers. Bennis has described organizations based on this model as "organizations without people."[30] March and Simon have also reflected on the lack of consideration that was given to individuals and the opportunity for them to have their higher order of needs satisfied. First, they observed a tendency to view the employees as just instruments to perform tasks and second, as givens rather than variables in the system.[31] There is little surprise that the machine model of organization was eventually confronted with several challenges because of its rigid approach, resulting in an inability to accommodate the human element of the organization.

The Human-Relations Period

During the human-relations period, a different model of organization was developed as a reaction to the machine model's lack of understanding and concern for the workers and because of its restricted perspective of the many sociological and psychological factors that influence the individual worker in his or her role in an organization. During this period many discoveries about human nature were made that challenged the assumptions upon which the machine model was built. It was learned that the amount of work that an individual accomplished is determined more by his or her social "capacity" than by his or her physical capacity; a person is not only motivated by economic rewards but also by noneconomic rewards; individuals in an organization react to stimuli not as an individual but as an actor in a role set; and the highest degree of specialization may not be the best way to organize the division of labor for the most efficient production. Such new understandings caused the human-relations school to consider the individual not as a given inert object but as a variable in the organization; a variable that does not always behave rationally and predictably. In fact, such knowledge resulted in increased attention being given to the place of participation, leadership, decision making, and communication in the organization.[32]

The Hawthorne studies had a powerful impact on organizational theories and practices.[33] Pfiffner and Sherwood have referred to the Hawthorne studies as "mark[ing] the beginning of an ideological revolution in organizational theory . . . . [They] established in the minds of the management people the concept of an organization as a social institution."[34] The irrational side of a person, and his or her need for affiliation in an informal human group, were vividly pointed out in the Hawthorne studies. No longer could *only* formal aspects of organization such as task and structure be considered when making changes in an organization. In analyzing an organization, it was not very apparent that the formal and informal organization could not be divorced. Technological changes in the future would have to be considered not only on their soundness but also on their impact on the informal organization.

Even though the organizational practices during the human-relations period did correct some of the shortsightedness of the classical period concerning sociological and psychological factors affecting human behavior in an organization, other serious limitations to organizational practices developed. In too many cases, the formal organization did not receive enough attention. Instead of producing a healthy organization, the practices of this period "cured" one organizational illness, but their side-effects produced another one. In either case the organization was not well. A new organizational prescription was needed in which organizational theories and practices would recognize and deal with all the interacting factors of an organization. Clearly, such a need to view the organization as a totality rather than as isolated fractured parts was indicated. Perhaps the notion that the forces on one part of an organization may have great impacts on the other parts of the organization was beginning to emerge as a crucial ingredient in a theory of organization. Some measure of the total organization is greater than that measure of the sum of its individual fractured parts[35]; therefore, how all the parts are related and balanced is an important factor in the total performance of the organization; hence, an organization is greater than the sum of its individual parts.

The Modern Period

The theories of the modern period generally have attempted to view an organization as an integrated whole.[36] No longer are decisions and practices considered on the basis of the kind of impact they will have on only the formal organization or the informal organization. Both are important. The theories of the modern period reflect a synthesis of the classic period (formal organization) and the human-relations period (informal organization)[37] or, as Owens has expressed in the Hegelian dialectic: thesis (classic period); antithesis (human-relations period); and synthesis (modern period).[38]

Many theorists of the modern period have reflected the influence of the classic and human-relations periods in that they have attempted to deal with both the needs of the individuals and the needs of the formal organization. Barnard has discussed the necessity of an organization to achieve both efficiency (personal relations) and effectiveness (productivity)[39]; Leavitt has used the concept of "pyramids and people"[40]; Likert has emphasized that the value of the human assets of an organization as well as the nonhuman assets are both very important and should be reflected in the accounting system of an organization[41]; and Argyris has emphasized the need to mediate the conflict between the formal and informal organizations, which he sees as being caused by restraints that the formal organization places on "self-actualization" of the individual members.[42] However, it should be emphasized that organizational theory today is by no means a united body of thought. A common element may be the attempt to view an organization in its totality, which, according to Scott, is the most common unifying aspect of modern organizational theory.[43] In this respect, modern organizational theory and general systems theory have much in common since both view an organization as a unified whole. As Scott has put it:

> The distinctive qualities of modern organization theory are its conceptual-analytical base, its reliance on empirical research data, and, above all, integrating nature. These qualities are framed in a philosophy which accepts

the premise that the only meaningful way to study organization is as a system.[44]

For the purpose of our discussion pertaining to educational planning, we shall say, after Kahn and others, that an organization is a dynamic and open system that is characterized by a continuing process of input, transformation, output and feedback. The openness of an organization in this context means that it depends on its environment to absorb its products and services, and to generate input that reactivates the process of transformation, thereby keeping the organization in existence.[45] Thus input into an organization includes individuals, energy, time, and materials that are transformed into services and goods output. The openness of the organization as a system implies that there are patterns of behavior that carry out the input-transformation-output cycle.[46]

Summary

Knowledge of organizational theories and practices is a necessary tool for the educational planner. Hence we have given a brief overview of the development of organizational thought identified under three classifications as classical, human relations, and modern. Evolving from the classical period was the machine model of the organization, bringing increased order, rationality, predictability, and impersonality to the organization. This rigid approach gave rise to the human-relations period, which saw the need for an understanding of the social capacity of the individual. Too much attention, however, was given to the individual at the expense of the total organization. Thus the resulting need for organizational theories and practices dealing with interacting forces of the organization evolved, giving way to the modern period. The theories of the modern period allowed the observers to view the organization as an integrated whole. We propose that this is one of the most important views an educational planner can have if he or she expects to see positive results from planning activities.

Notes

1. Warren G. Bennis, "The Coming Death of Bureaucracy," *Think* 32 (no. 6) (November–December 1966):30.
2. Fremont E. Kast and James E. Rosenzweig, *Organization and Management: A Systems Approach* (New York: McGraw-Hill, 1970), pp. 26–55.
3. James M. Lipham and James A. Hoeh, Jr., *The Principalship: Foundations and Functions* (New York: Harper and Row, 1974), pp. 106–107.

4. Amitai Etzioni, *Modern Organizations* (Englewood Cliffs, N.J.: Prentice-Hall, 1964), p. 20.

5. Leland H. Jenks, "Early Phases of the Management Movement," *Administrative Science Quarterly* 5 (no. 3) (December 1960):424.

6. Bennis, "The Coming Death of Bureaucracy," p. 32.

7. Wayne K. Hoy and Cecil G. Miskel, *Educational Administration: Theory, Research, and Practice* (New York: Random House, 1978), p. 3.

8. Felix A. Nigro, *Modern Public Administration* (New York: Harper and Row, 1970), pp. 84–87.

9. Frederick W. Taylor, *The Principles of Scientific Management* (New York: Harper and Brothers, 1911), p. 39.

10. Amitai Etzioni, *Modern Organizations,* © 1964, p. 20. Reprinted by permission of Prentice-Hall, Inc., Englewood Cliffs, New Jersey.

11. James G. March and Herbert Simon, *Organizations* (New York: Wiley, 1958), p. 13.

12. Nigro, *Modern Public Administration* p. 87.

13. Harold J. Leavitt, "Applied Organizational Change in Industry: Structural, Technical, and Human Approaches," *New Perspectives in Organizational Research,* vol. 2, edited by W.W. Cooper, H.J. Leavitt, and M.W. Shelly, (New York: Wiley, 1964), pp. 59–63.

14. Daniel E. Griffiths, "Some Assumptions Underlying the Use of Models in Research," *Educational Research: New Perspectives,* edited by Jack A. Culbertson and Stephen P. Hencley (Danville, Ill.: The Interstate Printers & Publishers, Inc., 1963), p. 128. Reprinted with permission.

15. Raymond Callahan, *Education and the Cult of Efficiency* (Chicago: The University of Chicago Press, 1962), p. 244. Reprinted from *Education and the Cult of Efficiency* by Raymond Callahan by permission of The University of Chicago Press, © 1962.

16. Warren G. Bennis, *Changing Organizations: Essays on the Development and Evolution of Human Organization* (New York: McGraw-Hill, 1966), p. 66.

17. Nigro, *Modern Public Administration,* p. 89.

18. Bennis, *Changing Organizations,* p. 66.

19. Hoy and Miskel, *Educational Administration,* p. 54.

20. Max Weber, *The Theory of Social and Economic Organizations,* translated by A.M. Henderson and Talcott Parsons (New York: Oxford University Press, 1947), p. 337.

21. Max Weber, *Essays in Sociology,* translated by H.H. Gerth and C. Wright Mills (New York: Oxford University Press, 1958), p. 214.

22. John M. Pfiffner and Robert Presthus, *Public Administration* (New York: The Ronald Press, 1967), pp. 41–42. Reprinted with permission.

23. Kast, and Rosenzweig, *Organization and Management,* p. 65.

24. Henri Fayol, *General and Industrial Management,* translated by Constance Storrs (London: Sir Isaac Pitman and Sons, 1949), p. 14.

25. John Franklin Mee, *A History of Twentieth Century Management Thought* (Ann Arbor, Mich.: University Microfilms, 1959), pp. 58–59.

26. Fayol, *General and Industrial Management,* p. 19.

27. Stephen P. Robbins, *The Administrative Process: Integrating Theory and Practice* (Englewood Cliffs, N.J.: Prentice-Hall, 1976), p. 37.

28. Etzioni, *Modern Organizations,* p. 22.

29. For a discussion of man's needs as conceptualized hierarchically, see A.H. Maslow, *Motivation and Personality* (New York: Harper and Row, 1954).

30. Warren G. Bennis, "Leadership Theory and Administrative Behavior," *Administrative Science Quarterly* 4 (no. 3) (December 1959): 263.

31. March and Simon, *Organizations,* p. 29.

32. Etzioni, *Modern Organizations,* pp. 32–39.

33. Fritz J. Roethlisberger and William J. Dickson, *Management and the Worker* (Cambridge, Mass.: Harvard University Press, 1939).

34. John M. Pfiffner and Frank P. Sherwood, *Administrative Organization,* © 1960, p. 101. Reprinted by permission of Prentice-Hall, Inc., Englewood Cliffs, New Jersey.

35. James G. Miller, "Living Systems: Basic Concepts," *Behavioral Science* 10 (July 1965):200–201.

36. William G. Scott, "Organizational Theory: An Overview and Appraisal," *Managerial Behavior and Organizational Demands: Management as a Linking of Levels of Interaction,* edited by Robert T. Golembiewski and Frank Gibson (Chicago: Rand McNally, 1967), pp. 22–30.

37. Etzioni, *Modern Organization,* p. 41.

38. Robert G. Owens, *Organizational Behavior in Schools* (Englewood Cliffs, N.J.: Prentice-Hall, 1970), pp. 14–15.

39. Chester I. Barnard, *The Functions of the Executive* (Cambridge, Mass.: Harvard University Press, 1950).

40. Harold J. Leavitt, *Managerial Psychology* (Chicago: University of Chicago Press, 1958), pp. 253–262.

41. Rensis Likert, *The Human Organization: Its Management and Value* (New York: McGraw-Hill, 1967).

42. Chris Argyris, "The Individual and Organization: Some Problems of Mutual Adjustment," *Administrative Science Quarterly* 2 (no. 2) (July 1957):24.

43. Scott, "Organizational Theory," p. 23.

44. Ibid., p. 22. Reprinted by permission.

45. Robert L. Kahn et al. *Organizational Stress: Studies in Role Conflict and Ambiguity* (New York: Wiley, 1964), pp. 12–13.

46. Ibid.

4 Systems Theories and Practices

The educational planner, by viewing the organization as a system of relationships among attitudes and among subunits, finds himself or herself with the perspective to prescribe successful interventions that effect change. Interventions in systems often require considerable time, and measurement of their effects also requires ample time. Later in this chapter *systems* will be defined, but initially we shall address organizational typologies and how the total organization influences behavior of its members.

Organizational Typologies

Rather than reviewing the contributions to modern organization theory of individual writers, the discussion focuses on a particular way to view organizations. Etzioni has constructed a typology, with a classification system based on compliance, in which he views one actor's power as supporting the behavior of another subordinate actor through a directive.[1] Blau and Scott have constructed a typology in which an organization is classified in terms of who primarily benefits from it.[2] For Parsons, the *primacy of orientation to the attainment of a specific goal* is actually the characteristic of a given organization that sets it apart from other social systems.[3]

The typology of organizations developed by Katz and Kahn is useful in studying organizations, and the concepts supporting this typology are adopted in this text as a basis for the organizational process approach to educational planning. Their typology was developed, based on their conceptualization of open, living social-system theory where a formal organization is classified in terms of the major type of function or activity in which it is engaged in the larger society. This typology has four categories, based on the particular genotypic function of the organization in the society at large. They are (1) maintenance organizations, (2) adaptive organizations, (3) productive or economic organizations, and (4) managerial-political organizations. These authors contend that schools are classified as maintenance organizations since their primary function in the society at large is socialization and training of individuals for particular roles in the larger society.[4]

An organization's functions and structure may be studied, analyzed, and described through basic subsystems. Hoy and Miskel have elaborated on how to understand an organization through the development of typologies, which allows for comparative study among schools, businesses, industry, and so on.[5] They focus on the four genotype functions, developed by Katz and Kahn. Here we shall present the subsystems developed by Katz and Kahn, and integrate them with the genotype functions outlined by Hoy and Miskel.

1. *Production or technical subsystem.* This subsystem is concerned with converting inputs into outputs and may also be classified as a *productive or economic organization,* which creates wealth, manufactures goods, and provides service, that is, an organization that provides output.

2. *Supportive subsystem.* Two major functions of concern here are: (a) procuring inputs and disposing of outputs; and (b) promoting and maintaining good relationship between the organization and its environment (for example, public relations, getting a school bond approved, and educating the public to a new curriculum project).

3. *Maintenance subsystem.* Activities of this subsystem deal with personnel in the organization in all facets (for example, role, arrangements, recruiting, selecting, motivating, disciplining, and socializing). The focus is on maintaining stability and preserving the organization through institutionalization of its personnel inputs and education of its larger society. The parallel genotype function may be thought of as a *maintenance organization,* which includes churches and schools, whose role is to socialize people by teaching them appropriate values to maintain social order.

4. *Adaptive subsystem.* The functions of this subsystem are designed to ensure that the organization can meet the changing needs of the environment (for example, research, planning, development, and so on). It is called *adaptive organizations* that may include educational organizations that are responsible for the development and testing of theories, the creation of knowledge, and for applying information in a limited extent to problems.

5. *Managerial subsystem.* The function of this subsystem is to coordinate the other subsystems, settle conflicts between subsystems and hierarchical levels, and relate the total organization to its environment. This subsystem cuts across all subsystems of the organization in its goal to encourage all the subsystems to obtain a concerted effort to achieve the highest level of functioning of the total system (for example, authority, regulations, policy, decision making, and communication). *Managerial or political organizations* adjudicate, coordinate, and control resources, including people, and other institutions. Included in this group are local, state, and federal governments and their related political structures.

Systems Defined

Before discussing an organization as a living, open, social system with many individual members interacting as actors in a particular role set, the term *system* should be defined since it has a number of special meanings that are often confused. *System* may refer to a number system, school system, air-conditioning system, and so on. Miller discusses a system as a set of units that have some definable relationships among them.[6] Hall and Fagan present material parallel to this definition but extend the notion of relationships to be between objects and their attributes.[7] Miller expands these definitions by focusing on the term *set*. Hence, *set* implies common properties among the units, and the state of each single unit influences the state of the other units within the system.[8] Therefore we may view a system as a set of units with the capacity to interact within the scope of their total environment.

All systems are either closed or open; thus according to Miller, an open system exchanges matter and energy with its environment, and a closed system has impervious boundaries through which no information, energy, or matter can traverse. Living systems are composed of energy, matter, and ordered by information. Some examples are organisms, organs, cells, societies, organizations, and groups. Living systems are open systems, and components of a living system do not have to be alive. Living systems may create artifacts that are objects made by man or animal and included in the system for some purpose. Some examples of artifacts are spider webs, prairie dog mounds, data-processing machines, airplanes, books, and so on.[9]

Robbins, in writing about the administrative process, has stated that open-systems thinking "recognizes that the organization is interdependent with its environment, is a subsystem of a larger system, is concerned basically with survival, and must deal with uncertainty."[10] He states that an open system is more flexible than a closed system, which ignores external conditions and makes no allowances for adapting to changes in the environment.

Open systems exhibit several common characteristics. The following characteristics common to open systems are based on the description of open systems by Katz and Kahn:

1. *Importation of energy.* An open system imports matter and energy[11] and information (inputs) from the external environment.

2. *The throughput.* Inputs into an open system are transformed into new forms, patterns, and products. For example, a school may create new knowledge, teaching materials, and other products from its inputs.

3. *The output.* An open system exports matter and energy and information into the environment. These outputs may be in the form of waste, services, new products, and so on.

4. *Systems as cycles of events.* An open system develops a cyclic pattern of activities. The necessary inputs to reinforce the system's cycle of activities are obtained from exchange of outputs with its external environment or derived directly from organizational activities. In the former case,

for example, a school may export the services of educating students for which it receives new inputs of money from the environment to sustain its cycle of activities. In the latter case, a voluntary organization may provide such a degree of satisfaction to its members that the inputs necessary to sustain its cycle of activities are derived directly from the activity.

5. *Negative entropy.* In order to survive, an open system must arrest entropy, a universal law of nature, by acquiring new inputs equal to or greater than its export of outputs.

6. *Information input, negative feedback, and coding process.* Selected bits of information[12] serve as signals to an open system concerning its functioning and the nature of its environment. Negative feedback is one type of information that helps a system regulate its functioning as conditions in its operation and environment change. Only information to which the system is attuned has meaning to the system. Coding is the selective mechanism of a system in which information is rejected or accepted and translated into meaning.

7. *The steady-state and dynamic homeostatis.* An open system that survives must maintain a balance in the exchange of matter and energy with information. This steady state is a dynamic equilibrium as opposed to a true equilibrium. In order to maintain a steady state, an open system may ingest or acquire control over external forces.

8. *Differentiation.* An open system tends to develop highly specialized subsystems to perform special system functions. In a school system, differentiation may be observed in the development of elaborated roles with special functions such as psychologist, reading teacher, accountant, bus driver, and dietician.

9. *Equifinality.* A final state of an open system may be reached in many different ways and from different initial conditions. That is, an open system is capable of achieving a given outcome or result in many ways.[13]

However, there are other important characteristics of open systems that differ. Katz and Kahn have observed that if this were not the case, we could simply obtain all our information regarding social organizations by studying biological organisms.[14]

In this book we shall explain some special types of system interventions (planned change) based on open-systems theory; thus it will be helpful if we look at a planner's point of view. Bell has outlined some basic concepts of open-systems theory applicable to higher education systems.[15] He points out that any organization or any part of an organization should be viewed as a system within a system. A college or university, for example, is a subsystem of its community and state just as a department is a subsystem of a college within the university. He points out that the interaction within the system reflects various layers of control and autonomy and that some subsystems have varying degrees of power over other subsystems. Another feature of open-systems theory is that it is nonreductionist. It does not try to break elements down to their lowest common denominator but tries to give perspective.[16]

However systems are viewed, they have usually been approached from one of two general avenues—process or structure. These two have often been confused, but, according to Miller, this confusion need not occur. He has made the distinction between process and structure where *process* is viewed as dynamic change in the matter and energy, information, of a given system, while structure is seen as a static arrangement of a system's parts in tridimensional space.[17]

An Organization as a Contrived Social System

Katz and Kahn have approached the study of an organization by conceptualizing it as a contrived social system in which the functioning or processes of the subsystem are analyzed. They perceive that the theoretical concepts of an organization depend more on the inputs, outputs, and functioning of the organization than on the rational purposes of its leaders.[18] Inputs from its environment are taken into the system and transformed into outputs. These organizational outputs then provide the necessary means through exchange processes for the organization to sustain itself and repeat the input-transformation-output cycle. Such an exchange process in the larger society is necessary because of differentiation and specialization of the large social system (society) into several subsystems such as schools, manufacturing plants, and so on, for the purpose of providing specific services and goods. Further, this exchange process is possible because of the "reciprocity principle," which means that that person should not injure others from whom they have received help and that in general people should help those who have helped them.[19]

Rogers, in discussing the reciprocity concept regarding leadership and supervision, has said that where both the subordinate and superior view each other under the same assumptions, there are three primary factors to consider.[20] The first factor deals with a supervisor's relationship with his or her superior, where a good relationship with the boss implies that group performance is superior to performance under opposite conditions. His second factor regarding the impact that leaders or superiors have on their subordinates emphasizes the competence of the superior in planning skills and technical knowledge. That is, the anxiety of the group is decreased if the superior is competent and vice versa. The superior's leadership pattern, factor 3, influences the subordinates' perception of their leader. If the leader is autocratic, decisions are made by the leader, while he or she permits the group to function independently within limits defined by the organization under the democratic pattern.

In a school system, the input of material resources, personnel, and labor enables the production of learning; for this service the larger social system (society) in which the school system exists provides new inputs (such as tax monies) so that the cycle can be repeated. These inputs are used for maintenance of the system as well as for production of services.

Organizations are contrived social systems, or, in other words, they are social inventions. They do not have the physical boundedness that characterizes the biological system. Social organizations do exist in physical space and "are tied into a concrete world of human beings, material resources, physical plants, and other artifacts, but these elements are not in any natural interaction with each other."[21] In fact, the physical proximity of parts of a system is not necessarily a good indicator of the intensity with which the parts may be interacting. Rather, an organization consists of the patterned activities of its members or "structuring of events or happenings rather than of physical parts and it therefore has no structure apart from its functioning."[22] It follows that the concept of an organization is dynamic rather than static. In contrast, the biological system has a more static, visible, and well-defined structure than an organization. Also social systems are more variable than biological systems, and the force that "holds them together is essentially psychological rather than biological. Social systems are anchored in the attitudes, perceptions, beliefs, motivations, habits, and expectations of human beings."[23] This being true, we emphasize the point that when these factors change or are modified in members of an organization and/or in individuals in its environment because of technological development, change in social values or whatever the cause, the organization will have stresses and strains placed on it to adapt or change the patterned activities of its members.

Hierarchical Relationships of Subsystem Functions in an Organization

In thinking about the subsystems and how they relate to each other, it is important to note that an organization is arranged in hierarchical levels and that its configuration, especially the relative position of a particular level in the hierarchy, may be determined by its major functioning. However, such is not necessarily the case since it is prevalent for functions of several subsystems to be performed at any one level. This is especially true in the case of the management subsystem, which is found at all levels and which cuts across all functions of the organization from top to bottom of the hierarchy. In fact, the major function of administration is to act as a "linking pin" between various subsystems that are performing special functions and between various groups of the organization in order to bond them as units of energy, matter, and information into a viable, integrated, and cooperative force for achieving the organization's major purpose for existing in the larger society.

In performing its special functions, the administrative or managerial subsystem, in addition to pervading every subsystem and level of the organization, both in influence and presence, also is specialized in decision making, vertically, so that a specific decision or task is assigned to a particular level of the organization that results in a pyramid or hierarchy of power and consequently authority.[24] Therefore, the degree of influence of a particular section of the administrative subsystem is usually greater the higher its location in the hierarchy. Such a division of power vertically in an organization, although it may not always have a high correlation with the hierarchical level because of various reasons from high expertise to personal charisma of certain individuals, does provide order to the organization's activities. Disputes between functioning groups that cannot be settled by the boundary agencies or the linking pins[25] of the conflicting groups can be referred to the next higher level for mediation.

Since the administrative subsystem cuts across all levels and all groups of an organization, it is likely that many dysfunctions and poor performances of an organization are often related directly to the quality of the functioning of the administrative subsystem. Therefore it is not surprising to find that many organizational studies have been aimed at improving the leadership and administration in organizations. In an educational organization, the administrative subsystem as it functions at the school level between principal and teacher and at the school-district level between superintendent and principal, to abstract only a few of the many important management relationships that exist in a school system, is a key point at which to focus intervention for improving the performance of the total educational organization. A program of planned change (see chapter 12) may be especially concerned with improving the teacher-pupil relationship and the general behavior of students as they interact in the organizational setting.

This is not to suggest that the achievement of planned change in an educational organization is not a complex phenomenon. It is complex because of all the delicate and intricate relationships that exist among a multitude of factors and because of the constantly changing patterns of interaction among these factors. Therefore, a dysfunction in an organization usually has no simple solution since there is normally not a one-to-one correspondence in the cause-and-effect relationship. Rather, the intervention and solution are likely to be complex because many factors underlie the cause-and-effect relationship.

Nevertheless, such complexities do not reduce the importance of the managerial relationships at various levels among groups at key points at which planned change strategies can be directed to improve organizational performance. This seems logical since it is the normal responsibility of the administration to plan, initiate, and guide change in an organization as it is needed to keep the organization functioning at a high level. Again the notion that the planner may be more helpful as an administrator than as a nonadministrator is of significance. However, it does not preclude other forces from initiating and guiding change if the administrative subsystem is derelect in discharging this planning function. Nor does this primary responsibility of administration to maintain a healthy, productive organization mean that experts from outside the organization, and members from other subsystems in the organization cannot or should not collaborate with the administration in bringing about needed constructive change. It does mean that if management's primary responsibility is not met, resulting in the organization's performance being low, the organization becoming "out of tune with the times," and so on, then it is likely that many forces will impinge upon the system resulting in an imbalance of forces that must be adjusted. Such an imbalanced situation is corrected when change occurs to equalize the imbalanced forces, resulting in a new equilibrium for the organization at a different level. Change occurring because of the default of the administrative subsystems of the organization to plan needed change is unplanned or natural change.

A system such as a school system, as Guessous has observed, is in equilibrium when its parts are compatible, and, excluding an outside interference, none of these components will change its relationship to the others in any notable way.[26] Such an equilibrium in an organization is not viewed as a static and smooth relationship but as a dynamic and continous struggle of many forces—a dynamic and shaky balance. Such a view of equilibrium in an organization means that one accepts the assumption that the organizations are bound to change. Such a change in an organization, if positive, is cumulative growth and is tolerated by the larger society only if it is at a rate that allows society to absorb it. Inherent in this relationship between the organization and the larger society, as open systems, is the ability and the reality of the two systems to exchange matter, energy, and information. This unplanned or natural change occurs in an organization in order to maintain a dynamic equilibrium. Gouldner views organizational structures as spontaneously and homeostatically maintained where any changes in patterns of organization are to be considered the direct results of unplanned reactions to threats to the equilibrium of the whole system.[27]

Unplanned change in an organization is important, but this work is primarily concerned with planned change in educational organizations aimed at improving relationships and functions at all levels, and *evaluating* its effects on the total educational system. Perhaps it should be emphasized that in any efforts of planned change, the support of the administrative subsystem is crucial to the organization's progress because of the unique functions that the administrative subsystem performs and because of the critical organizational space it occupies. Further, because of the specialization of the decision-making processes vertically in the organization, resulting in greater authority residing in each higher level of the hierarchy, it is important for any planning effort to have the sympathy and support of the highest levels of the administrative hierarchy. Hence, the notion of administrative planning has merit if the administrative planner has a sound knowledge of organizational and planning theories.

Summary

The educational planner should have a certain vantage point whereby he or she can take a hard look at the organization in which planning activities are conducted. We contend that by viewing the major functions or activities within the organization, the planner will better understand how relationships help or hinder the realization of goals. Awareness that the organization is interdependent with its environment may be the key to successful planning, but to overlook the fact that people make up organizations is the key to failure.

In this chapter we have shown that the management subsystem cuts across all hierarchical levels, yet individuals and groups comprise each level. Hence it is vitally important to know how individuals and groups influence each organizational subsystem. This problem is addressed in chapter 5.

Notes

1. Amitai Etzioni, *A Comparative Analysis of Complex Organizations* (New York: Free Press of Glencoe, 1961), p. 3.

2. Peter M. Blau and Richard Scott, *Formal Organizations: A Comparative Approach* (San Francisco: Chandler Publishing Company, 1962), pp. 40–57.

3. Talcott Parsons, "Suggestions for a Sociological Approach to the Theory of Organizations—I," *Administrative Science Quarterly* 1 (July 1956):64.

4. Daniel Katz and Robert Kahn, *The Social Psychology of Organizations* (New York: Wiley, 1966), pp. 110–148.

5. Wayne K. Hoy and Cecil G. Miskel, *Educational Administration: Theory, Research, and Practice* (New York: Random House, 1978), pp. 31–36.

6. James G. Miller, "Living Systems: Basic Concepts," *Behavioral Science* 10 (July 1965):200.

7. A.D. Hall and R.E. Fagen, "Definition of System," *General Systems—Yearbook of the Society for the Advancement of General Systems Research,* ed. Ludwig von Bertolanffy and Anatol Rapoport (Ann Arbor: Braun-Brumfield, 1956), p. 18.

8. Miller, "Living Systems," pp. 200–201.

9. Ibid., pp. 193–237.

10. Stephen P. Robbins, *The Administrative Process: Integrating Theory and Practice* (Englewood Cliffs, N.J.: Prentice-Hall, 1976), p. 270. Reprinted by permission of Prentice-Hall, Inc., Englewood Cliffs, New Jersey © 1976.

11. Katz and Kahn used only the term *energy* to describe all inputs; but the writers have chosen to use Miller's joint term *matter-energy* since it is more descriptive of the special relationship of the two in the strictest scientific sense. See Miller, "Living Systems," pp. 193–199.

12. The relationship in information and open systems has been explained in detail by Miller. He has discussed the influence of "information" on the operation of an open system, as well as "meaning" and "communication," which have a special relationship to information. See Miller, "Living Systems," pp. 193–199.

13. Katz and Kahn, *The Social Psychology of Organizations,* pp. 19–26.

14. Ibid., p. 19.

15. Edwin Bell, "Administrative Planning: Science or Art?" *Planning for Higher Education* 7 (no. 3) (December 1978):12–15.

16. J.E. Haas and T.E. Drabek, *Complex Organizations: A Sociological Perspective* (New York: The Macmillan Company, 1973). As quoted in Bell, "Administrative Planning."

17. Miller, "Living Systems," p. 211.

18. Katz and Kahn, *The Social Psychology of Organizations,* p. 16.

19. Ibid., p. 57.

20. Rolf E. Rogers, *Organizational Theory* (Boston, Mass.: Allyn and Bacon, 1974), pp. 143–145.

21. Katz and Kahn, *The Social Psychology of Organizations,* p. 30. Reprinted with permission.

22. Ibid., p. 31. Reprinted with permission.

23. Ibid., p. 33. Reprinted with permission.

24. Herbert A. Simon, *Administrative Behavior: A Study of Decision-Making Processes in Administrative Organization* (New York: The Free Press, 1957), p. 9.

25. For a discussion of the "linking pin" concept, seen Rensis Likert,

New Patterns of Management (New York: McGraw-Hill Book Company, 1961), especially pp. 97–118, 178–192.

26. Mohammed Guessous, "A General Critique of Equilibrium Theory," *Readings on Social Change,* eds. Wilbert E. Moore and Robert M. Cook (Englewood Cliffs, N.J.: Prentice-Hall, 1967), p. 23.

27. Alvin W. Gouldner, "Organizational Analysis," *Sociology Today,* eds. Robert K. Merton and Leonard W. Broom (New York: Basic Books, 1958), p. 405.

5

Individuals, Groups, and Leadership Within the Organization

Educational planners must take seriously the relationships among individuals within the organization and consider both the internal as well as the external forces of motivation. Two important interests of planners are: Are organizational objectives achieved more easily within the organization that provides a good climate, and does job satisfaction result from good organizational climate? Since each individual perceives situations in an individualistic way, we propose that each group also perceives circumstances in a unique way; hence what we know about individual psychology can also be applied to the group. Leadership of groups and organizations have common elements, and a leader is one who initiates certain procedures for achieving or changing organizational goals.

The educational planner is therefore a leader in that he or she focuses on planning strategies for changing the organization. We view planners ideally as administrators with some inherent decision-making function. Thus planners must know how situational variables and planning theories relate to the environment if effective planning and change is to be effected.

Individuals Within the Organization

To view an organization as a contrived social system provides an amenable framework in which to study the many planning actions and forces that constantly interact to bring change in an organization. Viewing an organization as an open system (discussed in chapter 4) existing in a larger social system, we observe the capability of accommodating conflict and rapid environmental change, especially through transactive planning. Because of this attribute, knowledge of open systems is becoming increasingly important to modern organization theorists.[1] Further, change that occurs in an organization does so in a social setting and is manifested through individuals acting as members in a particular role set; not as individuals acting in parallel in a social vacuum as it has often been treated.[2]

Educational planners must be aware of individual behavior, which is frequently reflected in a person's personality and in the way the individual reacts in a social setting. We must understand, with respect to the organization, that an individual's attitude toward others on his or her same level,

45

attitude toward immediate superior and subordinates, attitude toward the job, and attitude even toward the world in general are important variables in producing goods and providing services. An individual's attitude toward these variables in many respects is the result of where the person is located in the organization hierarchy, job pressures and requirements, and the attitudes and behavior of subordinates as well as superiors. Thus performance of the individual may be influenced by the complex organizational relationships and perhaps the degree of job satisfaction that develops in his or her organizational setting.

In an educational organization the "more satisfied educators perform at higher levels than dissatisfied educators"—at least this has been true at the intuitive levels of analysis, according to Hoy and Miskel.[3] But this contention may not be totally true since Hoy and Miskel have presented findings of several studies showing low positive relationships between job satisfaction and performance.[4] Nevertheless, we may view job satisfaction through performance and as a complex organizational phenomenon whereby both physiological and psychological factors influence a person's motivation and attitude toward the position.[5]

The way administrators of an organization perceive other employed individuals has been proposed as a key factor in motivation. The classic Theory X and Theory Y by Douglas McGregor provide some basic understanding of motivation of workers in an organization.[6] McGregor has shown through Theory Y that people have a basic psychological need to work including a drive for achievement and a desire for responsibility; hence man is basically good. Theory X formulates the picture of the worker as needing coercion for motivation, thereby lacking ambition and avoiding responsibility. That is, in terms of achieving organizational goals, man is lazy, seeing himself as more important than the group. Accepting Theory Y with its more proactive approach to motivation, we therefore subscribe to an administrative planning style amenable to arranging favorable conditions for change through encouraging cooperation among individuals and providing an atmosphere of support.

The basic assumptions of Theory Y are extracted from Maslow's theory of human motivation. Although the theory is concerned with human motivation, it may be adapted for an understanding of behavior in organizations.[7] Maslow suggested that there are basic physiological needs such as sex, thirst, and hunger. There is the need for security, or to feel safe, and the need to love and be accepted—the need for belonging. The need for respect, the esteem need, includes a desire for achievement, recognition, and prestige. Finally, there is the need to fulfill individual potential, or the self-actualization need.[8] These requirements are often perceived in a linear manner with the physiological need as basic followed by the others in order of presentation. However, for certain individuals these needs are not necessarily met in chronological order—hence a person may desire esteem more than security—yet professional people generally require the first three, physiological, security, and love or social needs.

Concerning the individual in the organization, Rogers contends that behavior results from internal and external factors.[9] Internal factors operate within an individual including, for example, attitudes, needs, and perceptions, while examples of external factors of motivation include but are not limited to job requirements, actions of subordinates, superiors, and fellow workers. Rogers presents an excellent discussion of McClelland's[10] theory of need achievement, which demonstrates the effects of the desire to excel.

Herzberg's two-factor theory—a theory explaining specific aspects of the job situation that enhance feelings of personal growth—deals with motivation.[11] On a job-satisfaction contiuum satisfiers or motivators have been identified through variables such as achievement, recognition, work, and responsibility, while dissatisfiers or hygienes have been revealed through such variables as salary, personal life, job security, possibility of growth, interpersonal relations that involve subordinates, peers, and superiors, status, working conditions, technical supervision, policy, and administration. Hoy and Miskel, in reporting research based on the two-factor theory, contend that a person operates from a neutral point, and there exists neither positive nor negative attitudes toward his or her job.[12] Yet when the gratification of certain factors increases, job satisfaction tends to be positive, while these motivators (factors) lead only to minimal dissatisfaction when they are not satisfied. Thus if the hygiene motivators are not gratified, job dissatisfaction results; however, the gratification of these same factors lead to minimal job gratification. Taken collectively, motivators tend to contribute more than hygiene factors to the complex scope of job satisfaction. By knowing that job satisfaction is a positive result of good organizational climate, the planner can logically assume that the individuals within this situation will work to achieve organizational goals and objectives.

In studying change in organizational behavior, it is important to be aware of the distinction between change that occurs in the individual members because of personality needs and values and change that occurs in the individual members because of their structured roles within the organization. The failure to make this distinction, according to Katz and Kahn, is the major error that researchers have made in studying organizational change. As these authors have stated: "The behavior of people in organizations is still the behavior of individuals, but it has a different set of determinants than behavior outside organizational roles."[13] For example, when an executive attends a sensitivity-training session away from his organization in a social group different from his usual role set in his organization, the method is powerful in producing change; but its focus is on the individual and not the organization.[14] When the executive returns to his organization, he must step back into a role set that has been unaltered by his experience. He may want to redefine his own way of doing things, but beliefs of superiors, subordinates, and colleagues are unchanged, and there has not been a change in organizational routine and rewards.[15] Mann perceives that the change process needs to focus on the forces within the individual as well as the organization immediately surrounding the individual.[16]

Change in an individual member of an organization and the influence that the member has with other members is greatly influenced by the larger organizational structure in which the members function. Pelz has discussed the importance of viewing the organization as a system when studying change and the inadequacies of methods in which the individual member of an organization is considered apart from other members' influence in the organization. The study of an individual supervisor's influence on his or her subordinates is not enough in itself. Rather, the relationship is more involved, and the analysis should also include the relationship of the supervisor with his or her own immediate superiors since that relationship will have profound influence on the relationship that the supervisor actually has with the subordinates at the lower level. According to Pelz, a supervisor who has considerable influence on his or her own superiors is likely to be more influential with his or her subordinates.[17]

Tannenbaum and Seashore have also recognized that in producing change in members of an organization, the total organizational structure as well as the individual must be considered. They stated:

> Our research was leading us slowly but surely up the organizational hierarchy. It now seemed apparent to us that to get supervisors to behave in optimum ways, one must create conditions in the organization as a whole which make it possible and easy for the supervisor to behave appropriately. Upon further investigation we found that the supervisor who pressures men may be following the example of a superior, and that some supervisors used pressure with subordinates because they believe their organization's norms required this. If it is desired to have supervisors treat their subordinates with consideration, to respect their men, it is not sufficient just to tell the supervisor to respect their men and to explain the rationale for this. Instead, it began to appear that the best way to get the supervisors to respect their men is *to make the men respectable*; that is, to change the organization in ways to give authority, responsibility, influence, control over significant aspects of their work life; to give them respectability.[18]

Parson's view of an organization also supports the importance of the total organizational structure with its established norms and roles in determining the actual behavior of its members. Parsons contends that a social system is also a behavioral system with an organized set of behaviors of individuals that are interacting. Hence this is a pattern of roles or units of a social system. We may speak of John Jones as the mail carrier or John Jones the husband of Jane Jones. When we speak of the mail carrier, however, we are abstracting him from the marriage relationship. Hence the mail carrier is a role and not a person.[19]

The concept of role, as just described, is central to Parsons' social-system theory; and he has emphasized the great influence that the total organizational environment has on the behavior of its members. He views a social system as a plurality of individual actors interacting in a situation where there is a tendency to optimize gratification.[20]

Newell believes that as social systems become more complex, roles constitute a highly complex phenomenon with role complexity resulting from an increase in the number of different roles performed by each member of society.[21] Furthermore, he contends, role complexity is a product of interrelationships between and among the various roles and role systems.

Getzels also recognized the power of the organization over its individual members' behavior and has noted that persons acting within the framework of that social system find their activities organized by the role structure of the system.[22]

Planned organizational intervention is indeed a complex undertaking because individual roles and behavior in an organization is multidimensional and multicausal. The relationship between cause and effect of organizational behavior is complex and not always possible to ascertain. In any case, the behavior of an individual in an organization is more than just the expression of the individual; it is the expression of the individual, but it is also influenced by the particular situation. *Behavior* therefore reflects the *person,* the aspects of the situation he or she is in, and the interactions among all three.[23] Hence, in considering planned change in an organization, it is insufficient to analyze only the individual's behavior without relating the analysis to the whole situation in which the behavior occurred. Such a requirement is challenging, thus demanding that a strong analytic-conceptual base such as social-systems theory undergirds planning efforts.

Groups Within the Organization

In this section we move from the individual to groups within the organization as a means of understanding more about educational planning through the organizational process aproach. We shall view a group as an open-interaction system in which actions and activities determine the system structure and successive interactions exert equal effects on the identity of the system.[24]

There are several classifications of groups in organizations. Two general classifications of groups are formal and informal, while command groups, task groups, interest groups, and friendship groups add to the specificity of classification whereby we can differentiate among those that are sanctioned by the organization. Rogers presents an overview of formal groups that are created to achieve specific goals and perform activities necessary for the organization to achieve its objectives. He has said that formal groups are established on the basis of rationality and logic and may be either permanent or temporary.[25] Two examples of permanent groups in an educational organization are departments of educational administration (higher education) and departments of school supervision (for example, instructional supervision, plant supervision, and transportation supervision in public schools). Temporary formal groups, those established to perform a one-time service, are known as ad hoc committees, task forces, and so on. Informal groups are neither designed or structured by the organization but arise out of a combination of human needs influenced by management philosophy of the formal organization or the need for social contact.

Additional group distinctions have been discussed by Robbins as a means to highlight those that are sanctioned by the organization.[26] He has outlined this subclassification by Sayles[27] as command, task, interest, and friendship. The command group, specified by the organization chart, is a group of subordinates that reports to a superior, for example, professors in a department who report to a specific department head. Task groups, the second classification, are sanctioned by the organization since they work cooperatively in completing a task. For example, the dissertation committee of a graduate student may be composed of members from several departments in a university where the dean of the graduate school has the final decision regarding acceptance of the dissertation. Interest groups, the third categorization, include persons who share a common interest in achieving an objective. An example of this categorization is a group of teachers attending a board meeting in support of a student who has been suspended from school. The fourth classification is friendship groups, characterized by social allegiances such as alumni groups working at the same school or university whose purpose may be to support an athletic team representing their alma mater. As noted by Robbins, these four classifications may have frequent overlap, and they are not necessarily dysfunctional because they are not sanctioned formally. He adds that an overdependence on formal-group functioning may be dysfunctional in achieving organizational objectives since the informal groups can provide such benefits as alleviating deficiencies in the formal structure.[28]

Behling and Schriesheim discuss the nature of groups in organizations pointing to the fact that relationships among group members influence their behavior on the job.[29] They approach the concept of group cohesion through the work of Elton Mayo,[30] Schacter,[31] and Thibaut and Kelley[32] by first emphasizing that the nature of our modern society has destroyed most of the sources of affiliative need satisfaction once available in more simple societies. They emphasize that Mayo's hypothesis of group behavior as an attempt to satisfy affiliative needs and expand this concept through Schacter's work, which focused on the concept that anxiety derived from deprivation or threats related to needs other than affiliation, thus endangering cohesion in work groups. Anxiety in work groups, they reveal, produces cohesion on the part of employees, stemming from the usefulness of coalitions as weapons in work competition for resources necessary for need satisfaction of individual members.

Prestige differentiation, another characteristic of work groups, often is revealed in pecking orders where certain individuals are deferred to. Prestige positions whether high or low, have certain rewards permitting the emergence of accepted rankings of individuals. Therefore, if the administrative planner understands the hierarchies within the groups he or she leads, important channels for influencing employee behavior may be revealed. Some prestige symbols are revealed through new office furniture or a new typewriter instead of hand-me-downs, first-name relationships with superiors, and the first to read the department copy of *The Chronicle of Higher Education*. These are ways of telling others where one stands within the group.

What forces affect groups and individuals? Perhaps this concern can help us understand how groups behave as well as how they develop goals and achieve cohesiveness and productivity. Newell [33] discusses the proposition by Schutz [34] that a group follows the same psychological laws as a person and a person follows the same psychological laws as a group. This theory, according to Newell, suggests that what is known about group psychology is also known about individual psychology and vice versa. Hence, "the theory implies . . . that since it is known that each person perceives situations and events in an individualistic and unique way, so each group perceives in a unique way . . . ." [35] Thus, according to this proposition we may say that what a planner knows about individual psychology can also be comparable to group psychology and the inverse is also true.

The intensity of the strength of forces that unites a group has been called *cohesion*. Robbins says that cohesion is the attraction that the group has to its members. [36] Cohesiveness depends on the alignment of the group with organizational goals. When the goals of a cohesive group parallel organizational goals, this groups will work toward organization goals, and a cohesive group will be more productive when it has confidence in the organization. [37] By holding high standards for entrance into a group, cohesiveness is maintained; on the other hand, when admission of poorly qualified members is allowed, cohesiveness may be affected.

If a group is hostile toward an organization, productivity or at least its quality will be affected negatively. Hostility by the group may cause goals different from those of the organization to evolve, resulting in less productivity. A group can reduce productivity as a united front, but the individual may be afraid to deviate from standards of behavior because of reduced security. If a member deviates from the group norm through social sanctions and rewards, the group can bring the deviant member into line.[38] Group influence, which causes the individual to align with group behavior, results in conformity.

In group situations, when people find that they are in the minority on an issue, many yield or conform to avoid going against the group. One reason for this is the fear of hostility or isolation from the group. A person in a group may also conform through observing leaders and following or imitating their actions.[39]

Leadership Within the Organization

Perhaps one of the best-known definitions of leadership has been presented by Hemphill, who regards leadership as initiating a structure-in-interaction as part of the process of solving problems.[40] In the group situation Fiedler observes that a leader is that person who has the task of directing and coordinating task-relevant group activities.[41] Lipham views a leader as one who initiates new procedures for achieving or changing organizational goals.[42] For the educational planner, whom we shall also define as a leader, there are the tasks of directing as well as coordinating problem-solving activities and initiating procedures for achieving organizational goals and objectives. If we can visualize the planner as an administrator, which is ideal in our thinking, then the dimension of decision making is inherent to our leadership concept. Hence, the planner would perhaps have more influence on planned intervention and on the selection of optimal alternatives in light of organizational complexities. By forwarding the notion that the planner is a leader and an administrator with decision-making powers, we may also think of him or her with the responsibility for establishing policies for the organization.

With the proposal that the planner is a leader, we shall now take a brief look at some theories of leadership that may assist our conceptualization of the educational planner.

The trait theory, one of the most widely studied theories of leadership, seeks to specify what definable traits make a successful leader. Thus, by possessing a certain number of desirable traits, it may be possible for these traits to predict natural leadership ability. Stogdill, however, in an extensive review of research through 1948, concluded that a person does not become a leader by virtue of possessing certain traits, but that the personal characteristics of the leader must have a relationship to the goals, activities, and characteristics of the followers.[43] Another thorough review of leadership studies by Stogdill, reported in 1974, showed that certain characteristics or traits considered independently have little predictive significance in determining a leader.[44] For example, some of these characteristics of the leader are identified as a strong drive for responsibility, a strong drive for task completion, and persistence in the pursuit of goals.

Based on studies such as those described here, it is perhaps a wise observation that the trait theory of leadership is limited, although it does provide a foundation from which to begin leadership conceptualization. There appears to be variables of interaction among individuals, organizational tasks, and other relevant elements involving human characteristics that also relate to leadership effectiveness. Some studies have been conducted under the assumption that production-centered and employee-centered aspects of leader behavior are single dimensional. Hence, as leaders became more person oriented, they are less production oriented with the inverse also being true. However, it was found that instead of a single dimension, there are two—one production oriented the other person oriented. Thus, it has been proposed that a leader may be production oriented and people oriented simultaneously.

From these two dimensions of leadership we have seen numerous concepts emerge, one of which is situational theory. Perhaps the most popular conceptualizations of two fundamental dimensions of leadership behavior has been presented by Halpin as initiating structure and consideration.[45] Initiating structure describes the relationship between the leader and the workgroup, while establishing patterns of organization, procedural methods, and channels of communication. On the other hand, consideration reflects friendly behavior, mutual trust, respect, and warmth in the relationship between the work group and the leader.

One of the most popular measures of leadership behavior emerging from the two-dimensional concept of leadership is the Leader Behavior Description Questionnaire (LBDQ) developed by Hemphill and Coons.[46] This instrument measures the dimensions entitled initiating structure and consideration. In his book on theory and research in administration, Halpin summarizes some major findings resulting from LBDQ studies.[47] He has shown that initiating structure and consideration are fundamentals of leader behavior and that the effective leader tends to be associated with high performance on both dimensions. Superiors tend to emphasize initiating structure, while subordinates are concerned more with consideration. Leadership style characterized as high on both dimensions is related to group characteristics such as intimacy, harmony, and procedural clarity. Furthermore, only a slight relationship was found between how leaders say they should behave and how subordinates say they do behave. However, different institutional settings tend to support different leadership styles.

According to Newell it appears that the type of leadership varies in accordance with the given situation.[48] Likewise, research indicates that to be effective, leadership style must be appropriate to the situation.

Approaches to leadership revealing that employee-centered supervision style may be the best have been illustrated by Likert.[49] His research efforts were based on rigorous quantitative approaches and in the place of the cruder methods available previously. Likert's methodology aimed at measuring dimensions of organizational functioning such as motivational forces, decision-making processes, and effectiveness of communication. He has conducted numerous studies to discover the organizational structure and the principles and methods of leadership and management that result in better overall performance. These studies have been designed to measure leadership in the best parts of the organization and compare their results with leadership used in the poorest components. Administrative effectiveness was also evaluated by Likert on variables such as job satisfaction, motivation, absence, productivity, and success in achieving organizational goals. He has concluded that leadership style is more important in influencing results than factors such as attitudes toward the organization and interest in the job.

Hersey and Blanchard, however, contend that this general trend toward employee-centered as the best model of leadership may not necessarily mean that there is one universally superior style of leadership.[50] Recognizing that leadership effectiveness depends on how leader behavior interrelates with a given situation, Hersey and Blanchard have tied to the task and relationships dimensions a third dimension called *effectiveness.* Thus their tridimensional, linear model attempts to integrate the concept of leader style with situational demands of an environment. According to their model, when a leader's style is right for a given environment measured by results, it is called "effective" and vice versa.

Out of the tridimensional model has grown the life-cycle theory. This theory is based on a curvilinear relationship between structure and consideration and maturity. The life-cycle theory provides the leader with some understanding of the relationship between an effective style of leadership and the level of maturity of the leader's followers. As the level of maturity of the followers increases, leader behavior requires less structure while consideration is increased and socioemotional support decreases. Hence, this theory suggests the right mix of relationship and task behaviors for the level of maturity of the followers.

There are two obvious limitations in these theories. First, it is implicit that individuals are flexible enough in their respective organizations to participate in the proper combination of behaviors at will. Hersey and Blanchard use the word *style* in describing their model when they actually discuss behavior. Fiedler has studied situational elements having the dimensions of interpersonal relationships, task definition, and power of the leader.[51] Perhaps the linearity of his model and others has caused confusion since task and human orientation have been placed on opposite ends of a continuum. An extension of the Fiedler model shows task behavior and relationship behavior as used to further describe initiating structure and consideration, which were discussed earlier in this chapter. Fiedler's contingency model falls into the interactional or situational approach. What he wanted to know is how one becomes an effective leader. Situational theory is aimed at discovering those variables that either allow or cause various behavior and leader characteristics to be effective.[52]

Fiedler's work has been directed toward discovering specific situations in which various leadership styles are most effective. Instead of discussing how an individual becomes a leader, Fiedler focuses on the assumption that given an individual is a leader, what behaviors or traits will make him or her a more effective leader? He deals with the underlying needs of the leader that motivate behavior, given the fact that leader behavior does not necessarily change as a situation changes.

Summary

Viewing the organization and its subsystems as contrived social systems allows the planner to be cognizant of forces that interact to bring about change. Yet these forces are brought about by individuals or groups acting in a given role set and not by persons in a social vacuum. Thus, it is important to know that individual behavior is often the result of the setting or atmosphere within the organization. Likewise group behavior may be influenced by organizational environment.

We are not surprised to learn that leadership is also a function of organizational situations, and in the latter part of this chapter we outlined some approaches to leadership. The trait theory has been presented as a way to explain leadership on the basis of what a leader is, while group and behavioral theory make an effort to delineate leadership on the basis of what a leader does. Situational theory, however, is directed toward discovering situational variables that permit a leader to be effective. There are in many cases considerable overlap as noted in tridimensional model and life-cycle theories where we note the overlap of situational and behavioral variables. In fact, in many cases we see spin-offs from the trait theory implanted in group, behavioral, and situational theories.

Notes

1. William G. Scott, "Organizational Theory: An Overview and Appraisal," *Managerial Behavior and Organizational Demands: Management as a Linking of Levels of Interaction,* eds. Robert T. Golembiewski

and Frank Gibson (Chicago: Rand McNally and Company, 1967), pp. 22–35.

2. Daniel Katz and Robert Kahn, *The Social Psychology of Organizations* (New York: Wiley, 1966).

3. Wayne K. Hoy and Cecil G. Miskel, *Educational Administration: Theory, Research and Practice* (New York: Random House, 1978), p. 123.

4. Ibid., pp. 135–136.

5. Ibid., p. 120.

6. Douglas McGregor, *The Human Side of Enterprise* (New York: McGraw-Hill, 1960), pp. 34–48.

7. Rolf E. Rogers, *Organizational Theory* (Boston, Mass.: Allyn and Bacon, 1975), p. 109.

8. Abraham H. Maslow, "A Theory of Human Motivation," *Psychological Review* 50 (1943):370–396.

9. Rogers, *Organizational Theory*, p. 115.

10. Ibid., pp. 104–105; 110–113; and D.C. McClelland, *The Achieving Society* (Princeton: Van Nostrand, 1961).

11. F. Herzberg, B. Mausner, and B. Snyderman, *The Motivation to Work*, 2d ed. (New York: Wiley, 1959).

12. Hoy and Miskel, *Educational Administration*, pp. 102–108.

13. Katz and Kahn, *The Social Psychology of Organizations*, p. 391. Reprinted with permission.

14. Ibid., p. 407.

15. Ibid.

16. Floyd C. Mann, "Studying and Creating Change," (Industrial Relations Research Association, Publication No. 17, 1957), pp. 146–147; as quoted by Paul C. Buchanan in "The Concept of Organization Development, or Self-Renewal, as a Form of Planned Change," ed. Goodwin Watson, *Concepts for Social Change* (Washington, D.C.: National Education Association, National Training Laboratories for Applied Behavioral Science, Cooperative Project for Educational Development, 1967), p. 5.

17. Donald C. Pelz, "Influence: A Key to Effective Leadership in the First-Line Supervisor," *Studies in Personnel and Industrial Psychology*, ed. Edwin A. Fleishman (Homewood, Ill.: The Dorsey Press, 1967), pp. 407–414.

18. From *Social Psychology of the Work Organization*, by A.S. Tannenbaum. Copyright © 1966 by Wadsworth, Inc. Reprinted by permission of the publisher, Brooks/Cole Publishing Company, Monterey, California and the author, p. 83.

19. Talcott Parsons, "Boundary Relations Between Sociocultural and Personality Systems," *Toward a Unified Theory of Human Behavior*, ed. Roy R. Grinker (New York: Basic Books, 1956), p. 328.

20. Talcott Parsons, *The Social System* (New York: The Free Press, 1951), pp. 5–6.

21. Clarence A. Newell, *Human Behavior in Educational Administration* (Englewood Cliffs, N.J.: Prentice-Hall, 1978) p. 154.

22. Jacob W. Getzels, James M. Lipham, and Roald F. Campbell, *Educational Administration as a Social Process* (New York: Harper and Row, 1968), p. 61.

23. Paul C. Buchanan, "The Concept of Organization Development, or Self-Renewal, as a Form of Planned Change," *Concepts for Social Change,* ed. Goodwin Watson (Washington, D.C.: National Education Association, National Training Laboratories for Applied Behavioral Science, 1967), p. 5.

24. Ralph M. Stogdill, *Individual Behavior and Group Achievement* (New York: Oxford University Press, 1959), p. 18.

25. Rogers, *Organizational Theory,* pp. 118–120.

26. Stephen P. Robbins, *The Administrative Process: Integrating Theory and Practice* (Englewood Cliffs, N.J.: Prentice-Hall, 1976), pp. 280–282.

27. Leonard R. Sayles, "Research in Industrial Human Relations," in *Industrial Relations Research Association* (New York: Harper and Row, 1957), pp. 131–145. As quoted in Robbins, *The Administrative Process.*

28. Robbins, *The Administrative Process*, p. 282.

29. Orlando Behling and Chester Schriesheim, *Organizational Behavior: Theory, Research, and Application* (Boston, Mass.: Allyn and Bacon, 1976), pp. 114–137.

30. Elton Mayo, *The Human Problems of an Industrial Civilization* (Cambridge, Mass.: Graduate School of Business Administration, Harvard University, 1933).

31. Stanley Schacter, *The Psychology of Affiliation* (Stanford, Calif.: Stanford University Press, 1959).

32. J.W. Thibaut and H.H. Kelley, *The Social Psychology of Groups* (New York: Wiley, 1959).

33. Newell, *Human Behavior,* p. 83.

34. William C. Schutz, "The Ego, FIRO Theory and the Leader as Completer," in *Leadership and Interpersonal Behavior,* eds. Luigi Petrullo and Barnard M. Bass (New York: Holt, Rinehart and Winston, 1961), pp. 48–65; Ibid., p. 83.

35. Clarence A. Newell, *Human Behavior in Educational Administration,* © 1978, p. 83. Reprinted by permission of Prentice-Hall, Inc., Englewood Cliffs, New Jersey.

36. Robbins, *The Administrative Process,* p. 290.

37. Stanley E. Seashore, *Group Cohesiveness in the Industrial Work Group* (Ann Arbor: University of Michigan, Survey Research Center, 1954), pp. 193–194.

38. Rogers, *Organizational Theory,* pp. 126–127.

39. Ibid., p. 128.

40. John K. Hemphill, "Administration as Problem Solving," in *Administrative Theory in Education* ed. Andrew W. Halpin, (New York: Macmillan, 1967), pp. 96–98.

41. Fred E. Fiedler, *A Theory of Leadership Effectiveness* (New York: McGraw-Hill, 1967), p. 8.

42. James M. Lipham, "Leadership and Administration," in Daniel E. Griffiths, ed., *Behavioral Science and Educational Administration,* Sixty-Third Yearbook, National Society for the Study of Education (Chicago: University of Chicago Press, 1964), pp. 120–123.

43. Ralph M. Stogdill, "Personal Factors Associated with Leadership: A Survey of the Literature," *The Journal of Psychology* 25 (1948):35–71.

44. Ralph M. Stogdill, *Handbook of Leadership: A Survey of Theory and Research* (New York: The Free Press, 1974).

45. Andrew W. Halpin, *Theory and Research in Administration* (New York: The Macmillan Company, 1966), pp. 86–90.

46. John K. Hemphill and Alvin E. Coons, *Leader Behavior Description* (Columbus: Personnel Research Board, Ohio State University, 1950). As cited in Hoy and Miskel, *Educational Administration,* p. 181.

47. Halpin, *Theory and Research*, pp. 97–98.

48. Newell, *Human Behavior,* p. 233.

49. Rensis Likert, *New Patterns of Management* (New York: McGraw-Hill Book Company, 1961), pp. 5–60.

50. Paul Hersey and Kenneth H. Blanchard, *Management of Organizational Behavior: Utilizing Human Resources,* 3d ed. (Englewood Cliffs, N.J.: Prentice-Hall, 1977), pp. 101–108.

51. Fiedler, *A Theory of Leadership Effectiveness,* p. 147.

52. Alan C. Filley and Robert J. House, *Managerial Processes and Organizational Behavior* (Glenview, Ill.: Scott, Foresman, 1969), p. 396.

6 Decision Making

How does the decision-making process function in an organization viewed as a contrived social system and just where do the administrative planners fit into the complex organizational change process? Since we are proposing a modification of the rationalist point of view that basically assumes a unitary decision maker, a comprehensive definition of the decision-making role is propsed. Hence, we turn to the concept of multiple decision makers described by Allison as "a constellation of loosely allied organizations on top of which . . . leaders sit; this constellation acts only when component organizations perform routines."[1] Hence, we may envision an environment in which decisions are made in an open, dynamic, contrived social system that is not purely a bureaucracy and not totally decentralized.

One basic assumption stemming from this apperception is that decisions are made by humans lacking complete knowledge—decisions affecting the behavior of other humans. If these decisions are to have relevance and value in effecting planned change in the organization and the environment where interaction is continuous, they must be implemented in the organization as it really operates. The description of an organization by Bozeman and Rossi as "a loosely coupled amalgram of units with increased differentiation and specialization leading to: (1) detailed, though highly segmented, views of problems; (2) parochial objectives and priorities; (3) diffuse power, and; (4) outcomes structured by form and routine,"[2] is also appropriate for our conceptualization of the educational organization.

Pervasive power in the organization, diffuse power, and Bennis's conceptualization of power distribution[3] are descriptors that we shall associate with power bases. In chapter 2 we introduced five power bases, proposed by French and Raven, as coercive power, reward power, referent power, legitimate power, and expert power.[4] These bases are characterized in table 6-1, and we shall assume that the various decision makers, leaders, or administrative planners within the organization shall have varying degrees of each distinction depending on their behavioral patterns, roles, and relationships among the interacting forces of the environment. Furthermore, we shall assume that these leaders are operating in an open system where authority is defined as the probability that a decision in the face of resistance will be adhered to by an individual or group.[5]

Empirical evidence leads us to believe that the two most appropriate power bases for administrative planners in educational organizations are

Table 6–1
Power Bases for Decision Making

Power-base Descriptor	General Characteristics
Coercive power	Used by leaders to cause required behavior; if decision is not adhered to, punishment is administered; if decision is adhered to, positive compensation is not necessarily the result.
Reward power	Used by leaders to effect desired behavior; when decisions are not adhered to, reward is diminished; if the maximum reward is not given or promised, the followers may not wish to conform; if overcompensation results, the followers may take advantage of the leaders whereby dysfunctions may result.
Reference power	Based on follower's identification with leader's decision; if if followers conform, it is a result of their desire to identify with the leaders; followers believe and perceive as leaders do; the followers have a desire to emulate and respect for the leaders.
Legitimate power	Based on willingness of the followers to ignore their own judgments in light of knowledge possessed by the leaders; if power in the contrived social system is perceived as legitimate by the followers and if the decision makers are also perceived as legitimate, then the decisions will be accepted as legitimate.
Expert power	Founded on expertise or decision makers' knowledge; if the leaders have special knowledge in a given area and do not exceed this limited range, the followers will accept the expert decisions.

Source: Adapted from John P. French, Jr., and Bertram Raven, "The Bases of Social Power," in *Group Dynamics: Research and Theory,* eds. Dorwin Cartwright and A.F. Zanders (New York: Row, Peterson, 1960).

expert and legitimate. Since expertise is highly desirable in the educational community, it would be difficult for us to speculate otherwise since academic accomplishment is a significant way of proving one's ability. Obviously, coercive, the least desirable power base, has been utilized in instances as the last resort to acquire group or individual approval of decisions. This unpopular approach may frequently be attached to insecure or careless decision makers who withhold information from their subordinates and work through hidden agendas. We did not wish to give the reader a false impression of power or suggest that power is undesirable for it is, indeed, necessary for the effective functioning of a contrived social system or organization. Power may best be perceived as a means for achieving organizational goals and hopefully planners in charge of decision making will work most frequently from the bases of power identified as expert or legitimate. We see diffuse power as being manifest through relationships among individuals as well as inherent in the administrative planner's positions of authority within the organization.

One role of administrative planners is indeed decision making; otherwise we see planners as those who plan for the sake of planning. Decision making leads to implementation for positive change when the planning has been done right. Yet even with good planning where the neighborhoods of alternatives are presented and even weighted quantitatively, we observe in some contexts that the decision is said to have been optimized. But in reality where administrators utilize knowledge of the organizational process, they tend to satisfice instead of optimize.[6] The result then is perhaps best described as the optimal "feasible" decision where "feasible" may indicate that the quantitatively optimal decision was not selected because of compromise or some anticipated problem tied to this choice. From this observation we can assume that totally rational decisions are frequently impossible because of organizational constraints and because complete knowledge of the environment is frequently incomplete. Thus we believe that it is important for educational planners to be knowledgeable of the organizational process in order to make better decisions.

Administrative planning, which includes but is not limited to the decision-making process, follows the general areas of administration identified by Litchfield as policy, resources, and execution.[7] Those activities encompassing the analysis, formulation, and implementation of the purpositive operations of the educational sector and the ideology supported by these actions, according to Levin, may be exemplified as policy.[8] Hoy and Miskel describe policy as objectives that actually guide the activities or actions of the total organization.[9] Underlying this definition is the assumption that the policy-making process is a major focus for specialized inquiry. However, according to Lindblom the method of inquiry into this process is still so new that no one seems to want to answer the question of what is included in it.[10] Hence, we may be led to believe that a policy is made through a sequence of well-defined steps, which may be true to a certain degree. Furthermore, to view policy making as though it were the product of one governing mind is simply not the case in a contrived social system such as public and higher education. The step-by-step method may overlook the political aspects of policy making, its apparent disorder, the consequent strikingly different ways in which policies emerge,[11] and the perspective of diffuse power bases.

A policy may be reached through political compromise among groups called policy makers functioning in a given organization. Policies may evolve from new opportunities, not necessarily from problems, and we must note that policies may just happen without any decision at all.[12] No one would say that the state governments planned the recent gasoline shortage; yet tolerating the shortage was established as policy without any explicit decision. The odd and even days for sales and maximum purchases were only devised to minimize frustrations. Because policy making is an extremely complex analytical as well as political process to which there is no beginning or end, the boundaries are most uncertain. Yet a complex set of forces we call "policy making," taken collectively, produces results we call "policies."[13]

Administrative planners may view policy making resulting from organizational problems as a function of transactive planning in an open system. Remembering Lewins' conceptualization of the change process over time,[14] perhaps the formal aspect of policy making can be characterized as illustrated in figure 6-1. This somewhat generic description reveals a dynamic interaction process whereby as the environment progresses through time (t_0 to t_n) certain value forces ($\longleftrightarrow$) act on and interact with the policy process. When needs arise, they are addressed through transformation into parochial objectives and priorities resulting in policy decisions for the implementation of change. In each of these three general categories, we should reemphasize how the value systems of the environment influence not only the conceptualization of the problems but also the transformation process and policy decisions as well. Again we shall inject the notion that policy decisions may not be optimal since the elements of competition, conflict, and compromise are present throughout the process. Reaction to policy implementation shall be interpreted as open sequence providing new insights into transformation, problems, and needs. Here we have avoided those policies that just happen without decision and those that evolve from what we shall call "common knowledge." For example, those unwritten policies of not openly criticizing the organization in the presence of outsiders or of contributing a percentage of income to a local charity are common knowledge and expectations in many educational organizations.

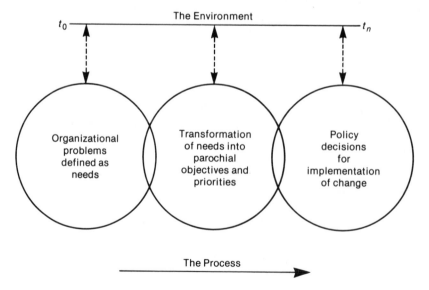

Figure 6-1. Policy Formulation Based on Problems

Litchfield's second functional area of administration, resource allocation, includes the commonly known elements such as money, supplies, facilities, materials, and people. However, since we are investigating the nature of decision making and how it relates to administrative planning, the assumption of diffuse power, presented earlier in this chapter, emerges as an important factor in the allocation of resources. The executive function then is designated as a means of integrating policy decisions with resource-allocation requirements while dealing with values and conflicts through compromise from some power base in the environment that is constantly changing and influencing human values. From this general classification of administrative functions, we shall add planning since it is present in each of the three classifications and ties the functions of administration to the administrative process.

Table 6-2 illustrates the connection between administrative functions and process. Policy making, allocating resources, and the executive function show the purpose or the intent of administration, while organizing, stimulating, and evaluation imply procedures or methods. Yet planning, as we see it, is administrative intent as well as a method or means of administration. Therefore, what is done and how it is done complement the decision-making process.

The Administrative Process

Some assumptions of power and authority and a general classification of administrative functions have been presented in order to lay the framework

Table 6-2
Planning as the Connection Between Functions and Process of Administration

Classification	Administrative Activity
	Policy Making
Functions	Allocating Resources
	Executive
	Planning
	Organizing
Process	Stimulating
	Evaluating

for four general classifications of the administrative process designated by Lipham and Hoeh as planning, organizing, stimulating, and evaluating.[15]

One basic assumption that we hold is that planning is a function of administration. *Planning* includes but is not limited to the development of objectives and the specification of how these objectives are to be reached. In the organizational context, we simply define objectives as the statements of direction toward which all organizational activities are aimed. Ideally, individual and group objectives complement organizational objectives.

Generally both the planning process and the administrative process have been viewed as ways conducive to determining goals, specifying objectives, developing strategies, and making long-range decisions.[16] Perhaps because of the overlap between these two processes, the concept of administrative planning has emerged. One way to exemplify administrative planning is through the study of the implementation process of management by objectives (MBO), which has been interpreted in light of the administrative process as administering through objectives. The MBO concept will be discussed in part III of this text.

Coordinating resources through the organizational structure for the purpose of achieving objectives has been described as *organizing*. Thus the common tie between planning and organizing is the thrust toward the achievement of organizational objectives. Lipham and Hoeh have characterized organizing as the process of making a plan operational.[17] Operational in this context implies implementation, an activity involving the statement of what task is to be completed, who is to complete the task, and specifying when the task is to be completed; and if necessary, delineating how much the implementation phase will cost.

The concept of a contrived social system's operating as an open system has been shown to be an element of importance in organizing. For example, the recognition that the organization, interdependent with its environment, may have difficulty in adapting to rapid environmental changes is paramount. Furthermore, the behaviors of individuals and groups must be harmonized if the organization achieves or gets close to achieving its objectives. Also power and authority relationships have their influence on whether or not the organization reaches its desired state or the neighborhood of objectives. Knowledge of power relationships and influence of groups and individuals within the organization provide administrative planners with the proper orientation for stimulating members to work toward objectives. *Stimulating* involves those decisions that are aimed at encouraging or motivating individuals to identify with planned objectives, enhancing job satisfaction, providing supportive relationships, and influencing organizational members to change.[18] This phase of the administrative process has been designated as leadership, which has been discussed in chapter 5.

The broad concept of evaluating is outlined here as the fourth phase of the administrative process. *Evaluating* may be broadly interpreted as the process of appraising the organizational inputs, process, and outputs in order to determine if certain specified standards have been met. Evaluating involves a continuous process of measuring the organizational achievements against organizational expectations. The gap between achievements and expectations has been called *need*. In chapter 12 we present an example of an intervention (a program of planned change) in an educational organization and show how the effectiveness of the intervention is measured.

The Rational Systems Approach

Decision processes based on plans resulting from the rational systems approach to problem solving have been abundant in recent years. Many of these processes have served to minimize the distance between purely rational methodology and the organizational and political models. A systems approach to problem solving that parallels the synoptic planning process in chapter 1 has been presented by Tanner,[19] which includes nine basic steps as follows:

1. Problem or subproblem definition
2. Data collection
3. Analysis
4. Solution design
5. Solution evaluation
6. Feasible solution? If yes, continue; If no, go to steps 1, 2, 3, 4, or 5.
7. Implement solution
8. Operate
9. New problems? Monitor or recycle to any step from 1 through 5.

These nine steps are straightforward where the process may be followed from the definition stage through the operational phase. Recycling and continuous testing for feasibility are integral components of this procedure. Largely ignored in this method were the political and organizational characteristics as well as incremental, transactive, advocacy, and radical planning theories.

The rational systems approach reached its highest level of popularity in the 1960s especially in the field of management science, and was introduced in educational organizations over a decade ago as a way of approaching decision making logically. Rational models emerged from works by Simon,[20] among others, as a response to the limitations of human capacity in dealing with large, complex organizations. The rational approach assumes maximum efficiency of decision making in light of expertise, abundant information, and a high degree of authority.

One major limitation of the rational-actor model when applied to an educational organization is in the assumption that decision making is unitary, which is not the case in decentralized operations. Another drawback is its assumption of a single set of objectives with decision-making functions centered on fitting alternatives to the highest returns. In the rational economic and highly centralized organization, the model is perhaps appropriate, but in a contrived and open social system, where we find the abundance of mixed motives, calculated ambiguities, and limited amounts of information, too frequently it is not appropriate in its purest form.[21] Under the rational systems model, decision making is straightforward, that is, steps progress and recycling occurs where maximization is the dominant criterion for choice.

Central to the appeal of the rational systems approach is the ease with which it is applied to structuring and quantifying alternatives. Models of choice permitting explicit comparisons associated with policy alternatives are not as understandable in the educational environment as in a closed, tight system. Objectives in the educational complex, at most are only parochial, subject to change with the environment, which means that rational models may be too simple and straightforward. Hence, with major constraints on the capacity of planning methodologies to examine all conceivable policy outcomes, where limited information is the rule rather than the exception, the model of rationality can lay claim at best to only limited rationality.[22]

We do not intend to mislead the reader and leave the impression that we are proposing to leap into the world of biorythms, drugs, ouija boards, mysticism, and idolatry, forsaking the systems approach and operations research. What we are emphasizing is the not-too-obvious limitations of our ambitious models. There is indeed a place in modern organizations for models such as MBO, program-evaluation-review technique (PERT), Delphi, needs assessment, and many, many others; however, these alone have left planners poorly equipped to deal with the complexities of the organizational process with its political interactions and conflict-ridden actions.

The Organizational-Process Model

One basic assumption of the organizational-process approach to decision making centers on the multitude of actors with fractional or dispersed power (multiple ratios and bases). These leading men and women working in an open and dynamic social system ensure specialized, diffuse problems including turf protection, organizational jealousies, matters of control, special interests, red-tape guidelines, coupled with frequently out-of-date reward systems.[23] The organizational-process approach adopts a predominantly proactive view of the organization and its environment, assuming interactive responses between the environment and the organization. We also observe that the organizational-process approach emphasizes transactive planning.

An example of diffuse power held by multiple actors employing transactive planning can be observed within a decentralized higher education system. For example, consider the College of Education, College of Liberal Arts, and College of Business in a university as a complex organization as shown in figure 6-2. Although the chart presents only one slice of the complex university setting, we can illustrate the diffuse power and authority relationships. Assume within the College of Education that a department goal is to propose a new program in educational planning. First, at the department level, elements of the program are specified (for example,

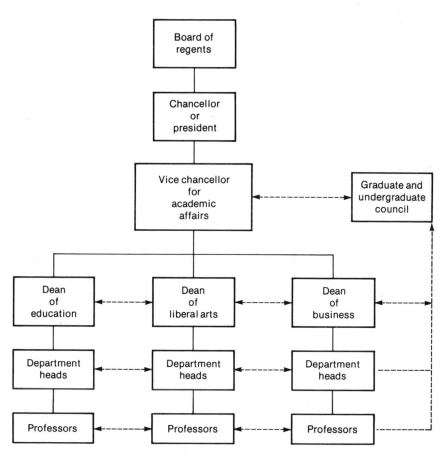

Figure 6-2. An Open Social System with Multiple Actors

courses, how the program complements the university objectives of service, research, and teaching; credit hours, prerequisites, and so on), often through compromise (because of turf protection among the departmental professors) and after several attempts, approval is gained. But the new program is simply a proposal at this phase since the professors in liberal arts and business must be consulted because the program may contain courses including statistics, operations research, organization theory, and politics. Here professors, department heads, and deans in all three colleges frequently represented by special interest or formal committees again scrutinize the proposal for process and content that may reflect among other things, intraorganizational jealousies, turf protection highlighted by red tape and power plays. Thus conflict, compromise, and games of action are employed in the name of academic excellence to modify the educational planning proposal once more before university approval is gained.

Through organizational routine the program finally reaches the graduate and undergraduate council. The program may now be a far cry from its initial inception, but again it may be changed, especially if there is the probability of more overlap than deemed necessary. At this stage of development and modification, the program may have been in the proposal stage for at least an academic year, and yet to be accepted and approved by the vice chancellor for academic affairs, who after review may forward it to the chancellor or send it back to the graduate council. Upon acceptance by the chancellor, the program proposal is forwarded to the governing body where final approval and adoption rests. Thus upon final approval by the board a new program involving policies is sent back in the form of a written document to the department for implementation.

We must admit that this complex trip from conceptualization to implementation is time consuming, but we are not saying that the process is bad. In fact, the final proposal may be much better in the end than in its original state. At least it has had the red-tape treatment, survived many power plays, and games, all of which are not only part of the organizational process but also functions of the bureaucratic politics model of action and transactive planning.

If the originating department adopts a proactive view of the university bureaucracy and its environment and is willing to put forth the effort and time, planned change can be effected. On the other hand, a purely reactive approach to planning by the department would possibly spell defeat for the program of planned change. It is therefore exceedingly wise for the administrative planner to understand at the outset where the conflicts may emerge and how the power bases of competing colleges, departments, and professors exist in the environment. It is not beyond comprehension to see either positive or negative forces from outside the university such as alumni groups acting on the organizational change.

From the preceding example we have observed not only process but output of a complex organization. Thus the planning process was "guided less by the maximization of definable goals than by the way the organization does things."[24] Hence, the objective was pursued as a function of organizational routines, taking into account matters of organizational health (Will my department be adversely affected?), as well as the values of the professors and deans (organizational actors) where the problem of control certainly entered the process through questions regarding student enrollment and additional costs.

The importance of standard operating procedures (SOPs)[25] must not be overlooked in the organizational process approach. SOPs may provide an enabling structure, lending some regularity to higher order tasks such as preparing policy responses by producing reports. In our example we noted that the output carried with it policy statements such as prerequisites and entrance requirements that were revealed in the production of a final document describing the new program. This document, in part a product of SOPs, served as an initial point for departmental implementation and operation. Although the SOPs were followed and conceivably seen as constraints (including special interests, matters of control, compromise, and so on), they may be perceived as adding sluggishness that is less common where more centralized and directed executive control exists.[26]

The politics of getting the decision of program approval in our example is an interesting yet important variable where compromises of special-interest groups were inevitable. According to Allison, "outcomes are the results of compromise, conflict, and confusion of officials with diverse interests and unequal influence."[27] He also contends that the assumption of competition may be fundamental and that SOPs or routines serve to aggregate parochial priorities and objectives that may be partially a result of political give and take. The decisional outcome in our example represents the fusion of politics and organizational process since both reflect the values of winning coalitions and routine procedure.

Our example illustrates that planned educational change depends on factors of organizational structure and political relationships that often respond slowly to rationality. The administrative planner must be able to adapt to the political process as well as the organizational process that are recognized infrequently and often poorly understood.

The Organizational Process and Planning Theories

Extensive knowledge of the decision-making functions employed in organizational process model is imperative for the educational planner. Furthermore, knowledge of actual practice in the organization and understanding of what ought to be are important. The administrative planner cannot be content to simply plan to maintain the organization, but he or she must be aware of the complex maze through which change is achieved. Thus we propose a model called *normative descriptive* (see figure 6-3) as an approach to decision making through the organizational process approach. Somewhere between "what is" happening and "what ought to be happening" is the neighborhood of where the decisions are made, and exactly where these choices are made depends on how important the decisions are to the actors and how each actor believes he or she will be affected. Based on the conceptualization of the organizational process, we contend that an organization is not exclusively one of humans but is also one of policies and politics.

From the literature reviewed for this text and our planning experiences, we propose eighteen major characteristics of the organizational process relative to planning and decision making. We also suggest the planning theories that are likely to complement as well as come in conflict with each of these traits in an open educational system. These categorizations, although general, are proposed as a means for understanding the relationships among the synoptic, incremental, transactive, advocacy, and radical planning traditions and the organizational process. This initial presentation may serve as a baseline for research on educational planning processes. Each organizational process descriptor is outlined first, and our comparison follows as presented below:

1. The organizational process (OP) is highly political. Because of the "give and take," "muddling through," and generally "wicked" problems dealt with in a highly political environment, the *incremental* planning tradition is suggested as the most complementary to the OP, while the synoptic approach may come in conflict with the politics of the OP because of the required interaction.

2. In the OP there are many decision makers at different levels of the organization. We contend that *transactive* planning theory is most amenable here because of its heavy emphasis on decentralized decision making. On the other hand, there is likely to be a more negative relationship between the OP and synoptic theory for the same reason.

3. Decision makers working through the OP operate from different power bases. The reasons cited in characteristic 2 above hold here as well, thus we see transactive planning as the most complementary and synoptic as having the most negative relationship with multiple power bases.

4. Decision makers involved in the OP approach have power to *influence* the opinion of others. This characteristic is perhaps a function of the individual and where he or she is in the organizational hierarchy. Hence, no clear theory classification exists for this trait.

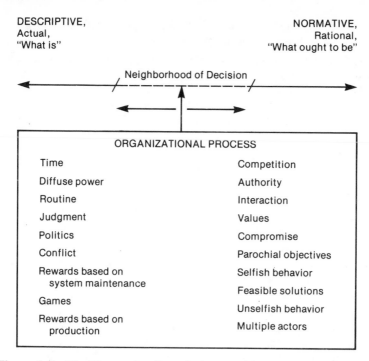

DESCRIPTIVE,   NORMATIVE,
Actual,   Rational,
"What is"   "What ought to be"

Neighborhood of Decision

ORGANIZATIONAL PROCESS

Time	Competition
Diffuse power	Authority
Routine	Interaction
Judgment	Values
Politics	Compromise
Conflict	Parochial objectives
Rewards based on system maintenance	Selfish behavior
	Feasible solutions
Games	Unselfish behavior
Rewards based on production	Multiple actors

Figure 6–3. The Normative-Descriptive Model for Decision Making

5. There is the element of *compromise* present in decision making in the OP. Both the transactive and advocacy traditions appear to be most beneficial here, and the synoptic theory is most likely to be less effective since it depends on the "best" alternative, largely ignoring individual and group reactions.

6. *Interaction* is a key ingredient of the OP. We see interaction as important ingredients in incremental, transactive, and advocacy planning theories. But this OP trait is largely ignored in the synoptic tradition.

7. The *optimal feasible solution* to a problem may be selected in the OP. This is also the case in incremental and transactive planning but not very probable under the synoptic theory.

8. The *optimal solution* to a problem may not be selected in the OP. Thus the *synoptic* approach is most appropriate in this situation. It is significant to note that the word *feasible* may be interpreted to mean less than ideal, even when expressed in quantitative terms.

9. The OP requires a considerable amount of *time*. Advocacy planning certainly parallels this characteristic, although radical, transactive, and

incremental planning require a great deal of time as well. Bargaining, inter-action, and group participation, highly characteristic of these approaches, imply the use of a considerable amount of time. Synoptic planning does not involve a huge quantity of time in comparison to the other planning approaches.

10. The OP encourages *competition* among participants. The element of competition is most readily recognized in transactive planning where face-to-face dialogue and interactive processes often prevail. Competition, however, is minimized through synoptic planning practices.

11. *Routine* is an important characteristic of the OP. Without ques-tion, the transactive approach to planning does not ignore organizational routine. This should not imply that all the SITAR traditions do, but the decentralized character of transactive planning is most conducive to rou-tine, while the synoptic theory is less dependent on standard operating pro-cedures than the other four theories.

12. *Conflict* is part of the OP. All planning theories are flavored with this trait but advocacy and radical planning exhibit this trait more fre-quently than the synoptic approach.

13. Playing *games* is a trait of the OP. First, because of the involve-ment in gaining control over the social process, we contend that transactive planning practices involve games, while this is also true to a lesser degree in incremental planning. Game playing is minimized under the synoptic tradi-tion, however.

14. In the OP *value judgments* are prevalent in establishing priorities. More value judgments are involved in incremental transactive, advocacy, and radical planning than in the synoptic or rational systems approach. This is true as much from the involvement of individuals and groups as from the lack of utilization of quantitative analysis.

15. The OP does not assume *complete information*. Synoptic planning methodologies rely heavily on "complete information," while the other four theories cannot make this claim.

16. *Parochial objectives* often result as a product of the OP. Both incremental and transactive planning theories parallel this OP trait. Col-laboration and compromise frequently yield objectives that are group norms instead of "ideal." The synoptic planning theory deplores parochial objectives since, among other things, it tends to maximize outcomes.

17. A *proactive view* of the organization is important in the OP. Taken in light of obtaining desired results in an organization, we contend that the transactive approach to planning is most amenable to the OP. Under the synoptic approach a proactive view of the OP is less important when optimization of objectives is considered.

18. The *reward system* in the OP is highly judgmental. Rewards under all planning approaches are perhaps judgmental, except synoptic. Here we

argue that reward is tied more to productivity than the "good old boy or girl" criterion.

The organizational process is indeed complex from the standpoints of reward and objectives. The reward system of an organization may not necessarily be correlated positively with the achievement of objectives, but may hinge on the maintenance of organizational norms. Furthermore, organizational objectives may be set at levels that are much lower than the ideal where maximum performance may not be required. Rewards through the rational systems approach (synoptic) may be restricted through politics and the organizational process.[28]

Is there one planning theory that can be recommended above all the others when confronted with the organizational process? We think not, given the fact that planning to effect change is often situational. Thus understanding the organizational process is vitally important to educational planning.

Summary

Decisions are made by humans, not by planning theories or models. Understanding how planning and organizational theories can help produce better decisions is, however, an important tool for any planner to have on hand. Knowing the power bases of the decision maker is also an asset of the planner; and if the planner is the decision maker, we see nothing wrong with that. But in complex organizations there are multiple decision makers that may cause malfunctions in our well-known rational systems approaches to decision making and planning. We must therefore view decision making as a process.

The decision-making process is a part of administrative planning that includes policy information. Policies may evolve, or they may emerge from problems defined as needs. Needs are transformed into parochial objectives and, through interaction with the environment policy decisions, are made for the purpose of implementing change. We advocate planning for change instead of letting change evolve haphazardly.

Planning is the common element included in administrative functions and the administrative process, both of which are inherent in an organization. Decisions, a product of the organizational process, are frequently made somewhere between the ideal and the real. When the organizational process is functioning at full capacity, we observe that frequently decisions are less than ideal when compared to the expected outcomes of rational systems thinking. This may not be "good" but we must live with it. Thus, by considering what we have outlined as the organizational process, we may better understand how and perhaps why certain decisions are made.

Notes

1. Graham T. Allison, *Essence of Decision: Explaining the Cuban Missile Crisis* (Boston: Little, Brown, 1971), p. 80.

2. Barry Bozeman and Frederick A. Rossini, "Technology Assessment and Political Decision-Making," *Technological Forecasting and Social Change* 15 (no. 1) (September 1979):29.

3. Warren G. Bennis; "A Typology of Change Processes" in *The Planning of Change: Readings in the Applied Behavioral Sciences* eds. Warren G. Bennis; Kenneth D. Benne; and Robert Chin (New York: Holt, Rinehart and Winston, 1961), p. 154.

4. John R.P. French, Jr., and Bertram Raven, "The Bases of Social Power," in *Group Dynamics: Research and Theory* eds. Dorwin Cartwright and A.F. Zander (New York: Row, Peterson, 1960), pp. 607–623.

5. Max Weber, *Theory of Social and Economic Organization,* translated by A.M. Henderson and Talcott Parsons (New York: Free Press, 1947), pp. 151–152.

6. Herbert A. Simon, *Administrative Behavior: A Study of Decision-Making Processes in Administrative Organization* (New York: The Macmillan Company, 1947), pp. 240–241.

7. Edward H. Litchfield, "Notes on a General Theory of Administration," *Administrative Science Quarterly* 1 (1956):3–29, as presented by Wayne K. Hoy and Cecil G. Miskel, *Educational Administration: Theory, Research, and Practice* (New York: Random House, 1978), pp. 215–216.

8. Henry M. Levin, "A Radical Critique of Educational Policy," *Journal of Education Finance* (no. 3) (Summer 1977):10.

9. Hoy and Miskel, *Educational Administration,* p. 215.

10. Charles E. Lindblom, *The Policy-Making Process* (Englewood Cliffs, N.J.: Prentice-Hall, 1968), p. 3.

11. Ibid., p. 4.

12. Ibid., p. 4.

13. Ibid., p. 4.

14. Kurt Lewin, "Frontiers in Group Dynamics," *Human Relations* (no. 1) (June 1947):34.

15. James M. Lipham and James A. Hoeh, Jr., *The Principalship: Foundations and Functions* (New York: Harper and Row, 1974), pp. 149–155.

16. E. Kirby Johnson, *Long-Range Planning: The Executive View Point* (Englewood Cliffs, N.J.: Prentice-Hall, 1966), p. 21; and George

C.F. Bereday and Joseph Lauwerys, *Educational Planning* (New York: Harcourt Brace Jovonovich, 1967), as discussed in Lipham and Hoeh, *The Principalship,* pp. 150–151.

17. Lipham and Hoeh, *The Principalship,* p. 151.

18. Ibid., p. 152.

19. C. Kenneth Tanner, *Designs for Educational Planning* (Lexington, Mass.: Lexington Books, D.C. Heath, 1971), pp. 19–22.

20. Herbert A. Simon, "Recent Advances in Organization Theory," in *Research Frontiers in Politics and Government* (Washington, D.C.: Brookings Institution, 1955), pp. 30–47; and Herbert A. Simon, *Administrative Behavior,* 2n ed. (New York: The Free Press, 1965).

21. Bozeman and Rossini, *Technology Assessment,* p. 27.

22. Robert L. Crowson, "Educational Planning and Models of Decision-Making," *Educational Planning* 2 (no. 1) (May 1975):58.

23. Ibid., p. 59.

24. Ibid.

25. Bozeman and Rossini, *Technology Assessment,* p. 29.

26. Ibid., p. 29.

27. Graham T. Allison, *Essence of Decision,* p. 162.

28. Tanner, *Designs for Educational Planning,* p. 258.

Part III
Process Models and Cases in Planning and Decision Making

From our discussion of organizational processes and the introduction to synoptic, incremental, transactive, advocacy, and radical planning (SATIR), we may perhaps begin to comprehend how complicated educational planning really is. If one conclusion were required regarding educational planning, we could say that it is at best situational. This is, given an organization that is highly centralized and given the task to effect change in that situation, we would suggest the rational systems or synoptic approach to planning. But given another less centralized organization, one or more of the SITAR traditions would be expected to yield the best results.

We have proposed that educational systems are generally more open than closed. Thus the organizational process approach to planning is considered best for an open system because things are more likely to get done under some well-selected combination of the synoptic, incremental, transactive, advocacy, or radical schools of thought. Yet even with the help of the SITAR theories, we cannot ignore the notion of situational planning. Hence to SITAR may be added situational (SITARS) because of the dynamics within the educational environment.

Table III-1 presents nine planning-action descriptors that are required in most planning situations. Obviously our list is only a limited illustration of planning actions, but our intent is to show the major or minor position of

Table III-1

A Comparison Between Planning-Action Descriptors and Planning Traditions

Action Descriptor	Rational Systems Approach			Descriptive Organizational Process	
	+2	+1	0	−1	−2
1. A priori goal setting		X		0	
2. Acquiring complete information		X		0	
3. Control over means		X		0	
4. Analytical analysis	X				0
5. Judgmental input			X		
6. Interaction and bargaining	0				X
7. Time and politics		0		X	
8. Cooperation		0		X	
9. Orientation toward the individual	0				X

X = Major position under major planning tradition.

0 = Minor position under major planning tradition.

these action descriptors under either the rational systems approach or the descriptive organizational process approach to planning. What we see in table III-1, for example, is the action of a priori goal setting where under the rational systems school of thought, it has a relative position value of $+1$, but when viewed from the organizational process perspective, it has a value of (-1). By extending this illustration to a third or n ($n = 1, 2, 3, 4, \ldots$) dimension, which we shall call an environmental situation (after the notion of situational leadership in chapter 5), we propose that the position value would change. Since we assume that the environmental situations are not necessarily linear, the new location of the position value of a priori goal setting can only be speculative. In fact, the reflective property of our comparison might be challenged as being greatly limited, but until there is research evidence to the contrary, the illustration will stand as a feasible point of departure.

Part III offers three processes and case studies as a means for exploring the nature of educational planning in organizations. We should emphasize that these processes have been selected for illustrating components of planning theories in operation and are not necessarily introduced as new ways to do things. In fact, we attempt to show how various components of these processes have sometimes failed. Their failure or lack of effectiveness, however, may be a result of the given situations where they were utilized. Again we note the environmental situations as important factors acting on expected results from these processes, and we reemphasize that there is not just one way to plan or effect change.

Table III-2 outlines nine planning-action descriptors indicating their degree of existence in the evaluative-research process, the MBO process, and the Delphi process, respectively. For example, we see that analytical analysis is used to a greater degree in evaluative research than in MBO or Delphi. Under certain environmental situations, we are quick to admit that an equal weight might be appropriate in each of the three processes.

Chapters 8 and 10 provide examples of the MBO process. In chapter 8 we outline what is perhaps an ideal setting for MBO in higher education. We are not offering MBO as something new, necessarily, but we are taking a look at the total process from the organizational-process point of view, emphasizing incremental and transactive planning theories as opposed to the rational systems approach where MBO really initiated. The limitations are obvious as the reader follows the process, but the reader should gain a new respect for the complexities of the organizational process and the time required to implement a new concept or program.

There is an obvious failure reported in chapter 10. This could in many ways be attributed to the planners. However, we contend that learning better ways of planning from a failure is better than remaining ignorant about the process. Chapter 10 is heavily flavored with the rational systems

Table III–2
The Relationship Between Three Process Models and Planning-Action Descriptors

Action Descriptors	Evaluative Research Process	MBO Process	Delphi Process
1. A priori goal setting	*	X	X
2. Acquiring complete information	*	X	X
3. Control over means	*	X	X
4. Analytical analysis	*	X	X
5. Judgmental input	X	X	*
6. Interaction and bargaining	X	*	X
7. Time and politics	X	*	X
8. Cooperation	X	*	X
9. Oriented toward the individual	X	*	X

* = Exists to a greater degree in the process.

X = Exists to a lesser degree in the process.

concept since the order to implement MBO came from the top down. The feeble attempts to utilize incremental and transactive planning strategies did not produce a good positive textbook example of how an organization lived happily ever after once it knew that MBO was the right thing to do. We speculate on the reasons for this apparent failure and hope that administrative planners can profit from the shortcomings that are exposed.

In the last two chapters we reveal several complexities of working with organizations to effect change. There are hints of advocacy and radical planning in the planned intervention in an urban high school. However, we see the incremental and transactive traditions in collaborative and face-to-face bargaining. Also some muddling through may characterize the way officials managed the tense situation initially. The positive results of our rational systems approach or synoptic planning activities are minimal. Yet since our involvement extended to little more than one year, we can say that perhaps we did not have enough time.

In all of our examples throughout this text, we have stressed the need for time to effect change, at least to the point where results can be witnessed and operationalized. Lack of time for study and implementation of planned change may be the greatest enemy of the administrative planner. When results are not quick to emerge, there appears to be the tendency to blame the planner or his or her techniques instead of admitting that not enough time has been allowed.

7

The Management-by-Objectives Process

Chapter 6 discussed the administrative process as planning, organizing, stimulating, and evaluating—all of which facilitate organizational change. Action-initiating structure for achieving objectives was defined as "stimulating," which has been further described as leadership and involves methodology for motivating change in groups and individuals. To motivate positive behavior, we shall assume that individuals have desires for achievement and responsibility, personal and organizational growth and increased social awareness leading to personal satisfaction. Therefore, we accept McGregor's Theory *Y* as a proactive approach to administrative planning whereby individuals, when committed to objectives, will exercise self-control and self-direction in working to achieve them.[1] The commitment to change process has been perceived as a function of rewards attached to achievement of objectives and linked to the self-actualization needs and ego satisfaction described by Maslow.[2]

Out of theories relative to need satisfaction and motivation has come the philosophy of planning and administration known as "management by objectives" (MBO). Seeking to improve motivation through mutual goal setting while minimizing external control, we envision MBO as a process of involving individuals and groups in the organizational and planning processes. Several classifications of objectives are expected in a complex organization beginning with the individual. Thus the MBO process involves objectives amenable to self-actualization, self-esteem, security, and physiological needs.

We are not surprised therefore to see individual objectives in educational organizations that include advancing rank, achieving tenure, and receiving recognition relative to productivity, leadership, satisfaction, and awareness. Specifically, in higher education these are complementary to the organizational objectives of teaching, research, and service. One may be rewarded a higher rank and salary if he or she is a good teacher, performs service to the state and community, and becomes proficient in research and service. This achievement, of course, is ideal and assumes the proactive approach. However, what we have discovered about the organizational process leads us to conclude that there is "the good old boy or girl" (GOB/G) group, be it ever so small, that achieves certain rewards regardless of productivity. Just how this little group reconciles minimal productivity and accomplishments tied to maximum reward shall be left to the speculation of the reader. Occasionally there are members of the GOB/G classification who are highly productive, and thus we see nothing wrong with their receiving rewards. Regardless of how we may classify individuals in an organization with its multiple objectives, it is imperative that individual, group, and organizational objectives be complementary.

We shall look to the organizational process and planning theories as a place from which to move into the MBO process. From the problem definition stage in the synoptic approach emerges *developing alternatives* for achieving objectives—a logical place, we believe, to begin.

An Overview of MBO

The development of alternatives for operationalizing the practice of MBO was introduced by Drucker.[3] As a philosophy of management, MBO focuses on cooperative goal setting among superiors and subordinates. Odiorne describes MBO as a process for facilitating the identification of organizational goals. But more than this is involved since interaction between the subordinate and the superior is required whereby each individual specifies his or her major responsibilities and attaches measurable expectations as operating guides.[4] He expounded on the top-down and the bottom-up approaches to MBO and highlighted the crucial aspects of objective setting. Some implications evolving from this definition are that those individuals at the top within the organization are committed to the concept of MBO, that there are clearly delineated overall goals for the organization within which those in the organization can work and with which they can identify, and there is total involvement by all of those within the organization; that there will be sufficient time and resources available to give the concept an opportunity to become established and operational.

These four implications we see as essential for a successful MBO program. Total and active commitment by those of authority within the organization is of vital importance to the success of such a concept as MBO, and without this commitment the concept is in trouble before it is started. We should always be aware of the need for this commitment, and it has been suggested that top-level managers be included in appraisals at the start to see what makes them work. This experience shows that top management is behind this performance-appraisal method.[5]

Rosenfeld and Smith have commented that the organization must be committed to a fair test for implementing a participation program. Members of the organization must also believe that the organization is as committed to the program as they are asked to be.[6]

Individuals at the top levels of the organization have within their hands

the final power of decision making, and without the decision of total commitment from those with the power to make such a commitment, this concept is doomed to failure. These are the people who must lead in setting the
overall goals of the organization. We propose, however, that there should
be input from individuals at all levels of the organization regarding general
goals and objectives that express the raison d'etre of the organization, but
there must also be standard operating procedures established within which
the input from all levels must work.

One vital reason for commitment by those at the top of the hierarchical
structure is the time requirement. The literature underlines frequently an
observation by Howell that it takes at least five years to achieve a fully
effective MBO system.[7] Successful implementation of MBO is a slow process. It takes time to change an organization that has operated under Tay-
lorian concepts of authoritarian management as compared to one that operates by Barnardian ideas and takes into consideration the goals of the
employee and improving the efficiency and effectiveness of the overall
operation. As Levinson has noted, top management has often assumed that
it has the responsibility for setting objectives, providing appropriate
rewards, and controlling anyone who is employed by the organization.
However, this reward-and-punishment way of thinking leads the MBO process to failure.[8]

Individuals unaccustomed to MBO may find it difficult to see the total
framework at first or to justify its implementation. Besides overcoming this
difficulty, there is another misunderstanding that must be overcome and
that takes time. Most early attempts to use MBO ran into problems because
administrators, often too impatient, wanted to show quick results.[9]

Howell has emphasized that the failure to allow sufficient time for
development is the major downfall of most objective-setting systems.[10] This
warning carries with it the factor concerning involvement of all those within
the organization. Howell tied this factor to the time factor when he pointed
out that three years of concentrated efforts are needed on the part of management just to introduce MBO in an organization.[11] This time projection
we believe is not unrealistic because our experiences show that it takes considerable time to define objectives, orient the whole organization to a new
way of thinking, as well as to test, evaluate, and begin to achieve an inner-
organizational confidence among individuals both horizontally and vertically.

The essence of the MBO process lies in participation of all individuals
in the organization. Studies have shown that to be effective—that is, to be
more than just a hollow management device—MBO must have this input.
Token participation by the workers or empty gestures by management at
allowing participation do not work. Burke and Wilcox have indicated that

the beliefs and ideas of subordinates are necessary if they are to feel that reasonable objectives are being set and that certain job-related problems are being solved.[12]

This opinion is sanctioned by Gill and Molander, who believe that objectives to which individuals will be most committed are those that are cooperatively worked out on a group basis rather than by those persons of authority.[13] Furthermore, unless target setting is done through group participation, resulting objectives may lead to the organization's failure to achieve its goals.[14]

We see the free interplay of all organizational elements as determining the success of the program. We also believe that the objectives of the larger unit must be clear to those of the smaller parts. Thus we note the importance of such ideas as Likert's linking-pin theory where in successful organizations it is the leader of a lower group who is also a member of the next highest group. In order for MBO to be successful, organizations have found that this kind of structure, in which there is an avenue for free vertical interchange, is very helpful. Within this type of structure the objectives of the organization as well as the ideas and goals being sought by the MBO process can better be transmitted throughout the organization. This is important because the process involves individuals on the bottom of the organizational ladder in the formulation of their objectives within the context of the overall objectives of the organization and in functional terms as required by the tenets of MBO.

Humble has stressed the importance of involvement and of preparing people to accept MBO. He noted that MBO at (lower) levels quickly proves whether strategic company objectives are already clear, where there are gaps and whether present thinking is sufficiently broad.[15]

Thus each person has a discussion with his or her immediate supervisor in order to understand the overall goals of the organization as well as the general and specific objectives of his or her unit. As Gaither has noted, this is the point at which if there are any misunderstandings or disagreements regarding these objectives, resolution of the conflict should be attained through the communication process.[16]

Individual job descriptions and the objectives resulting from this consultation are put in writing for future reference and evaluation, which requires specific and measurable statements. This procedure is then followed on up the hierarchical scale within the organization until the top is reached. It is hoped that when this point is attained, there is a better understanding all along the hierarchy of the workings of the whole. Consequently, each person can visualize himself or herself as a manager, with the ability to manage planned change improvements more effectively, eligibility to set priorities, and perceptions to see the consequences of individual actions and goals of the organization.

In industrial organizations this is the point at which the MBO process leads to what Jenkins has described as a system of work, planning, and review, conducted by all managers every three months.[17] The time involved between review sessions has been shown to vary from two months to annually, but a majority of the literature reveals that a quarterly review is fairly standard, at least in the first two to five years of the establishment of an MBO system.

Jenkins has further described this review session as one during which each person develops and prioritizes objectives for the job, then discusses them with his or her immediate superior. Following is a period of negotiation during which agreement is reached on such attributes as attainability and feasibility.[18] Priorities are then established, the objectives written up, and another time period between review sessions is entered.

Some of the time periods for review vary. Furthermore the methods of establishing goals vary. For example, one approach is known as "peer goal setting." This procedure invovles individuals at a given level in the organization in the development of their objectives cooperatively.[19] Here we see the transactive theory of planning complementing the MBO process. This general outline is frequently followed by organizations that have successfully employed MBO. But it is simply an outline enabling hard work and dedication to be better channeled toward the successful accomplishment of objectives. MBO is no panacea, and according to Humble, MBO may not live up to its claims when viewed as only an appraisal mechanism. Thus the MBO procedure may not only help reveal problems that an organization has to deal with but it may also frequently provide a tool for solving problems. Furthermore, one positive consequence of MBO is that it may motivate managers to higher performance.[20]

This motivation is very important if an evaluation system is to operate in any educational organization. Studies by Weiland[21] and by Raven and Rietsma[22] have illustrated that clarity of the goals of an educational organization was of utmost importance if cooperation was to be expected of those within the organization in the pursuit of the achievement of those goals. Since the days of Chester Barnard, research has shown that efficiency and accountability within an organization are much higher when those who make up the organization can identify their personal goals within the general goals of the organization. MBO is designed to bring about this kind of identification, and according to Humble, MBO is a dynamic system for integrating the company's need to clarify and achieve its profit-and-growth goals with the manager's need for contributing.[23]

In the identification and development of goals, an educational institution cannot think simply in terms of units such as dollars, or items produced or sold. Consequently, since MBO has evolved from the rational systems point of view, we see the need to tie together the unique value systems of education and educators. When analyzing an organization such as an educational institution, one must see the total process of inputs, activities, and outputs more than just separate units that make up the system of administration.[24] Or, as Robert Lahti has succinctly described it, "nonquantifiable objectives, . . . can be established by describing a condition which will exist when the objective has been reached."[25] In the educational institution the use of MBO requires the formulation of well-defined plans and activities that culminate with the comparison of the actual with the expected results. MBO, as Olson has observed, provides a logical framework for focusing attention on whether or not an objective has been achieved[26]; yet, we must note that objectives themselves are products of the persons within the organization communicating and interacting freely with each other.

MBO in Education

Business and industrial organizations have spent several years and considerable sums of money in the development of MBO systems, and educational organizations that have implemented MBO systems perhaps have profited by utilizing business and industry's experiences. MBO has become a popular administrative approach, especially on college campuses, as illustrated in work by McConkey, Lahti and Collins.[27] Some reasons for the increased movement toward the MBO concept as a means of more effective management are decreased financial support, declining enrollments, collective bargaining, and increasing administrative accountability.

Spin-offs of the MBO process have been discovered in secondary education as well. For example, the development of objectives known as "behavioral objectives" or "performance objectives" has been advanced by Bloom, Mager, and Popham,[28] among many others. Furthermore, several state education agencies have moved in the direction of MBO; for example, an entire series of monographs for planning revolving around objectives has been produced by the Alabama State Department of Education.[29] This seven-part series focuses on: establishing goals, assessing needs, identifying resources and constraints and prioritizing needs, developing objectives, alternative strategies, implementation, and operating and evaluating the program.

MBO appears to be highly suited for higher education organizations since it allows for centralization of instructional objectives by decentralized decision making to meet those objectives. Several organizational attributes of academic institutions suggest MBO's utility in management and budgeting and especially in academic planning. Because faculty members generally have some experience with self-governance, MBO is amenable to the concept of self-management. Thus self-evaluation is recognized primarily as a faculty responsibility and the decentralized nature of an educational institution increases the need for cooperation, participation, and consensual decision making.[30]

The MBO process, however, may conflict with our conceptualization of the organizational process. Although MBO, as we present it, has some ties to Theory Y, the fact that MBO shows signs of the rational systems approach and the rationality of human behavior may conflict with diffuse power and authority, and organization routine. This is true if MBO is basically a top-down approach. Whereas MBO seeks precise statements of institutional objectives, the organizational-process approach frequently allows for parochial objectives set at levels that are much lower than the ideal. Presumably the most troublesome of the MBO assumptions is that organizations are essentially "closed systems" with unitary decision making. This comes in direct conflict with the organizational-process characteristics such as multiple decision makers, open systems, and politics. Yet, because the decision-making function fluctuates between the descriptive and the normative ends of the normative-descriptive decision model, this conflict may not be sufficient to destroy the MBO process altogether. Hence, what is really taking place in educational organizations is the adoption of an adapted rational MBO process.

Given these general concerns for implementation of MBO in educational organizations, there are some methods and procedures that could lend themselves well to ensuring better MBO operation in open systems. For example, Hoy and Miskel have summarized the major steps in developing an MBO program for an educational organization as the development of goals on a system or districtwide basis. This is followed by the delineation of objectives for each job area and the integration of objectives with goals. Establishing procedures for measuring objectives tied to control is their fourth general step for the MBO program.[31] A similar procedure stated in general terminology shows that the MBO process is made up of four steps that according to Robbins are:

1. Setting goals
2. Action planning
3. Self-control
4. Periodic progress reviews[32]

These may be generically interpreted to be about the same as those presented by Hoy and Miskel. Both references imply monitoring and measuring performance. Phillips has outlined a comprehensive procedure utilizing primarily the transactive planning approach for implementing MBO in an educational organization.[33] Four basic assumptions for this procedure shown in table 7–1 are as follows:

Table 7-1
A Transactive Procedure for Implementing MBO

		Involvement
Phase I	Information dissemination and education	Total organization

A. Phase I helps to answer the following questions:
   1. What is MBO?
   2. How does it work?
   3. What are its advantages, limitations?
   4. Does MBO take more time?
   5. What are its outcomes?
   6. How will evaluation be affected?

B. Some activities to help answer these questions are:
   1. Conferences
   2. Seminars
   3. Retreats
   4. Symposiums
   5. Committee meetings
   6. Conferences between superiors and subordinates
   7. Faculty and staff meetings

Phase II	Establishing organizational objectives	Total organization

A. Program objectives should be clearly stated, flexible; activities should focus on improvement that is observable, and should be monitored and evaluated on a scheduled basis. Cost of reaching the objective should be stated.

B. Guidelines presented in A may be categorized according to program, activities, and resources.

C. An acceptable level of productivity should be established for the organization, and the conditions under which they are to be reached should be clarified.

D. All objectives should be written and published within the organization.

Phase III	Establish objectives for each unit (e.g., college and department)	Subunits of the organization

A. Objectives should follow those guidelines in phase II.

B. Objectives are stated with minimum ambiguity and understood by participants.

C. Objectives are to be operational in that clear guidelines can be delineated and activities specified to reach the objectives.

D. Departmental objectives should tie in with the next level, etc.

E. Resources are available or attainable to reach objectives

Table 7–1 continued

		Involvement
Phase IV	Formulation of individual objectives	Interaction between subordinates and superiors
	A. Each department establishes general objectives as noted above.	
	B. Each individual specifies objectives and indicates how each objective complements departmental objectives.	
Phase V	Periodic review at all levels (e.g., university, college, department)	Total organization
	A. Measure achievement according to statements of objectives.	
	B. If appropriate, set new levels (higher or lower) and continue the MBO process.	

1. Goals and objectives are poorly defined within the organization.
2. The order has come from the top-down to implement MBO.
3. Few individuals within the organization are aware of the MBO concept.
4. The MBO process is continuous.

Total involvement of all members of the organization is necessary before completion of phase I because MBO depends on continuous and total involvement of all members of the organization before it can be successfully implemented. Consequently, any measures that could be taken to present the concept to the whole organization at once (or to as large a size group as is feasible) should be taken. This method of introduction would provide less chance for misrepresentation of the concept in its introductory stages and would better enable the presentation of MBO as a concept applicable to the total organization.

The first activity in phase II involves the formulation of overall objectives for the total organization. Consequently, the process of overall objectives formulation might be facilitated by a gathering of all the members of the organization, whether this be in a single conference involving everyone or in several conferences necessitated because of physical size of the organization, commitments, or geographical spread.

However its introduction is accomplished, the Information Dissemination and Education Phase is one of the most important elements of the MBO process. This phase involves the establishment of overall objectives or goals for the organization as a whole that are functional, measurable to a degree in most cases, and clear to all those within the organization. This set of overall objectives is the base from which all the separate parts of the organization can formulate their own objectives. This base can be returned to for clarification or restructuring of the goals of some part of the organization.

It is important that the reasons for implementing MBO be understood by all those within the organization. Consequently, some time would have to be spent giving a background of MBO itself and the formulation of objectives so that an understanding of how the whole concept evolves could be obtained.

Besides the establishment of the idea of setting objectives, the first phase is also important in that it must be structured to help the persons within the organization view themselves as managers. We believe that individuals in any organization who have the responsibility of performing functions related to problem solving can be defined as managers. In an educational system, those in administration, instruction, and all other functions perform problem-solving activities as a large part of their daily routine. This phase involves the rearrangement of thinking that is firmly implanted on a proven past. The rearrangement involved would establish what should be in the future and then would focus thought on the achievement of that future with a minimum of reliance on the past.

Once the concept is introduced, phases II and III can be entered, and the process of actually formulating objectives can be undertaken. In industry, the president, the board, or in some cases the stockholders, formulate the company's overall objectives. In an educational system this same process operates to some extent but requires modification. Educational systems depend on public monies to survive, and consequently the public feels it should help formulate the goals of the system. The students within the system want a voice in the process that is going to shape their careers. Teachers feel that their voice too is important since they are the ones directly responsible for the finished product. Consequently, when overall objectives for an educational institution are formulated, many internal and external factors must be taken into consideration.

In order to establish a point of departure and a systematic orderliness to an MBO procedure, the beginning point should be the presentation of the mission of the organization as seen by the designated person of authority in charge of the organization. Whether this is the principal, superintendent, president, commissioner, or chancellor does not matter, as long as he or she can be viewed by the body of the organization as the leader. This individual's suggestions will carry the weight of having been selected out of all those that come from public demand, requests from within the organization, the latest research, governmental legislation, and other sources.

The mission that the leader of the organization presents should be outlined as suggestions and not as authoritive demands. Almost everyone within an educational institution is aware of the need for diplomacy when trying to evoke action from members. MBO is at most a developing concept in education, and the beginning stages of any new concept requires careful handling.[34]

With the presentation of the mission and objectives (we use the terms *objectives* and *goals* interchangeably) of the organization as they are seen by the person recognized as the leader, the transactive procedures as seen in table 7-1 call for general input by the rest of those within the organization concerning their views as to the organization's overall objectives. In order to prevent this from being a chaotic process where everyone seeks to be heard at once, or to prevent the one-to-one situation whereby a supervisor seeks (and thereby could influence) responses from those under him or her, a planning procedure such as the Delphi technique can be used for gathering the member's views. We shall deal with Delphi in chapter 9.

Summary

MBO can be a positive component of an organization's operating procedures. Yet there are limitations that must be overcome. In this chapter we have presented an overview of MBO and how the concept is perceived in education. We have discussed a transactive procedure for implementing MBO in an educational organization in this chapter as a means for minimizing unitary decision making. In chapter 8 we focus on some additional advantages and limitations by presenting an example of MBO in higher education.

Notes

1. Douglas McGregor, *The Human Side of Enterprise* (New York: McGraw-Hill, 1960).

2. Abraham H. Maslow, *Motivation and Personality,* 2d. ed. (New York: Harper and Row, 1970).

3. Peter F. Drucker, *The Practice of Management* (New York: Harper and Row, 1954).

4. George S. Odiorne, *Management by Objectives: A System of Managerial Leadership* (New York: Pitman, 1965), p. 55.

5. J.D. Baxter, "Management by Objectives Surfaces," *Iron Age* (September 25, 1969):100.

6. Joel M. Rosenfeld and Matthew J. Smith, "Participative Management: An Overview," *Personnel Journal* 46 (no. 2) (February 1967):102.

7. Robert A. Howell, "Managing by Objectives—A Three State System," *Business Horizons* (February 1970):25.

8. Harry Levinson, "Management by Whose Objectives?" *Harvard Business Review* (July–August 1970):130.

9. Samuel W. Jenkins, "Management by Objectives," a paper prepared for presentation at Management Seminars at Plovdiv, Bulgaria, and Sofia, Bulgaria, September 21–28, 1970, p. 2.

10. Robert A. Howell, "A Fresh Look at Management by Objectives," *Business Horizons* (Fall 1967):54.

11. Ibid., p. 57.

12. Ronald J. Burke and Douglas S. Wilcox, "Characteristics of Effective Employee Performance Reviews and Developmental Interviews," *Personal Psychology* 22 (no. 3) (1969):291.

13. J. Gill and C.F. Molander, "Beyond Management by Objectives," *Personnel Management* (August 1970):20.

14. Ibid.

15. J.W. Humble, *Improving Management Performance* (London: Management Publications, 1970), p. 19.

16. Gerald Gaither, "Guidelines for Implementation of MBO" (unpublished paper at The University of Tennessee, 1970), p. 1.

17. Jenkins, "Management by Objectives," p. 5.

18. Ibid.

19. Howell, "A Fresh Look at Management by Objectives," p. 51.

20. Humble, *Improving Management Performance,* p. 1.

21. George F. Wieland, "The Determinants of Clarity in Organization Goals," *Human Relations* 22 (November 1969):161–172.

22. B.H. Raven and J. Rietsma, "The Effects of Varied Clarity of Group Goal and Group Path Upon the Individual and His Relation to His Group," *Human Relations* 10 (May 1957):29–45.

23. Humble, *Improving Management Performance,* p. 1.

24. Gerald G. Mansergh, ed., *Dynamics of Management by Objectives for School Administrators* (Danville, Ill.: The Interstate Printers and Publishers, 1971), p. 5.

25. Robert E. Lahti, "Management by Objectives," *College and University Business* (July 1971):33.

26. David E. Olson, *Management by Objectives* (Palo Alto, Calif.: Pacific Book Publishers, 1968), p. 2.

27. Dale D. McConkey, *MBO for Nonprofit Organizations* (New York: American Management Association, 1975); Robert E. Lahti, *Innovative College Management* (San Francisco: Jossey-Bass, 1973); and R.W. Collins, *Management by Objectives: Advantages, Problems, Implications for Community Colleges* (Los Angeles: University of California, 1971).

28. Benjamin S. Bloom, ed., *Taxonomy of Educational Objectives*

Handbook I: Cognitive Domain (New York: David McKay, 1956); Robert F. Mager, *Preparing Instructional Objectives* (Palo Alto, Calif.: Fearon Publishers, 1962); and W. James Popham, "Objectives and Instruction," in *Instructional Objectives, American Education Research Association Series on Curriculum Evaluation* (no. 3) (Chicago: Rand McNally, 1969).

29. Lee Boone, Guy Meade, and Jackie Walsh, *Systematic Planning Series for Local Education Agencies,* The Office of Planning and Evaluation, Alabama State Department of Education, Montgomery, Ala., 1977.

30. Beverly A. Cigler, "Management by Objectives: Practice, Pitfalls and Utility for Small Colleges," *Planning for Higher Education* 7 (no. 5) (April 1979):2.

31. Wayne K. Hoy and Cecil G. Miskel, *Educational Administration: Theory, Research and Practice* (New York: Random House, 1978), p. 127.

32. Stephen P. Robbins, *The Administrative Process: Integrating Theory and Practice* (Englewood Cliffs, N.J.: Prentice-Hall, Inc., 1976), p. 138. Reprinted with permission.

33. James B. Phillips, "Application of an Educational Management by Objectives Model." (unpublished doctoral dissertation, The University of Tennessee, 1973), pp. 41–43. Reprinted with permission.

34. Ibid., p. 47. Reprinted with permission.

8 Management by Objectives in a Complex Organization: An Example from Higher Education

In this section we shall build on the concepts of the organizational process and illustrate management by objectives (MBO) through a hypothetical example in a university with special emphasis on the departmental and college levels. The example is a result of our personal experiences, a review of the literature, and personal visits and interviews at nine colleges and universities. One basic assumption underlying this hypothetical example is an open educational environment. For this example we shall also assume a decetralized organization, with many levels of decision makers, ample interaction, and politics freely operating throughout the total system.

The context of our example is the hypothetical educational organization illustrated in figure 8–1, where the MBO cycle is assumed to be continuous whereby external variables interact with all four levels. Clients of the system may be exemplified as school systems, businesses, industries, politicians, and certain organized groups, while graduates may provide external as well as internal inputs into the MBO cycle. State and federal agencies

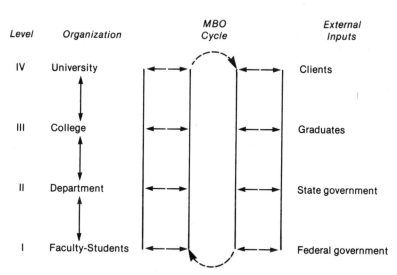

Figure 8–1. The Context of MBO in an Educational Organization

may effect inputs through legislation and guidelines. Although this illustration is general, it provides a framework to explore the nature of the MBO process that we shall assume is aimed at improvement of communications among several variables and performance evaluation—not only faculty evaluation but also departmental and college evaluations. We shall also assume that the mission statement has been developed through some procedure such as Delphi with total organizational involvement. For a more comprehensive understanding of what the ideal organization entails, we shall now state the mission and objectives[1] for our hypothetical educational organization.

Mission of the University

Statement of mission: State University. State University is the major comprehensive university of this state, with one central campus and four regional campuses. With various programs the university serves the entire state, and, as a major land-grant university, it is also a natural resource. The fundamental purpose of the university is to improve the quality of life by developing the capacity for better understanding, thinking, and taking action. Hence, these goals are to be accomplished through teaching, research, and public service. Furthermore, the dissemination of knowledge serves the individual as well as acts as a force to shape society for the common good; dissemination also allows for a significant international resource.[2]

The general mission statement continues by outlining the various degree programs, indicating the university role in generation of new knowledge, and stating the opportunities for clients resulting from quality programs. Emphasis is placed on equal opportunity as a basic philosophy, and respect for human commitment and aspirations is acknowledged.

The *primary objectives* of a university are instruction; research, scholarship and creative work; and public service. Support objectives may be categorized under faculty and staff; academic program; students; and governance, administration and financing. An outline for an ideal mission statement developed from the Ohio State University model is as follows:[3]

Primary Goals

    I. *Instruction:* To continue as well as enrich the quality of instruction, certification, and evaluation:
       A. Undergraduate and graduate
       B. General professional
       C. Community and continuing education

II. *Research and scholarship:* To enhance the discovery of knowledge as well as its interpretation and application through relevant programs:
   A. Discovery of knowledge
   B. Interpretation of findings
   C. Application of knowledge

III. *Public Service:* To sustain and also enlarge advisory, planning, evaluation, and implementation services to clients outside the university:
   A. Advisory and consulting services
   B. Planning and evaluation services
   C. Implementation activities

Support Goals

I. *Faculty:* To carry forward and enlarge support for individual rights and appropriate environment:
   A. Institutional environment
   B. Extra support
   C. Individual rights
   D. Individual benefits

II. *Academic offerings:* To sustain and enrich the number and quality of academic support systems, easy access to, and assistance in using:
   A. Computer services
   B. Other technical support systems
   C. Library materials
   D. Artistic support services

III. *Students:* To maintain and increase individual development, access to counseling, student support services, support of academic goals:
   A. Faculty access
   B. Developmental activities
   C. Counseling services
   D. Health care
   E. Allowing student access
   F. Providing financial services

IV. *Governance and administration:* To sustain and improve process for participative decentralized decision making; effective support of program; efficient administrative operations; and acquisition of financial support necessary for effective programs:
   A. Participation
   B. Cost/effectiveness
   C. Evaluation
   D. Financing

In keeping with our organizational-process approach, we suggest the Ohio State University mission statement because of the emphasis on participation as specified below.

Participation

A. To provide for involvement of clients, faculty, administrators, staff, trustees, and students in planning and policy-making activities of the university.
B. Ensure individuals the opportunities for participating in decentralized decision-making activities that affect them.
C. To sustain an open system of communications with students, staff and governing bodies of the university.[4]

Here we note several characteristics of the organizational process evidenced through key phrases such as: "involvement . . . in planning and policy-making activities . . . ; . . . opportunities for participating in decentralized decision-making activities . . .; and . . . an open system of communications with . . . governing bodies . . . ." These statements acknowledge the external as well as internal variables evidenced by statements such as "involvement of clients, faculty . . . ," making this mission statement ideal for the MBO process.

Mission of a Hypothetical College of Education

The parameters of the mission of our hypothetical college of education have been established by the university mission statement of *primary* and *support* objectives. Needs of students, faculty needs and interests and needs of other clients are addressed through program content and scope. We shall define a program as a coherent set of activities with specified objectives. It is assumed that program activities reflect efforts to implement the mission of the college within certification requirements of the accrediting agencies and state regulations—external inputs. It is also assumed that the objectives within the mission statement have been developed and prioritized by a procedure such as Delphi with total faculty participation.

Mission Statement

College of Education. The mission of the college of education is to provide instruction, promote research, scholarship, and creative work, and furnish public services that maintain and contribute to the improvement of education. The faculty and staff strive to help students become more effective teachers, administrators, planners, researchers, and supporters of education. The college mission is concerned with improving education in rural, suburban, and urban areas of the state. This comprehensive mission requires that the college of education provide programs with a wide scope, full of depth and focusing on research and service activities and up-to-date teaching skills and delivery systems.

The college of education emphasizes the preparation and retraining of individuals for school-based roles and the continuous study of educational problems that includes vocational-technical education, community colleges, health-delivery programs, and higher education. Thus the mission of the college is to prepare educational leaders as well as human services professionals who perform educational roles in other settings.

The college mission statement continues according to the university mission statement. Now we shall move into the departmental level illustrating how objectives at the four levels shown in figure 8-1 complement each other.

University Mission

Research

Priority 1. To encourage basic research, descriptive research, evaluative research, and applied research in all colleges (education) for the purpose of problem solving and the discovery of new knowledge.

College mission

Research

Priority 1. Allocate faculty resources to provide maximum time for conducting basic research within the parameters established by teaching and service objectives.

Operational Objectives
A. Provide released time to faculty for assignment to state or local research projects.
B. Provide secretarial assistance necessary to support faculty scholarship.
C. Utilize university computing center to facilitate research and scholarship.

Costs	*1982–1983*	*1983–1984*
Two secretaries	$24,000	$25,000
Computer services	2,000	2,500
Released time	9,000	9,500
	$35,000	$37,000

Departmental Objectives

Research

Priority 1. To encourage, initiate, and engage in research activities (knowledge production), individually, as a department, with students, with and for practitioners, and jointly with others in higher education.

Operational Objectives

A. Provide released time to faculty for assignment to state or local research projects.

B. Utilize university computing center to facilitate research and scholarship.

Costs	1982–1983	1983–1984
Computer services	$ 500	$ 600
Released time	2,000	2,300
	$2,500	$2,900

Transferred from college budget to departmental budget.

Research Objective of One Faculty Member

Priority 1. Active involvement in Covington County staff-evaluation project and State Department of Education MBO study— includes two publications that can be considered of substantial magnitude to be completed by 1984. (This means *active* participation, not just advisement.)

Several important characteristics are evident in this example. First we note how the mission statements are refined at the college level and observe that even more specific constraints are attached as we approach level 1 (faculty member). The factors of cost and time are acknowledged in the operational stages, and our staff member indicates that he or she will engage in two specific research-and-development activities that will also be considered as service. Hence one of the staff member's service objectives is addressed as follows:

Service

Priority 2. Engage actively in at least one field-oriented activity of a sufficient duration to warrant intensive student involvement. Student involvement will be a significant component in performance evaluation of attainment of this objective. (State MBO project to be completed in 1984.)

Although the MBO process appears to be from the top down in many organizations, we contend that this approach alone cannot work effectively in our hypothetical example. Faculty members who interact with all levels of local and state governments provide direct and indirect input at many levels of the MBO cycle. For example, if the staff member cited previously works on a significant research-and-development project at the state level, then clients of the university through direct and indirect communications channels will make favorable or unfavorable input at the departmental level, the college level, and at the top level of the organization. We may now ask questions relative to how is the staff performance evaluated and rewarded in the MBO cycle.

Staff Evaluation

In a decentralized organization operating under the MBO process, the department head and staff member agrees in advance on the individual performance objectives. As shown in the previous section, these objectives relate to departmental, college, and university objectives described as research, service, and teaching. The College of Education at The University of Tennessee, operating under the MBO process for more than ten years, has developed a comprehensive evaluation form as illustrated in table 8-1. We shall utilize this form in our example to represent the comprehensiveness of MBO. This form represents an annual summary that is submitted by the department head and signed by both the faculty member and the department head. It accompanies the departmental budget request for faculty reward to the office of the dean who recommends the reward specifications to level IV.

For each course taught by the staff member, a validated questionnaire is completed by students and administered through the office of the department head. The staff member is not allowed to tabulate student responses to the eleven categories of teaching. Examination of table 8-1 reveals that student evaluation accounts for approximately 33 percent of the final rating the staff member receives. The teaching component of the evaluation is adjusted according to assignment (for example, if twelve courses per year is a normal teaching load and the staff member teaches only six, the weight is reduced by one half). The weights are assigned according to percentage distribution fo time shown on page 1 of table 8-1.

Student advising cuts across the percentage distribution of time since research service and teaching are often accomplished as a function of advising. This is a strong feature of the performance evaluation and correlates with the support goals in our mission statement for the hypothetical university.

In the final evaluation each faculty member is allowed to rate himself or herself independently. This rating is carried to the final MBO conference where a comparison is made between department head assessment and the evaluation that each faculty member assigns to himself or herself. Several hours are sometimes required in the final session since negotiations may be necessary before final agreement is reached. Obviously, our hypothetical university setting provides for decentralized decision making since, for example, in this final evaluation the department head recommends a percentage for salary raise. Similar procedures are followed between the various levels of the organization.

Some of the positive spin-offs we observe from the MBO or transactive planning process are improved communications. This is evidenced by knowing what is expected and how much time is required to achieve an objective and by having been involved in determining expectations. Performance-evaluation criteria are subject to change as the mission and objectives of the college and university changes; hence, MBO is not only continuous across the levels of the organization but the process is congruent with environmental changes over time.

Table 8–1
College of Education Academic-Evaluation Form

Name _____ Department _____ Rank _____

Appointment date _____ Date appointed to present rank _____

Percentage distribution of time: A. Last or current year:

                Teaching _____ Advising _____ Research _____ Service

           B. Next year:

                Teaching _____ Advising _____ Research _____ Service

Rationale agreed upon for this distribution of time:

Approved _____   _____
               Department Head   Date

Table 8–1 continued

	(5) Outstanding	(4) Highly satisfactory	(3) Satisfactory	(2) Below average	(1) Unsatisfactory	Not applicable	No chance to observe
A. Teaching							
1. Assists students to achieve the instructional objectives.							
a. Clarifies objectives.							
b. Utilizes subject matter in an organized manner; is well prepared.							
c. Expresses thoughts clearly, and helps others to do so.							
d. Creates a learning environment that encourages an interchange of ideas.							
2. Evaluates extent to which objectives have been met.							
3. Relates the subject to other fields and to its practical applications.							
4. Develops a good climate for learning: stimulates interest, arouses curiosity, has an enthusiastic interest in teaching.							
5. Demonstrates a thorough knowledge of the subject.							
6. Demonstrates growth in subject mastery.							
7. Demonstrates emotional stability, enthusiasm, openmindedness, flexibility, self-confidence, and friendliness.							
8. Assists students to relate content to realistic learning situations.							
9. Adapts and uses materials and methods developed through research and/or other creative effort.							
10. Participates in nonthesis committees and direction of graduate research.							
11. Presents evidence of student evaluation of their experiences.							

Summary _____

_____

_____

Table 8-1 continued

	(5) Outstanding	(4) Highly satisfactory	(3) Satisfactory	(2) Below average	(1) Unsatisfactory	Not applicable	No chance to observe
B. Advisement							
1. Assists students in exploring career goals: type of careers, need for graduate work or professional school; competence and prospect.							
2. Assists students in assessing program status and progress; areas of difficulty, deficiencies, and projected graduation date.							
3. Assists students in planning programs, areas needing attention, courses requiring prerequisites, areas to strengthen goals, and suggested electives.							
4. Explores problems the students may share: living conditions, health, financial, scheduling pressures, how to withdraw from school, drop, add, or audit a course, take a course in the evening school or by correspondence, make substitutions in a prescribed curriculum, change majors or college, check on graduate status, and remove *I* grade.							
5. Suggests special consultation: counseling center, writing lab, housing, admissions and records, financial aid, placement and career planning, reading and study skills, tutorial assistance, and so on.							
6. Explores possible extracurricula activities, special interests, professional clubs, and so on.							
7. Makes oneself accessible to students.							

Table 8-1 continued

	(5) Outstanding	(4) Highly satisfactory	(3) Satisfactory	(2) Below average	(1) Unsatisfactory	Not applicable	No chance to observe
C. Research, development, or other creative work							
1. Publishes articles, or reports that incorporate or coordinate scholarly writings, research, or new ideas.							
2. Develops innovative approaches to solve education problems.							
3. Performs or creates for the general public in the field of his or her specific teaching speciality, i.e., art shows, piano or vocal performances, conducting, acting, dance.							
4. Develops research proposals.							
5. Attracts research funds.							
6. Is actively involved in conducting research in one's subject or interest area.							
7. Achieves professional recognition.							

Summary _____

_____

D . Leadership and service activities: To educational agencies							
1. Develops new organizational structures: e.g., team teaching, departmentalization, new administrative structures.							
2. Initiates staff-development programs: e.g., interservice programs, retreats, visitations.							
3. Develops new instructional and curricular designs; e.g., programmed material, contract approaches, individual learning packets, classroom meetings, group counseling, interdisciplinary curricula, career education, etc.							

Table 8-1 continued

	(5) Outstanding	(4) Highly satisfactory	(3) Satisfactory	(2) Below average	(1) Unsatisfactory	Not applicable	No chance to observe
4. Develops cooperative work arrangements: e.g., training grants, educational cooperatives, internships, school surveys, exchanging teaching or work assignments between university and other groups.							
5. Develops liaison activities between university and educational or other agency personnel: e.g., continuing dialogues on a person-to-person basis, speeches for PTA, FTA, career days, teacher groups.							
6. Develops field experiences in schools and related community agencies: e.g., student teaching, practica, internships, student-tutor program, regular field experience.							
7. Publishes textbooks, monographs, and other teaching materials.							

Summary _____

_____

D . Leadership and service activities: To professional associations

1. Is actively involved in professional organizations.							
2. Contributes to professional programs: e.g., program organizer, program presenter.							
3. Develops innovative approaches to solving professional problems: e.g., developing training standards, position papers, conducting symposia.							

Summary _____

_____

Table 8-1 continued

	(5) Outstanding	(4) Highly satisfactory	(3) Satisfactory	(2) Below average	(1) Unsatisfactory	Not applicable	No chance to observe
D . Leadership and service activities: To the university							
1. Accepts additional responsibilities; participates in staff meetings and committees; is prompt in carrying out instructions; is involved in appropriate faculty and/or student committees and activities; special assignments, etc.							
2. Accepts and follows departmental, college, and university policies; criticizes constructively through proper channels; works as a change agent for departmental, college, and university goals and commitments.							
3. Seeks professional self-improvement: special related study; participation in seminars and workshops; independent study service with professional programs or organizations.							

Summary _____

_____

_____

Evaluate items proportionately to time distribution; attach the faculty member's annual report. (Use back of page for comments, additional items, and so on.)

Final rating _____

The professor's signature denotes that he or she has had a conference with the department head and that he or she is aware of the rating being turned in to the Dean. The faculty signature does not necessarily denote an agreement with these ratings.

Date   Faculty Signature   Department Head Signature

Used by permission of Dr. Robert K. Roney, Professor, Educational Administration and Supervision, College of Education, The University of Tennessee.

Reward Through MBO: A Limiting Factor

As with any evaluation procedure, there is the concern for the relationship between MBO ratings and salary treatment. At the budgetary level where performance is converted into dollars or other benefits, we may witness external variables that are more a result of the organizational process than any other single factor. The supply and demand among various disciplines may be the most obvious. It is not uncommon to hear the question, "Why aren't professors of education paid on the same scale as professors of law or medicine?" They should be, but the environmental constraints dictate otherwise. Such constraints as estimated potential for future performance may be considered in the reward system or even past performance. We see these as functions of the organizational process that come in conflict with MBO. We must not forget that MBO, although humanistic, does have roots in the rational systems approach.

Then there are the rater differences across the system. Even when ratings are agreed on by superior and subordinate, there are those superiors who are more lenient than others. Or, there may be a superior who used the "good old boy or girl approach yielding high rewards for some who have perhaps performed poorly. Even the lack of training in performance appraisal and the limitations of the rating scale certainly influence overall outcome. Yet in looking at trends, we note that ratings account for no more than 50 percent of the variation in salary increases. Consequently, here is another point where the orgnizational process moves in to cloud the synoptic MBO picture. Accordingly, there are those that would argue that pay is not the foremost motivator. We must not forget our readings from Weber who contended that money is a motivator if the individual believes that increased effort will lead to better performance and raises result from better performance.[5] Individuals in academic settings may be motivated less by pay than those in other organizations.

Another limitation of the MBO process as we have outlined it for the hypothetical university is that student ratings as a measure of teacher effectiveness may include many inherent weaknesses.[6][7] Furthermore, many raters may have limited ability to judge the quality of research, publication, and public-service activities. The faculty member giving the best grades may also receive better student ratings. The grumpy faculty member, although a good teacher, may fall below his or her colleagues. Hence, we can conclude that performance appraisal i sone of the most difficult tasks for administrators, just as assigning grades to student performance is one of the most difficult jobs of teachers.

Conclusion

For MBO to achieve its ambitious outcomes, there must be support for the concept at every level of the organization. Support is gained if there is confidence in the organizational leadership and a willingness on the part of the decision makers to reward each individual on the basis of measured results. MBO can be a superior method to illustrate how transactive planning theory can be put into practice. With the proper support in terms of time, money, and reward, the process can be a cohesive force within a complex organization.

Notes

1. For a complete version of a superior statement of mission, see *Guide for Program Reviewers* (The Ohio State University, Columbus, 1978), p. 17.

2. Ibid., p. 17.

3. Ibid., pp. 18–23.

4. Ibid., p. 22.

5. Max Weber. *The Theory of Social and Economic Organization* trans. T. Parsons (New York: Free Press, 1947).

6. Betty Lou Raskin and Patricia R. Plante, "The Student Devaluation of Teachers," *ACADEME* 65 (October 1979):381–383.

7. Wilbert J. McKeachie, "Student Ratings of Faculty: A Reprise," *ACADEME* 65 (October 1979):384–397.

9 The Delphi Process

The development of objectives may be considered as a function of the organizational process and approached in several different ways. For example, Newell has outlined eight processes for developing objectives as follows: (1) the group conference, (2) the confrontation meeting, (3) the objective-strategy-tactics system, (4) the school of the future, (5) constraints, (6) questionnaires, (7) individual conferences, and (8) peer evaluation.[1] In this chapter we shall deal exclusively with the use of questionnaires as a process for setting objectives. Because of its highly judgmental input process, we shall discuss the procedure known as Delphi, which has synoptic as well as incremental and transactive properties amenable to educational planning. Delphi was developed by Olaf Helmer and his colleagues at the Rand Corporation in the early 1950s.[2]

Several modifications of Helmer's original Delphi process have emerged recently that are useful in administrative planning. Two of these adjusted Delphi processes have been classified as the inductive or the deductive[3] approaches. Like the original approach, these modifications also serve as means of working toward the consensus of issues, but procedures for establishing objectives and developing priorities have been augmented. In the inductive approach, which depends on incremental and transactive theories, we note that the initial probe does not specify any objective; thus probe I may be formulated as follows: "In the decade ahead this organization should concentrate its efforts and resources on the following objectives . . . ." The semantical analysis is required with this approach as opposed to the deductive process by which probe I specifies a list of objectives with participants being requested to prioritize each objective according to some predetermined value scale. In administrative planning, we recommend the inductive process based to a great extent on transactive planning theory because direct input from individuals is an important factor in the process. Each participant can see his or her ideas prioritized through the Delphi process, thereby allowing a greater probability of the individuals' working toward achievement of objectives on implementation. When the objectives are determined prior to seeking consensus (the synoptic approach), there exists the danger that individuals in the organization may perceive the administration as trying to force outcomes from the top down. Hence, resistance is to be expected more in the implementation than in the developmental phases.

111

As presented earlier, the proposed process for developing organizational objectives may best be described as modified Delphi technique since in it the selection of a panel of experts in a particular field is not required. Because we seek to obtain inputs from everyone within the organization, there is little concern for who is an expert. In chapter 10 of this text, we illustrate how a modified Delphi approach was used in a total organization for establishing objectives. We are not suggesting, however, that the only acceptable approach in establishing a system's mission and general objectives requires the inclusion of everyone within the organization. But it is indeed ideal if every member can be a participant in the Delphi process. For example, to establish or modify the general objectives of a university, we visualize that the deans and department heads might contribute to the overall mission statements where several faculty members assist both administrative levels in formulating acceptable objectives. At the departmental level, when objectives are developed, all faculty members would contribute throughout the entire process, however. This process is illustrated in figure 9-1 and may be in some conflict with the top-down approach to the management by objectives process outlined by Drucker.[4]

We have introduced this general process that could either include a public school system or an institution of higher education. Inputs from the public, school boards, and/or state governing or support agencies could be provided through each level depending how the Delphi process is con-

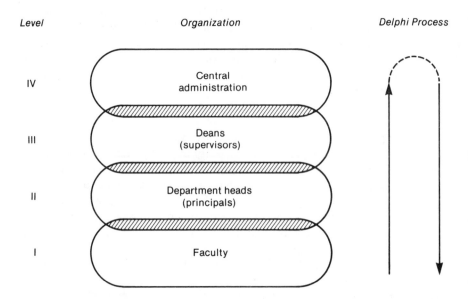

Figure 9–1. Establishing Objectives in an Educational Organization

ducted. If, for example, a department is establishing objectives, it is expected that its former clients as well as the present student body would be represented in the Delphi process.

Anonymity is an important characteristic of the Delphi process, and through the appropriate use of questionnaires, specific responses are not associated with individuals. Dalkey proposes that anonymous responses reduce undesirable interaction through the influence of dominant individuals.[5] Yet when the group process is used for formulating objectives, dominant individuals may try to influence others in discussion; but since the questionnaire is a secret ballot, this influence may not be as effective as through other group process.

Apart from the development of objectives, other applications of Delphi have been through forecasting, strategy, or preference probes.[6] Delphi studies have been used to predict alternative futures where minimal "hard" data exist from which to make predictions. This was the approach originally developed by Helmer to identify defense technology needs for the future. Klein and Alkin used the strategy probe (similar to the forecasting probe) to describe program alternatives in terms of cost feasibility and likelihood of success.[7] Collins followed a futuristic mode in defining components of administrative competency for school superintendents.[8] Each competency of the future was judged according to importance and utilization by a panel of twenty-three respondents.

A typical application of Delphi has been in the setting of institutional goals. Weatherman and Swenson[9] report on Helmer's[10] study to establish priorities for planning the distribution of federal education funds. Eliciting preferences regarding the future direction of teacher education in a school of education has been accomplished through the Delphi procedure by Cyphert and Gant.[11] Following a similar pattern, Phillips conducted a study to develop and prioritize objectives for a division of a state department of education.[12] His procedures are presented in chapter 10 of this text. A comprehensive faculty-performance-evaluation model was developed by Yoda that utilizes the Delphi process in establishing priorities tied to criteria for teacher effectiveness in the university setting.[13] Thus in educational organizations we have observed a trend more toward the use of Delphi in establishing priorities and objectives than in forecasting the future.

Assumptions of the Inductive Delphi Process

There are various documents presenting assumptions of the Delphi technique for forecasting (for example, see Helmer,[2] Dalkey,[5] and Weatherman and Swenson[6]). Here we shall deal with the assumptions relative to establishing priorities and objectives in an educational organization.

Organizational Variables

Since we are devoting our attention to the organizational-process approach to educational planning, there are several assumptions that may deviate from those shown in the current literature on Delphi. In chapter 6 we described eighteen general characteristics of the organization, and here we shall extract some of those we see as having relevance to the assumptions of the inductive Delphi process. We have identified five organizational variables that may affect the outcomes as follows:

1. Objectives may be set that have priorities lower than the ideal. When rankings occur through several Delphi probes, the middle 50-percent range frequently eliminates exceedingly high or low priorities. Hence, several parochial objectives are expected on the final Delphi round.

2. Compromise through the swaying the opinion for consensus may also tend to lead to more parochial objectives.

3. More time is required in the inductive Delphi process than in the deductive approach. This is true in any inductive Delphi approach regardless of the size of the panel. However, because of the inclusion of all members of the organization, the semantical analysis of probe I will require a considerable amount of time.

4. More work is required on the part of the planner in charge of the process because of the magnitude of the study (approximately 160 man-hours in the conference setting reported by Phillips[12]). Thus feedback may be returned more slowly.

5. Interaction among participants may give special-interest groups an advantage.

Participant Variables

There are seven general assumptions that emerge through working with a total organization. These are as follows:

1. The inductive Delphi process will yield normative results in large groups. The panel of experts is the total organization.

2. Because the total organization is utilized, there will be a large number of representative experts.

3. Participants within certain interest areas may stay outside the range of consensus. For example, in a college of education where there may be a heavy concentration of generalists, it may be difficult to get consensus on the use of computers in management. This is especially true if the objectives related to technology tend to threaten certain jobs.

4. Most participants will remain in the Delphi study if they are able to identify their input and if they understand the purpose of the study. Furthermore, the semantical analysis of round 1 is important, and care should be taken to keep original statements close to the intent of the contributor.

5. Narrative manipulation of feedback from probe I will be minimized through the elimination of ambiguity of statements.[14] Thus, participants will remain in the study when face validity is maximized.

6. The planners in charge of the Delphi analysis will not manipulate statistical feedback to support their own biases. It would be tragic to develop objectives that were outside the mission of an organization if they focused on destroying vital organizational components; therefore, it is important to note that if a "bogus" objective is included, this objective must be highly scrutinized.

7. All responders will receive feedback on all probes and remain in the study. Whether they participate throughout the entire study is of concern, but on rounds where individuals fail to participate, it can be assumed that their perceptions were within the domain of the responders.

Procedural Variables

There are five general assumptions concerning procedure that we believe to be important for the administrative planners who conduct Delphi studies in the context of an organization. One chief assumption is that the planners must remain unbiased. Other assumptions are:

1. Each participant must understand the purposes of the Delphi process. In a large organization ample time must be taken to advertise the importance of developing objectives as well as the necessity of remaining in the study until its completion. Here the importance of the results should be stressed over the characteristics of the Delphi process itself.

2. In the inductive process the initial probe is openended. Objectives by nature are futuristic in that they provide direction; consequently a statement such as "In the decade ahead, this organization should concentrate its energies and resources on . . ." is appropriate.

3. The judgmental approach in analyzing probe I yields better semantic similarity than the analytic approach. For example, Rubenstein has reported that the judgment approaches (scaling, sorting, and substituting) have generally been found to have a rank correlation of .92 between groups judging semantic similarity, while analytical approaches (verbal context, association, semantic generalization and Thesaurus information) produced correlations of .85 or less.[15]

4. Consensus is reached on any objective when stability between two probes occurs; and unanimity is achieved when more than 50 percent of the respondents are found to be within predetermined limits. [16]

5. Responders participating in a Delphi study can be manipulated to produce significant changes in their responses. [17]

An Overview of the Delphi Process

We present the Delphi technique as an intuitive methodology for eliciting, refining, and gaining consensus from individuals within an organization regarding a given issue. Delphi is a technique for gaining information and an opinion feedback through sequential interrogations of any number of individuals. The data become useful in making more rational judgments. [18] Typically, the procedure includes a questionnaire (probe I) sent to a panel of experts who are anonymous to each other (as far as the questionnaire being sent) and asked to make independent judgments about an assigned topic (note we have deviated from this approach in the organizational process). From probe I in the inductive (openended) approach, the semantical analysis is conducted.

The semantical analysis proceeds as follows: From all statements submitted, a list of key words or word combinations is constructed. Multiple objective statements are divided. Statements representing similar issues are studied by using the technique of substitution, a single statement representing the objective is developed. Further reduction is accomplished by substituting one word synonyms to represent underlying concepts. This process is conducted by using the following decision rules in a sequential manner:

1. Determine the main idea underlying each statement.
2. Examine each statement to determine if there is more than one major idea.
3. Create two or more separate statements if more than one major idea exists.
4. When the examination of several statements reveals that they represent one idea, one statement is developed representing all others.
5. If a problem of interpretation is encountered, the respondent is contacted and asked to revise his or her statement. [19]

From the semantic analysis of the first questionnaire, a second questionnaire (probe II) is formulated from responses of the first and returned to the same panel of responders who are invited to revise their responses if they feel it necessary. If interquartile ranges are provided, those in the first and fourth quartiles are asked to reconsider in regards to their deviance from the group. In probe III the previous responses are again tabulated and returned to the panel for reconsideration. The polling, aggregation, and feedback continue until stability and consensus of the group are gained.

Before we accept the fact that consensus has been reached between two consecutive rounds, it is necessary to determine stability. Stability occurs when the responses in two consecutive rounds are found to be alike at some level of statistical significance, regardless of whether a convergent opinion occurs.[20] The Chi-square statistic is perhaps the most popular technique for making the decision about stability although the coefficient of variation has also been used as a stopping criterion.[21]

The Delphi technique has at times been expanded to ask for the rating of the desirability of the events, what impacts the events might have if they occur, and any possible interventions that could enhance or reduce the probability of occurrence.

Weatherman and Swenson point out the advantages of Delphi:

1. Delphi is a means for obtaining information from a large number of persons, without having restrictions imposed by geography.
2. It is easy to administer and relatively low in cost.
3. It provides a means of obtaining information about problems that are often difficult to conceptualize.
4. It allows attention to be focused on the desired problem areas.
5. It permits a high degree of control by the administrator of the study.[22]

Bernstein, however, has criticized the Delphi technique for its difficulties in mail communication, and possible distortions by not having selected appropriate participants. There always exists the lack of assurance that a particular consensus will be reached.[23] The semantic analysis of probe I (inductive approach) always presents a problem of intepretation and proper statement diagnosis for the following probes. Thus the Delphi technique seems to be effective as a method for studying the process of thinking about the future and a planning tool that may aid in probing priorities held by members and constituencies of an organization.[24]

Utilizing Delphi in Establishing Objectives

Here we shall present a hypothetical example and assume that we are administrative planners in a college of education working with a department having eleven members. The purpose of the study was to establish and prioritize service objectives. Following this phase the department could then work toward time and cost estimations for each objective in order that the implementation and operation phases might begin. Probe I was an openended statement as follows: "In the next five years this department's service objectives should be . . . ."

After a semantical analysis, probe II was developed as shown in table 9–1. This table indicates the response by one group member, while table 9–2 reveals a summary of group responses from probe II indicated in the column entitled "Group Response Median and Centile 50% Range." We have utilized the responses of one individual (columns 3 and 4) throughout this example and on each probe a copy of objectives (probe II) was returned to each of the eleven participants; however, variations of this approach may be taken such as printing copies of the objectives on each probe. Probe III was returned to each of the eleven responders (see table 9–2 as an example of one person's feedback). Probe IV (table 9–3) resulted from analysis of probe III, and at this point a check for stability was conducted.

Table 9–1
Delphi Probe II

Research, teaching, and service are the major responsibilities of the State College of Education. The following strategic objectives for our department regarding service have been developed from probe I. Please consider each objective carefully and rate it in terms of importance on the Likert-type scale of 10, intensely important, to 1, not important.

Not *Important*									*Intensely* *Important*
1	2	3	4	5	6	7	8	9	10

Rank

2	*Strategic Objective 1.* Allocate staff resources to provide time for service activities within the parameters established by the mission of the college.
8	*Strategic Objective 2.* Provide inservice offerings and consultative services for client that are within the scope of college expertise and mission.
5	*Strategic Objective 3.* Expand the service domain of the College of Education whereby more attention is focused on educational concerns of community agencies.
6	*Strategic Objective 4.* Encourage a tie of service efforts with instruction, research, and publication activities.
6	*Strategic Objective 5.* Sponsor annual conferences as a service to the educational profession.
7	*Strategic Objective 6.* Recognize the contributions of faculty in college and university governance and in professional organizations.

Table 9–2
Delphi Probe III

Thank you for your response to round II. The group responses are recorded in column 2 (Median and "Centile 50% Range"). Column 3 shows your response to round II. If your response to round II per objective is outside the range and you do not wish to change, please state your reason in column 5. Your new response should be placed in column 4 based on the scale below. Thank you.

Not
Important

| 1 | 2 | 3 | 4 | 5 | 6 | 7 | 8 | 9 | 10 |

Intensely
Important

Strategic Objective	Group Response Median and Centile 50% Range	Your Response to Round II	Your New Response	Reason for Not Changing Your Response If Outside the Range
1	9–10	2	9	
2	7–9	8	8	
3	8–9	5	5	I am not interested in nonschool agencies
4	5–8	6	6	
5	6	6	6	
6	6–8	7	7	
(1)	(2)	(3)	(4)	(5)

In order to determine stability for *strategic objective 3,* used as an example of operations conducted on all six objectives, we tested the following hypotheses at the .05 level of significance with the Chi-square statistic.

H_0:   Probes III and IV are equal (independent)
H_1:   Probes III and IV are not equal (dependent)

A summary of the frequency distribution is shown for strategic objective 3 in figure 9–2.

When the expected frequencies were calculated for the 2-×-5 contingency table in figure 9–2, we found that more than 20 percent of the cells had expected frequencies of less than 5. In fact, all cells had expected frequencies less than 5. It was therefore necessary to collapse cells. Consequently, in order to meet the Chi-square criterion regarding expected frequencies, the only possible combination was as shown in figure 9–3.

Table 9–3
Delphi Probe IV

Thank you for your response to round III. The groups responses are recorded in column 2 (Median and "Centile 50% Range"). Column 3 shows your response to round III. If your response to round III per objective is outside the range and you do not wish to change, please state your reason in column 5. Your new response should be placed in column 4 based on the scale below. Thank you.

Not Important									Intensely Important
1	2	3	4	5	6	7	8	9	10

Strategic Objective	Group Response Median and Centile 50% Range	Your Response to Round III	Your New Response	Reason for not Changing Your Response if Outside the Range
1	9–10	9	9	—
2	8–9	8	8	
3	8–9	5	5	I am not interested
4	5–8	6	6	in nonschool
5	6	6	6	agencies
6	6–7	7	7	
(1)	(2)	(3)	(4)	(5)

Since the expected and observed are identical, the calculated $X^2 = 0$. With one degree of freedom a Chi-square value of 3.841 was needed for significance at the .05 level. Therefore, we accepted the hypothesis that probe III is independent of probe IV and concluded that stability had been achieved. Next we observed that approximately 73 percent of the responders were within the centile 50-percent range (8–9) on probe IV for strategic objective 3. With these two criteria being met, we concluded that it was appropriate to terminate the Delphi study for this objective. In fact, this was the case for all objectives, and the study was terminated.

In the event that the stability criterion had not been met, a decision would have been made to continue the study until stability and consensus were achieved. Those individuals commenting as to why they remained outside the group consensus range were reported in the analysis of the study for the purpose of informing the group about the disagreement concerning certain objectives. This information could prove to be a valuable source of

		Scale				Row total
	3	5	8	9	10	
Probe III	1	2	2	3	3	11
Probe IV	1	1	3	5	1	11
Column total	2	3	5	8	4	

Figure 9-2. Frequencies for Probes III and IV on Strategic Objective 3

	Scale		Row total
	3–8	9–10	
Probe III	5	6	11
Probe IV	5	6	11
Column total	10	12	22

Figure 9-3. Expected Frequencies When Figure 9-2 Was Collapsed

information when individual objectives were compared to departmental objectives in the management-by-objectives evaluation sessions between department head and staff members.

Summary

The Delphi process is complementary to activities aimed at developing objectives through the consensus of opinion. It is obviously based on judgment flavored with expert knowledge about the problem to which it is applied. This planning procedure also helps us take a photograph of the future. If we have confidence in the experts who are participating in the process, the futuristic outcomes of the Delphi process can become goals that we may wish to achieve or avoid.

Notes

1. Clarence A. Newell, *Human Behavior in Educational Administration* (Englewood Cliffs, N.J.: Prentice-Hall, Inc., 1978), pp. 136–138. Reprinted with permission.

2. Olaf Helmer, *Analysis of the Future: The Delphi Method* (Santa Monica, Calif.: Rand Corp., 1967), pp. 7–36.

3. Gail D. Thornton, C. Kenneth Tanner, and Henry H. Cooper, "Decision Making with Delphi Techniques, Bayesian Procedures and Monte Carlo Simulations," *Planning and Changing* 6 (no. 1) (Spring 1975): 50–51.

4. Peter F. Drucker, *The Practice of Management* (New York: Harper and Row, 1954). See also chapter 7 in this text.

5. N.C. Dalkey, *Delphi* (Santa Monica, Calif.: Rand Corp., 1967).

6. Richard Weatherman and Karen Swenson, "Delphi Technique," in *Futurism in Education* eds. Stephen P. Hencley and James R. Yates (Berkeley, Calif.: McCutchan Publishing, 1974), pp. 99–102.

7. S. Klein and M.C. Alkin, "Program Planning Tools and Procedures," in *Evaluation Workshop I: An Orientation* eds. S. Klein; J. Banny; D. Churchman; and M. Nadeau (Monterey, Calif.: CTB/McGraw-Hill, 1971).

8. William Eugene Collins, Jr., "Components of Administrative Competency as Determined by Tennessee Superintendents" (unpublished doctoral dissertation, The Graduate School, The University of Tennessee, Knoxville, 1974).

9. Weatherman and Swenson, "Delphi Technique," p. 101.

10. Helmer, *Analysis of the Future.*

11. F. Cyphert and W. Gant, "The Delphi Technique: A Tool for Collecting Opinions in Teacher Education," *Journal of Teacher Education* 21 (no. 3) (Fall 1970):417–425.

12. James B. Phillips, "Application of an Educational Management by Objectives Model" (unpublished doctoral dissertation, The Graduate School, The University of Tennessee, Knoxville, 1973).

13. Koji Yoda, "An Application of Computer-Aided Delphi and Cost/Effectiveness Concepts to University Personnel Administration" (unpublished doctoral dissertation, The Graduate School, The University of Tennessee, Knoxville, 1973).

14. Bradley W. Nelson, "Statistical Manipulation of Delphi Statements: Its Success and Effects on Convergence and Stability," *Technological Forecasting and Social Change* 12 (no. 1) (June 1978):41–60.

15. Herbert Rubenstein, "Some Problems of Meaning in Natural Languages," in *Handbook of Communication,* eds. Ithiel deSola Pool and Wilber Schramn (Chicago, Ill.: Rand McNally College Publishing, 1973).

16. Jarir S. Dajani, Michael Z. Sincoff, and Wayne K. Talley, "Stability and Agreement Criteria for the Termination of Delphi Studies," *Technological Forecasting and Social Change* 13 (no. 1) (January 1979):85.

17. Nelson, "Statistical Manipulation," p. 57.

18. Helmer, *Analysis of the Future.*

19. Collins, "Components of Administrative Competency," p. 35. Reprinted with permission.

20. Dajani, Sincoff, and Talley, "Stability and Agreement Criteria," p. 84.

21. J. Morley English and Gerald L. Kerman, "The Prediction of Air Travel and Aircraft Technology to the Year 2000 Using the Delphi Method," *Transport. Res.* 10 (1976):1–8; and quoted in Dajani, Sincoff, and Talley, "Stability and Agreement Criteria," p. 86.

22. Weatherman and Swenson, "Delphi Technique," pp. 111–112.

23. G. Bernstein, *A Fifteen Year Forecast of Information Processing Technology* (Washington, D.C.: Naval Supply Systems Command, Government Printing Office, 1969).

24. Thornton, Tanner, and Cooper, "Decision Making with Delphi Techniques," p. 51.

10 Initiating MBO Through the Delphi Process in a Conference Setting: A Case Study

James B. Phillips and
C. Kenneth Tanner

Introduction

In this section we present a case study of conference activities focusing on how management by objectives (MBO) was introduced in a division of vocational-technical education at the state level. These activities were conducted within the constraints of a conference designed to

> bring together state staff personnel and educators for the purpose of exploring the process of management by objectives and its application to all fields of vocational education. Bringing together all of the state staff and the teacher educators at one time for a concentrated effort is deemed desirable as opposed to having fragmented sessions for a few . . . . [1]

The objectives for this conference were listed under two headings. The general objectives were specified as follows:

1. To familiarize the staff with the concept of MBO and educate the group in order that it may apply the process.
2. To facilitate the redirection or restructuring of the department and the entire teacher-training program.

As specific objectives, to be met by the end of the conference, the following were listed:

1. Each participant will have defined his or her responsibility and function within the State Division of Vocational-Technical Education more clearly.
2. Each participant will have stated his or her responsibility and function within the State Division of Vocational-Technical Education more precisely.

Dr. James B. Phillips is program coordinator, Department of Conferences, The University of Tennessee, Knoxville.

3. Each participant will find organizational restructuring alternatives that that will enhance his or her ability to perform given responsibilities and functions leading to a state program of vocational-technical education that operates through the process of management of objectives.

The Management by Objectives Conference was held at a location with ample facilities. One hundred and thirteen persons registered for the conference, representing the state vocational-technical education staff and vocational teacher educators from the universities and colleges within the state.

First Day's Activities

The conference opened at 1:30 p.m. with an introduction and welcome, and a short talk was given about what was already being carried out as a part of MBO by the state department of education and especially the division of vocational-technical education. This discussion was aimed at orienting the participants' thoughts so that they would better understand that MBO was not something strange, but instead was primarily made up of concepts that had been used for a number of years, demonstrating that some of the concepts with which they were familiar and used regularly were very applicable to the overall process of MBO. Accordingly, the participants were expected to be more comfortable about listening to a concept that was directing them to change the way in which they thought about their jobs.

This orientation was followed by an overview of personal job objectives and MBO as a concept. The primary purpose of this survey session was introductory since the participants were going to be asked to construct working departmental objectives by the end of the conference, and to have a basic understanding of MBO. As part of this introduction a pretest was given. This pretest (table 10–1) was designed to give the conference coordinators feedback regarding what the participants really knew about MBO and to find out how many participants could construct clear, concise objectives. In order to judge how much the participants knew about the concept, they were asked to define MBO. Of the 99 persons who returned the pretest, 11 (or 11 percent) submitted definitions that revealed some familiarity with the concept of management by objectives.

The process of determining how many participants could construct clear, concise objectives involved following the criteria that a job-performance objective statement had to:

1. Be designed for periodic revision, if necessary
2. Focus on reasonable improvement
3. Be stated whereby accomplishments could be measured

Table 10–1
Worksheet 1

Name _____ Date _____

1. Participants in this workshop undoubtedly vary considerably in their knowledge and understanding of MBO. In the space below and on the back of this sheet, please explain in one or two paragraphs what you perceive to be the elements essential for MBO in vocational-technical education.

_____

_____

_____

_____

_____

2. The preparation of job-performance objectives is central to any vocational-technical MBO system. In the space provided below, please write three job-performance objectives that you believe are legitimate to your present job.

1. _____

_____

2. _____

_____

3. _____

_____

4. And meet the following criteria for evaluation:
   A. Contain an acceptable performance level
   B. Delineate job-performance conditions
   C. Specify time constraints and quantities when appropriate

After careful evaluation of the 99 returned pretests according to the preceding outline, it was determined that 8 (or 8 percent) of the participants could construct job-performance objectives that would be usable in an MBO system. While these evaluations were being made by the conference coordinators, discussions were presented to the participants regarding the federal regulations and state legislation that had direct bearing on the division and its use of MBO. These discussions were designed to give the participants a better idea of the structure within which they were required to work and were followed up with an oral presentation by the superintendent for vocational-technical education who articulated a list of state objectives and priorities.

The superintendent of VTE was asked to present this list for several reasons. First, his presence and participation was thought to be a necessary part of the program. Also, having held this position for several years, this forum gave him an opportunity to reflect the objectives and priorities as they were beginning to become evident to him from his dealings with other departments of state government, with the people of the state, and with both the state and federal departments of education. His presentation of priorities gave them an air of being closer to the outcomes the U.S. Office of Education (and consequently federal legislation) was going to push for in the near future. In spite of these implications, the superintendent took caution to present these objectives and priorities as his point of view and not as commands or demands of the division as a whole. This note of caution was very important because the priorities as presented by the superintendent were to only serve as baseline examples for the rest of the participants. From these priorities and objectives, the other participants could get a better idea of what was intended of them when they were asked to present their own lists of general, overall objectives for the division.

Following the superintendent's presentation, a film was shown to illustrate the role of the manager and to better help the participants see themselves as managers. In order for MBO to be really effective, every person involved in the process should see himself or herself as having a managerial role no matter where their position existed on an organizational chart. When the film was completed, the first day's activities ended by having the participants provide two or more endings to the following sentence: "In the decade ahead, the state Division of Vocational-Technical Education should concentrate its energies and resources on . . . ." One hundred and one responses (table 10-2, workshop 2) were collected.

This worksheet was Delphi probe I. The participants were allowed enough time only to complete the worksheet without having time to discuss their responses with their coparticipants. This was accomplished by having several monitors moving throughout the group collecting worksheets as soon as participants completed them. The participants were then dismissed for the day, and the conference coordinators proceeded with the semantical analysis in order to provide a manageable list of overall objectives from all the items supplied by the participants who completed worksheet 2.

In order to obtain this list, each item was evaluated separately and carefully to determine whether or not it could fit into any of the more general categories that began to take shape as the semantical analysis proceeded. Any item that could not legitimately be included with any other items already listed was given its own place on the list. It must be emphasized that this careful evaluation or semantical analysis was absolutely necessary in order to legitimize use of the Delphi technique. Literature reveals that a weakness of the Delphi technique can surface at this point because there may be a temptation to omit items, especially if the list is becoming lengthy and the items are suggested by only one person. Special care was taken to

Table 10–2
Worksheet 2 (Probe I)

Please provide two or more endings to the following sentence:

In the decade ahead, the State Division of Vocational-Technical Education should concentrate its energies and resources on:

1. _____
   _____
   _____

2. _____
   _____
   _____

3. _____
   _____
   _____

Note: Use back of worksheet if necessary.

assure the inclusion of every isolated item of each participant so that each participant could identify each of his or her suggestions on the resulting second probe, whether or not the items were merged with other very similar suggestions into a listing, or whether the item had to be listed separately.

At this particular conference approximately 58 manhours were spent on the process of evaluating probe I and producing worksheet 3, as shown in table 10–3. Perhaps we should note that at this point in the MBO process the objectives were very general. Thus we were beginning to be concerned for the effectiveness of our initial conference efforts, but in the organizational process, change does move slowly, as we have pointed out frequently throughout the text.

Second Day's Activities

On Tuesday morning the second session began at 8:30 a.m. with the initiation of probe II. This probe consisted of distributing worksheet 3 (table 10–3), which contained the results of probe I ordered in random manner. Participants were asked to indicate the priority they would give each of the 22 items without giving the same priority number to any two items and with using the number 23 to designate any item that they felt should be eliminated. The participants were asked to retain a listing of the numbers as they assigned them to the items so that individual comparisons could be made on the next probe. The worksheets were then taken up and evaluations were made to determine the priority distribution favored by the participants for each item. While this evaluation was being made, the conference was structured to provide a presentation that described the use of the MBO method by the Ohio State Vocational-Technical Education Department, followed by a presentation of the applications of MBO by industry.

Table 10–3
Worksheet 3 (Probe II)

Instructions: Following the statement of each objective, indicate the priority you would attach to it by using the following key:

1. Top priority	13. Thirteenth priority
2. Second priority	14. Fourteenth priority
3. Third priority	15. Fifteenth priority
4. Fourth priority	16. Sixteenth priority
5. Fifth priority	17. Seventeenth priority
6. Sixth priority	18. Eighteenth priority
7. Seventh priority	19. Nineteenth priority
8. Eighth priority	20. Twentieth priority
9. Ninth priority	21. Twenty-first priority
10. Tenth priority	22. Twenty-second priority
11. Eleventh priority	23. Eliminate this objective
12. Twelfth priority	

Statement of State Objectives	*Priority*
Develop consumer-education programs for junior high school.	_____
Build a career-education base in junior and senior high VTE programs.	_____
Develop work-study programs for all students fifteen years old and older who need aid.	_____
Increase communications to improve the public image of VTE.	_____
Expand inservice programs to meet specific needs of specific groups.	_____
Prepare job training for at least half of those sixteen years and older, with concentration on the handicapped.	_____
Initiate an increased degree of cooperation between VTE and general education.	_____
Develop a data-collection system for evaluation and improvement or elimination of existing programs.	_____
Institute four residential schools for at least 2,000 youths.	_____
Initiate adequate vocational-guidance, placement, and follow-up programs.	_____
Build elementary-level programs to encourage favorable vocational attitudes.	_____

Table 10–3 continued

Statement of State Objectives	Priority
Improve and initiate retraining and up-grading of programs for eighteen years and older.	_____
Provide better coordination of the total state VTE program by improved communications.	_____
Develop consumer-education programs for adult women in culturally deprived areas.	_____
An increased responsibility of VTE for the rounding out of the student's education beyond the lab or shop.	_____
Build occupational programs for dropouts under sixteen years old.	_____
Place an increased emphasis on youth organizations.	_____
Develop vocational home-economics programs for all girls and adult women to prepare for dual (homemaker and worker) roles.	_____
Update teacher-training programs for more relevance.	_____
Increase postsecondary programs for the eighteen to twenty-four-year-old group.	_____
By a set date, change the name of VTE to Career Education.	_____
Develop a research system for the development of new programs and comprehensive schools: i.e., manpower programs, curriculum development, facility expansion, etc.	_____

Approximately 20 manhours were required to produce worksheet 4 (table 10–4). Following a lunch break, this worksheet was presented to the participants as probe III. The participants were divided into units beginning with this session. These units were: Group A, divided into two groups including persons involved in program services and training, and teacher education; Group B, consisted of participants from the area vocational-technical schools; and Group C, was divided into two groups consisting of field-service personnel from two districts within the state. Because of this division of the groups, it was possible to determine not only how a groups as a whole ordered the overall objectives but also to determine how the five groups within the division ordered the objectives.

Stability and consensus were reached between probes II and III; hence, probe III was the final probe concerned with overall division objectives. Eighty-six persons completed and returned a usable worksheet 4 (probe III). Of this number 18 were in Group A, 19 were in Group B, and 49 were in Groups C–1 and C–2. The results of this probe are revealed in table 10–5. It should be noted that six items received a priority of 4 or higher, with the call

Table 10-4
Worksheet 4 (Probe III)

Instructions: Shown in column B is the priority most frequently assigned by respondents in worksheet 3. Column C contains your previous response. Indicate your new response in column D and the reason (column E) for the difference between your new response and the most frequently assigned priority in column B. For your new response (column D), please use the following key:

1. Top priority	13. Thirteenth priority
2. Second priority	14. Fourteenth priority
3. Third priority	15. Fifteenth priority
4. Fourth priority	16. Sixteenth priority
5. Fifth priority	17. Seventeenth priority
6. Sixth priority	18. Eighteenth priority
7. Seventh priority	19. Nineteenth priority
8. Eighth priority	20. Twentieth priority
9. Ninth priority	21. Twenty-first priority
10. Tenth priority	22. Twenty-second priority
11. Eleventh priority	23. Eliminate this objective
12. Twelfth priority	

Statement of State Objectives	B	C	D	E
Develop consumer-education programs for junior high school.	20			
Build a career-education base in junior and senior high VTE programs.	1			
Develop work-study programs for all students fifteen years old and older who need aid.	15			
Increase communications to improve the public image of VTE.	2			
Expand inservice programs to meet specific needs of specific groups through group involvement.	10			
Prepare job training for at least half of those sixteen years and older, with concentration on the handicapped.	13			
Initiate an increased degree of cooperation between VTE and general education.	10			
Develop a data-collection system for evaluation and improvement or elimination of existing programs.	2			
Institute four residential schools for at least 2,000 youths.	22			
Initiate adequate vocational-guidance, placement, and follow-up programs.	3			

Table 10–4 continued

Statement of State Objectives	B	C	D	E
Build elementary-level programs to encourage favorable vocational attitudes.	6			
Improve and initiate retraining and upgrading of programs for eighteen years and older.	13			
Provide better coordination of the total state VTE program by improved communications.	1			
Develop consumer-education programs for adult women in culturally deprived areas.	18			
Increase responsibility of VTE for the rounding out of the student's education beyond the lab or shop.	19			
Build occupational programs for dropouts under sixteen years old.	11			
Place an increased emphasis on youth organizations.	22			
Develop vocational home-economics programs for all girls and adult women to prepare for dual (homemaker and worker) roles.	17			
Update teacher-training programs for more relevancy (includes preservice and inservice).	6			
Increase postsecondary programs for the eighteen to twenty-four years group.	14			
Change the name of VTE to Career Education.	4			
Develop a research system for the development of new programs and comprehensive schools: i.e., manpower programs, curriculum development, facility expansion, etc.	2			

for "better coordination of the total state program by way of improved communications: receiving the highest priority of one. "Building a career education base in junior and senior high," "development of a data collection system," and "development of a research system for new programs," all three received a priority of 2. "Initiate adequate vocational-guidance placement, and follow-up programs," received a priority of 3, and "increasing communications to improve the public image," received a priority rating of 4.

Table 10–5

Priorities Assigned Overall Objectives by the Units of the Division

Instructions: Following the statement of each objective, indicate the priority you would attach to it by using the following key:

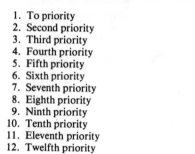

1. To priority
2. Second priority
3. Third priority
4. Fourth priority
5. Fifth priority
6. Sixth priority
7. Seventh priority
8. Eighth priority
9. Ninth priority
10. Tenth priority
11. Eleventh priority
12. Twelfth priority

13. Thirteenth priority
14. Fourteenth priority
15. Fifteenth priority
16. Sixteenth priority
17. Seventeenth priority
18. Eighteenth priority
19. Nineteenth priority
20. Twentieth priority
21. Twenty-first priority
22. Twenty-second priority
23. Elminiate this objective

Statement of State Objectives	Modal Priorities Assigned by the Units of the Division				
	A	B	C-1	C-2	Overall Modes
Develop consumer-education programs for junior high school.	20	22	20	18	20
Build a career-education base in junior and senior high VTE programs.	1	2	8	3	2
Develop work-study programs for all students fifteen years old and older who need aid.	15	12	15	15	15
Increase communications to improve the public image of VTE.	9	7	4	2	4
Expand inservice programs to meet specific needs of specific groups.	4	8	10	10	10
Prepare job training for at least half of those sixteen years and older, with concentration on the handicapped.	13	13	13	12	12
Initiate an increased degree of cooperation between VTE and general education.	12	10	7	7	8
Develop a data-collection system for evaluation and improvement or elimination of existing programs.	2	8	7	1	2
Institute four residential schools for at least 2,000 youths.	22	22	22	15	22
Initiate adequate vocational-guidance, placement, and follow-up programs.	3	7	2	3	3
Build elementary-level programs to encourage favorable vocational attitudes.	7	6	5	10	6
Improve and initiate retraining and up-grading of programs for eighteen years and older.	11	14	13	13	13

Table 10–5 continued

Statement of State Objectives	Modal Priorities Assigned by the Units of the Division				
	A	B	C-1	C-2	Overall Modes
Provide better coordination of the total state VTE program by improved communications.	6	1	1	5	1
Develop consumer-education programs for adult women in culturally deprived areas.	18	15	18	12	18
An increased responsibility of VTE for the rounding out of the student's education beyond the lab or shop.	19	15	17	16	16
Building occupational programs for dropouts under sixteen years old.	11	11	9	13	11
Place an increased emphasis on youth organizations.	18	20	16	22	22
Develop vocational home-economics programs for all girls and adult women to prepare for dual (homemaker and worker) roles.	17	15	18	17	17
Update teacher-training programs for more relevancy.	8	9	6	8	6
Increase postsecondary programs for the eighteen to twenty-four years group.	14	14	16	14	14
By a set date, change the name of VTE to Career Education.	23	21	23	20	23
Develop a research system for the new programs and comprehensive schools: i.e., manpower programs, curriculum development, facility expansion, etc.	7	6	2	7	2

Column A includes program services and program planning and teacher educators.
Column B represents area vocational-technical school personnel.
Column C-1 includes field-service personnel.
Column C-2 includes field-service personnel (divided into two groups because of size).

At the bottom end of the scale, there were four items that received a rating of 20 or above. "Developing consumer-education programs for junior high" was rated 20. Both the "Institution of four residential schools," and "Place increased emphasis on youth organizations," received the lowest priority rating of 22.

One item, "By a set date, changed the name of VTE to Career Education," received a rating of 23. This rating meant that the participants thought that this item should be eliminated as an objective. On worksheet 2 this item had been suggested by three participants. It was not listed by the superintendent as an objective, but he did use the term "career education" several times. When worksheet 3 was returned, this item was rated as 23; consequently the coordinators of the conference, who had been discussing the possibility of using a "bogus" entry and assigning it a high priority to determine if the opinions of the participants could be swayed, decided to use this item. On worksheet 4, this item was listed as having a priority rating of 4. However, when the results of the ratings of worksheet 4 were tabulated, this item was again returned to its original rating of 23 by the participants. In the column that asked for their reasons for differing from the rating of 4, they listed such reasons as, "the name is not that important," "if something is illegitimate, giving it a different name does not legitimatize it," and "a rose by any other name."

Following the final feedback on overall, general objectives, each group had a discussion session that culminated in the completion of worksheet 5 (probe IV) shown in table 10-6. This worksheet was very similar to worksheet 2. It called for two or more endings for the following sentence: "In the decade ahead, [the name of the unit] should concentrate its energies and resources on . . . ." This was the final written activity for the participants for the second afternoon. The conference closed the second afternoon following two discussions. The first discussion was on the unit level concerning the tying together of unit-level objectives with individual objectives, and the second discussion involved a presentation to the group as a whole concerning MBO at the institutional level.

Third Day's Activities

Wednesday morning's activities started at 8:30 a.m. with feedback (probe V) of probe IV to each of the five groups. Feedback was given in the format similar to that of worksheet 3 (table 10-3). As had been done in the evaluation of probe I, all night had been allowed, if necessary, to develop probe V, to evaluate the objectives of each unit, and to compile the resulting list to be presented to the participants the following morning. It was found that slightly over 60 manhours were required for this process. The actual evaluation time spent was about the same as required for probe I; however, producing six different forms required more time for clerical duties.

This feedback session was followed by three sessions that involved the group as a whole. Presentations at these sessions concentrated on further actual application of MBO to vocational education, and the development and writing of job-performance objectives on an individual basis. The third session immediately followed lunch and concentrated on presenting MBO as it was viewed by the teacher educators.

Table 10-6
Worksheet 5 (Probe IV)

Please provide two or more endings to the following sentence:

In the decade ahead, the *Program Services Section*[a] should concentrate its energies and resources on:

1. _____

_____

_____

_____

_____

2. _____

_____

_____

_____

_____

3. _____

_____

_____

_____

_____

Note: Use back of this paper if necessary.
[a]One of the five groups.

While these sessions were in progress, a tabulation of probe V was made. This tabulation focused on each of the five groups separately and was returned to the participants at the afternoon session (see table 10-7) for a final ordering of unit objectives. From this probe, priorities representing consensus were obtained (stability and consensus were obtained as illustrated in chapter 9).

Fourth Day's Activities

Feedback (for example, see table 10-8) was given to the participants in each of the five groups on Thursday morning at 8:30 a.m. Following this feedback, the groups continued to work on personal performance objectives. This session ended at 10:30., and a concluding statement was made in which

Table 10–7
Worksheet 7 (C) (Group A, Probe V)

Instructions: Shown in column B is the priority most frequently assigned by respondents in worksheet 3. Column C contains your previous response. Indicate your new response in column D and the reason column E for the difference between your new response and the most frequently assigned priority in column B. For your new response, column D, please use the following key:

1. Top priority
2. Second priority
3. Third priority
4. Fourth priority

5. Fifth priority
6. Eliminate this objective

Statement of Program Service Objectives	B	C	D	E
To give direction and leadership to help build a career-education base for K–12.	1			
Initiate adequate vocational-guidance, placement, and follow-up programs.	2			
Prepare job training for at least half of those sixteen years and older with concentration on handicapped and disadvantaged.	3			
Provide leadership, cooperation, and help in the development of a data-collection system to include curriculum development	4			
Develop and implement work-study programs for all students fifteen years old and older who need aid.	5			

Table 10–8
Objectives and Final Priorities of Field Services, Group C–1

1. Top priority
2. Second priority
3. Third priority
4. Fourth priority
5. Fifth priority
6. Sixth priority
7. Seventh priority
8. Eighth priority
9. Ninth priority

10. Tenth priority
11. Eleventh priority
12. Twelfth priority
13. Thirteenth priority
14. Fourteenth priority
15. Fifteenth priority
16. Sixteenth priority
17. Eliminate this objective

Table 10–8 continued

Statement of Field-Services Objectives	Priority Rating
Identify and interpret the role of the regional office in relation to local and state educational agencies.	3
Design and implement a process of program planning and evaluation (accountability) at both the regional office and local program level.	3
Improve classroom and class-related instruction at the local level through inservice-training activities and through the dissemination of innovative teaching techniques.	1
Facilitate and improve communications within and without the educational environment	5
Expand the breadth of program offerings commensurate with student and community needs.	12
Coordinate program-administration activities at all program levels.	7
Improve the image of vocational education.	9
Develop a job-placement capability at the local program level.	12
Improve local vocational-education program facilities.	10
Evaluate, modify, and promote youth organizations affiliated with vocational-education programs.	10
Evaluate the scope and effectiveness of work-experience programs.	9
Facilitate the redirection of teacher education to assure that its courses are relevant to and consistent with the professional- and technical-competency requirements of teachers.	8
Develop and disseminate instructional materials.	14
Improve and expand the financial professional assistance services of the regional office to the local educational agency.	12
Design and operationalize a management information system that will provide accurate up-to-date information for decision-making purposes.	16
Evaluate and improve vocational-education program standards.	6

the participants were encouraged to return to their respective offices and continue to work toward completion of personal performance objectives with a total MBO system in mind. They were informed that a follow-up session would be held within four months.

Continuing Activities

The follow-up sessions were designed to take the form of half-day sessions at four locations within the state. These were scheduled at intervals for the remainder of the fiscal year.

Conclusion

At the completion of this intensive conference, several questionnaires were foremost in the minds of the authors. Was bringing the group together a good idea? Did the conference redirect the group? Did the participants view themselves as managers? Was enough time given to adequately explain MBO?

The first impression was that bringing the group together was good. But, for motivating the group toward MBO, the answer was not clear. At least this was not evidenced in the formulation of objectives. As evidenced by the example of group priorities in table 10-8, the objectives were, indeed, parochial and perhaps too flexible for our concept of MBO—especially at the departmental level (for example, table 10-7). The entire set of objectives would be extremely difficult to utilize in performance evaluation. Perhaps we could write this off as participants' not having enough time to understand the MBO process. The reason for the poor objectives (in MBO terms) could not have been a function of the presentations since three experts at the national level were presented, made several presentations, and worked with the five groups individually. It can be speculated that the problem was well defined in priority 1 (table 10-4); "provide better coordination of the total state VTE program by way of improved communications."

Did participants see the objectives presented by the superintendent as final? Was the group ambivalent? Our answers can only be guesses. However, if we look at the organizational process at the state level, some interesting generalizations are of value. Participants apparently did not see themselves as managers. By keeping the objectives vague and general, no one could point to failure or success. Since the elected governor appoints the state superintendent of education in this state and since he in turn may elect a new superintendent for VTE, soon the state political situation might change. Elections are never more than four years away; therefore being lost in the bureaucracy at the departmental level apparently was comfortable for the majority, organization maintenance was foremost, and power was more centralized than decentralized. Hence, living by directives was more the rule than the exception. One obvious conclusion was that the system was more closed than open. Interaction was limited between division heads and department heads, although interaction within the groups appeared to be good. Communications were from the top down.

If anything was proved in this case study, we illustrated that immediate feedback could be provided. But, providing immediate feedback did not appear to be a motivation for change. However, we were made to realize once again that change is a slow process and willingness to change is perhaps more sluggish. Were the participants unwilling to accept MBO in light of the organizational constraints? Did our instrument (table 10-6) lead participants in a direction that was "too general"?

Note

1. C. Kenneth Tanner, "How to Initiate MBO" (unpublished conference presentation, 1976), p. 2.

11 The Process of Evaluating Planned Change

We noted in chapter 6 that *evaluating* is central to the administrative-planning process. In this chapter we shall deal with some background information related to evaluative research and then present an evaluative research model amenable to the measurement of planned interventions in an educational organization.

The evaluative-research process is a means of observing planned change in an organization. A basic assumption underlying this primarily synoptic planning approach is that in a client system, educational planners can plan desirable changes in advance, and through deliberate rational and incremental efforts, they can move the organization toward the goals of the program of planned change. Evaluative research then involves, ascertaining through controlled measurements what changes actually occurred, what caused them, and why. Since an organization is a contrived social system, it is necessary to use a multicausal model in measuring and evaluating change and establishing causal and contributory factors, as opposed to a single-cause model that may be appropriate for a closed system.

A multicausal model of change is based on the assumption that an event is caused by many interdependent forces rather than a single one. Thus an event may be a symptom of a "wicked" problem because of the many forces that actually cause it. Further, the effects of these forces may be expressed through intervening events rather than directly on the event being studied. This multicausal model is therefore complementary to the whole idea of open-systems theory as suggested in our earlier discussion of open systems.

Evaluative research may begin with the statement of a relationship suspected between two variables independent and dependent.[1] Evaluative research is applied research in that it is concerned with testing knowledge through application rather than primarily being concerned with discovering knowledge.[2] Evaluative research may serve many specific purposes, and as Tyler has suggested, it may be used to monitor the quality of ongoing educational programs. Thus new data are gained that administrative planners can use to plan and revise programs. A further purpose may be to disseminate information to the general public.[3] Cargo has pointed out that evaluative research may provide accounting information for funding sources;[4] while Mann has suggested that the most immediate objective of evaluative research, but not necessarily the most important, is to assist an organization in making a decision whether or not to adopt some new program.[5]

The evaluative-research design must accommodate actual events as they occur in a particular situation, not just in a hypothetical situation. Further, the data-gathering instruments and techniques must be geared to the specific evaluative-research design in order to function effectively and obtain desired measurements of what changes actually occurred in the dependent variables (goals). Suchman has stated that the goals of the program are not expected to be achieved completely; rather, the amount of change toward stated goals can be measured and expressed along a scale or continuum.[6] Measurements may be shown by the use of a Likert-type scale.[7] For example, in a preexperimental research design in which a group serves as its own control, a measurement could be taken of the group's performance of stated goals in a program of planned change (the intervention or dependent variables) prior to conducting the program. A posttest measurement of the group's performance on the same items following the treatment (program of planned change) could be taken and compared to a previous measurement. The results of these measurements, if shown on a scale such as a Likert-type scale, would indicate the relative degree to which the desired goals had been achieved based on some normative standard, while the posttest measurement, when compared to the pretest measurement, would indicate what direction the value of the group relative to the goals had moved and how far.

Not only are clear indications of what happened to the dependent variable (goals) necessary, but the independent variable (program of planned change) must be adequately described so that it is clear what the program included and how it was conducted. Suchman has stated that it is crucial to evaluative research that these two problems be adequately resolved. The first problem area is the isolation of the program elements that are suspect of producing change, and the second category deals with the specification of criteria that will actually show if change occurred.[8]

Mann has suggested that to adequately describe the independent variable, it is necessary to state the nature of overall design, followed by the total population and its characteristics, the size and characteristics of the sample, where and perhaps when the method was tested, the change strategies used, the findings, and the possible methodological errors present.[9] With a well-defined independent variable and adequate measurement of change in the dependent variables (goals), it should be possible to establish causal and contributory factors of the changes that occurred. Further, as Weiss has pointed out, unexpected changes may develop that have even more significances than the goals being sought; yet without an adequate description of the independent variable in a manner similar to that suggested by Mann, it may be impossible to determine why or how they occurred.[10]

Since evaluative research in social sciences occurs under actual field conditions and is concerned with complex human behavior, precise measurements are obviously more difficult to obtain than in the physical sciences where measurements are more quantitative. Accordingly, as Seashore has noted, changes in organizational processes develop rather slowly, and because of the long period of time needed for the changes to occur, it may become difficult for the researcher to control conditions and circumstances.[11]

Despite the trying conditions under which evaluation and research occurs, they are clearly inquiry activities. Worthen and Sanders have noted that both evaluation and research are systematic inquiry techniques, but the discovery of new knowledge is the chief characteristic of research while evaluation is a judgment of worth or social utility.[12] Certain standards must be met in order for evaluation to be classified as research. Cargo believes that for evaluation to quality as research, measurements must be based on some set of verifiable (and preferably quantitative) observations.[13] Suchman has taken a similar position. He has made a distinction between "evaluation" and "evaluative research." He views evaluation as a judgment of worth concerning a program, and evaluative research as confined to the utilization of research procedures for the purpose of making an evaluation.[14] Scriven further characterizes evaluation as being unlike typical research in that evaluative design takes into consideration problems of role and threat, focuses on credibility beyond reliability, and is influenced by the extent that audiences control the actual format of reports.[15] Evaluative research is therefore closely allied with the scientific method that utilizes the experimental model with control and experimental groups subjected to before-after measurements, judgment, reliability, and credibility of the researcher.

However, Lake found in a review of research on planned change in organizations that most of the studies he surveyed lacked thorough or meaningful research foundations.[16] In reflecting on the possible reasons for this apparent shortcoming among researchers in the field, he commented that our traditional models of research—those of a highly controlled and experimental nature—need reexamination.[17] Guba, commenting on the type of research design appropriate for evaluating change programs, has stated that researchers in the field have difficulty in meeting the various assumptions of classical systems and design,[18] and he has proposed the use of what he terms an "experimental approach," distinguished from the experimental approach in what the experimental asks "what if" as opposed to the aexperimental approach that asks "what actually happens."[19]

Others have pointed to the difficulties encountered in conducting experimental research with formal organizations in a natural field setting because of various situational constraints—ranging from difficult to control variables to problems with obtaining reliable measurements of change in dependent variables.[20]

However, the question is not whether "shoddy" nonscientific procedures should be allowed since evaluative research certainly must stick to the canons of the scientific methods as closely as possible in research design and in procedures for collecting and analyzing data.[21] The appropriate question seems to be how available research design and techniques can be put to the best use in accomplishing high-quality evaluative research. The design that is finally selected will probably emerge as a result of a combination of factors: the unusual circumstances in the situation, special administrative needs, and resources available.

Campbell has reviewed several research designs that are available in the social setting. Many of these designs are what he terms "preexperimental" and others are true experimental designs.[22] The preexperimental designs deviate in some manner from the true experimental designs. Under certain circumstances, a preexperimental design may be the one that best fits the particular evaluative research being conducted.

This may be true for several reasons and in the field setting, one important reason for going to a preexperimental design is the difficulty of finding organizational units that can be "matched." Even if this requirement is achieved, it is very difficult to keep them matched over a long period of time,[23] and most organizational change programs do extend over a long period. Mann has noted that in the organizational setting, influence of an innovative program in an experimental group may spread like a disease to other parts of the organization.[24] Wherever the situation dictates that one must deviate from the classical experimental-research design, a choice of several research designs is available for use.[25]

The preexperimental design, "One-Group, Pretest, Posttest Design" that allows a group to be its own control is one evaluative-research design that can solve the problems of unavailable matched groups and contamination of control groups because of the spread of influence from an innovative program elsewhere in the organization. It is true that this design, as Campbell has pointed out, does not provide for control of certain extraneous variables.[26] But in an organizational setting, in some cases this design may be superior to the experimental design since, as Barnes has indicated, the assumptions of the experimental design that the groups are equal, that the control group is not influenced by the program of change in the experimental group, and so on, place more faith in the experimental design than it deserves under such conditions.

Suchman emphasized that a longitudinal study, an extension of the one-group, pretest, posttest design discussed earlier, is useful for studying change in a group over a period of time. This design provides for measurements of a group over a period of time with each successive measurement being compared to a previous measurement(s). This is similar to a clinical-evaluation design in that the subject is its own control and the researcher can compare changes in the subject at different points in time. Such a research design is especially well suited to the demands of an ongoing program since the feedback obtained at various points provides needed data for the program administrator to use in making necessary adjustments in the program. [27]

An Evaluative-Research Model

In a social system, because of the interdependent nature of one variable with others, a single causal effect is not viewed as having only one resulting effect. Rather, a change program in an organization is viewed as a "causal" sequence; that is, it produces a chain of events that occurs over a period of time. Because of this, an evaluative researcher studying the results of a change program on a set of objectives (dependent variable) may focus not only on measuring changes in the components of the program but may also want to measure change in the intervening events or variables as well. The conceptualization of change occurring through a chain of events and through time is illustrated in figure 11-1.

Figure 11-1 shows that a program of planned changed does not have a direct and immediate effect on the desired objectives. Also changes (effects)

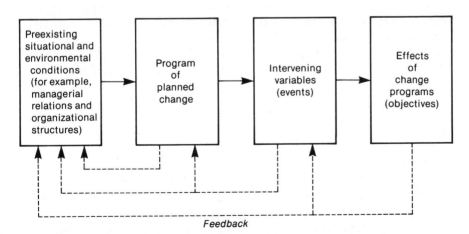

Figure 11-1. Multicauses and Multieffects of Change Program

that do occur along the chain of events produce feedback affecting other prior events. It should be stressed that there is a time lag in the feedback processes. The time required for feedback from an event to have an effect on other events, as suggested by the longer dotted line in figure 6-1 showing feedback from "effects of change program" to "program of change," is not immediate as it is for other events occurring closer to the "program of planned change."

A planned change program is one way to help an organization in the improvement of its production (output). However, the effects of the change program do not necessarily have a direct and immediate impact on the final production of the organization. Change occurs through a chain of intervening variables, and such change may take some time to be expressed in the output variables of the organization. Therefore, in evaluating a change program, a researcher may want to measure all changes that have occurred, not only in the production, but changes that have occurred in the intervening variables as well. Therefore the measuring instrument used to evaluate the program of planned change may be designed not only to measure changes at the same point in time but also at different points along the chain of events—causal, intervening, and end-result variables.

Not only may the measurements of the effects of the change program be focused at several points along the resulting chain of events but the change program may also direct its efforts at specific points along such a chain of events. A program may direct its efforts to produce change in its end-result variable by intervening at any one of several points in the chain of events leading up to the final end-result variable.

Likert has discussed the chain of events that occurs in an organization in its efforts to produce goods and/or services. This chain of events is based on the concepts of interacting causal, intervening, and end-result variables impinging one on the other. The intervening variables are what he terms the "interaction-influence system" of the organization (the operating behavior of organizational members in their role set in terms of peer leadership, communication patterns, teamwork, trust in leaders, and so on). The interaction-influence system or the intervening variables of the organization are viewed as a set of interdependent and interrelated variables that influence the end-result variables (output). Since the usual measurements in an organization of the end-result variables (student achievement, teacher turnover, student dropout, absenteeism, waste or damage to school, and so on) cannot possibly indicate the current status of the organization's intervening variables, Likert has suggested that they be measured also.[28]

A program of planned change, as outlined in figure 11-2 may extend over a period of time (first phase, twelve months). The program's impact on the end-result variables (organization output) of the school probably may or may not be felt during these first twelve months. Therefore, as figure 11-2 shows, the evaluative measurements are to be focused at three points along

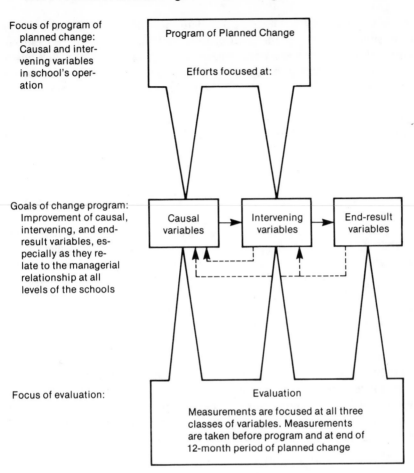

Figure 11-2. Program of Planned Change at an Urban High School

the continuum of the change processes in order to obtain a more complete picture of what may actually happen in the organization. At the end of phase I, the school system may make a decision from a choice of three alternatives: continue the program unaltered; continue the program but in a modified form; or drop the program completely.

Summary

This chapter has focused on evaluating change as it occurs in a contrived social organization. A school system is conceptualized as being a subsystem of the larger society in which it exists, and therefore its continued existence is possible only through the process of exchanging its special services (output) with the larger society for necessary resources (input). In such a conceptualization, the school is viewed as continually changing, and its very existence is possible only through the maintenance of a dynamic equilibrium.

Even though educational systems are constantly changing, they have historically lagged behind the current best practices and those changes that have occurred usually have come in spurts as a reaction to some event in the larger society. Therefore, it is proposed, especially in view of the rapid acceleration of social and technological changes in today's society, that a school system must constantly renew itself through planned change in order to be a viable system.

The effects of a planned change program are not immediately and directly felt in the organization output, but rather the changes occur through a chain of events. This chain of events is conceptualized as occurring through time and manifesting itself through several phases or stages.

A program of planned change has several basic elements. In order to study any planned change, it is deemed essential that these elements be described adequately and their effects be measured in terms of relative change, not total achievement, toward stated goals of the program. The evaluation of a program of planned change must be made on measurements taken over a period of time. Further, these measurements, in order to show a complete picture of what has occurred in the organization, must be directed at several points along the chain of intervening events as well as at the final desired improvement in the organization's output variables. In chapter 13 we deal specifically with the evaluation of a program of planned change.

Notes

1. Edward A. Suchman, *Evaluative Research* (New York: Russell Sage Foundation, 1967), p. 84.

2. Ibid., p. 75.

3. Ralph W. Tyler, "The Problems and Possibilities of Educational Evaluation," *The School and the Challenge of Innovation* (New York: McGraw-Hill Book Company, 1969), pp. 76–78.

4. Francis G. Cargo, "Approaches to Evaluative Research: A Review," *Human Organization* (Summer 1969):89.

5. John Mann, *Changing Human Behavior* (New York: Charles Scribner's Sons, 1965), p. 188.

6. Suchman, *Evaluative Research,* p. 85.

7. Rensis Likert, "A Technique for the Measurement of Attitudes," *Archives of Psychology,* 22 (October 1932–1933):140–146; and Bernard S. Phillips, *Social Research: Strategy and Tactics* (New York: The Macmillan Company, 1966), p. 184.

8. Suchman, *Evaluative Research,* p. 172.

9. Mann, *Changing Human Behavior,* p. 193.

10. Robert Weiss and Martin Rein, "The Evaluation of Broad-aim Programs: Experimental Design, Its Difficulties, and Alternatives," *Administrative Science Quarterly* 5 (no. 1) (March 1970):102.

11. Stanely E. Seashore, "Field Experiments with Formal Organizations," *Human Organization* 23 (no. 2) (Summer 1964):167.

12. Blaine R. Worthen and James R. Sanders, *Educational Evaluation: Theory and Practice* (Worthington, Ohio: Charles A. Jones, 1973), p. 14.

13. Cargo, "Approaches to Evaluative Research," p. 87. Reprinted by permission of the Society for Applied Anthropology.

14. Suchman, *Evaluative Research,* p. 7.

15. Michael Scriven, "Evaluation Perspectives and Procedures," in *Evaluation in Education,* ed. W. James Popham (Berkeley, Calif.: McCutchan Publishing, 1974), pp. 3–4.

16. Dale G. Lake, "Concepts of Change and Innovation in 1966," *Journal of Applied Behavioral Science* 4 (no. 1) (January–February–March 1968):21.

17. Ibid.

18. Egon Guba, "Methodological Strategies for Educational Change," a paper presented to the Conference on Strategies for Educational Change, Washington, D.C., November 9, 1965, p. 4; cited in *Perspectives on Educational Change,* ed. Richard Miller (New York: Appleton-Century-Crofts, 1967), p. 380.

19. Ibid.

20. Some examples are Louis B. Barnes, "Organizational Change and Field Experiment Methods," *Methods of Organizational Research,* ed. Victor H. Vroom (Pittsburgh: University of Pittsburgh Press, 1967), pp. 57–111; John R. French, Jr., "Experiments in Field Settings," *Research Methods in the Behavioral Sciences,* ed. L. Festinger and D. Katz (New York: Dryden Press, 1953), pp. 98–135; Seashore, "Field Experiments," pp. 164–170; and Frank B. Baker, "Experimental Design Considerations Associated with Large-Scale Research Projects," *Improving Experimental Design and Statistical Analysis,* ed. Julian Stanley (Chicago: Rand McNally and Company, 1967), pp. 206–227.

21. Brian MacMahon, Thomas F. Pugh, and George B. Hutchinson, "Principles in the Evaluation of Community Mental Health Programs," *American Journal of Public Health* 51 (July 1961):963–968.

22. Donald T. Campbell, "Factors Relevant to the Validity of Experi-

ments in Social Settings," *Psychological Bulletin* 54 (no. 4) (July 1957): 297–312.

23. Barnes, "Organizational Change," pp. 95–96.

24. Mann, *Changing Human Behavior,* pp. 186–187.

25. Campbell, "Factors Relevant to the Validity," pp. 297–312; and Donald Campbell and Julian Stanley, *Experimental and Quasi-Experimental Designs for Research* (Chicago: Rand McNally, 1963).

26. Campbell, "Factors Relevant to the Validity," pp. 298–299.

27. Suchman, *Evaluative Research,* pp. 100–102.

28. Rensis Likert, *New Patterns of Management* (New York: McGraw-Hill, 1961), p. 202.

12

A Planned Intervention in an Urban High School: A Case Study

Nature of the Problem

This case study describes and analyzes a phase of the life history of an educational organization. First, we shall describe the environment of an urban high school in Chattanooga, Tennessee, that is, Brainerd High School, as it existed in the academic year 1970–1971.

Describing Brainerd High School has been made more complex by the fact that it was not a physical object with only a little interaction with its environment; rather, it existed as a social institution embedded in the cultural environment of the larger Chattanooga society, and between the two, constant interaction was present. This interaction, a two-way affair, definitely revealed an effect. Therefore, in order to understand Brainerd, a social institution formed by the patterned activities of its members, it was also necessary to have some understanding of its environment.

Katz and Kahn have emphasized the importance of understanding and relating to the system's functioning and the forces from its external environment that impinge upon it. They contend that the notion that irregularities in the functioning of a system due to environmental influences should be treated as error variances is a misconception. Hence, arguing that they should be controlled out of studies of organizations is improper. On the other hand, open-system theory maintains that environmental influences are not sources of error variance. Thus we must also study the forces that impinge on a social system.[1]

The Chattanooga metropolitan area, the setting in which Brainerd functioned, could be thought of as a large wheel with the city of Chattanooga as its hub and Hamilton County comprising its outer area. Within the Chattanooga metropolitan area, there were two separate school systems—the Chattanooga City School System and the Hamilton County School System.

There were some interesting population patterns in the Chattanooga metropolitan area. Census figures for 1970 indicated that since 1960 the city of Chattanooga, Tennessee's fourth largest city with a population of 121,000, had lost 10,000 people, while Hamilton County gained 16,000. These changes reflected a pattern in which people had moved outward from the city to surrounding areas. Consequently, the population changes in the metropolitan area generally involved very little growth. The major changes in population resulted from a redistribution of the existing population.

Perhaps the most striking feature of the population in the metropolitan area was the geographic distribution of the public school students by race. In the Chattanooga City School System, there were 27,000 students of which 13,000 were black. Hamilton County School System had a student population of 28,391 of which only 930 were black. The black population of the metropolitan area then was predominantly located in the Chattanooga School System and concentrated toward the hub of the metropolitan area.

Another condition that had permeated the entire social fabric of the Chattanooga area was that dual schools by race were operated in the Chattanooga School System until 1966. Since that time, a "freedom-of-choice plan" had been used to assign students to individual schools. However, in 1971 the five senior high schools of the Chattanooga School System had a student body that was predominantly composed of one race.

The desegregation of school faculties by race had been a slow process. The tactic employed was one of filling vacancies as they occurred with teachers from the opposite race. As one administrator of the Chattanooga City Schools explained, "Because of a commitment for desegregating the schools . . . when a black teacher retires or resigns, a white teacher is assigned to fill the vacancy, and vice versa."[2] Thus there was no large-scale movement or forced reassignment of teachers and/or students to effect a racial balance in the individual schools.

Brainerd Senior High School was a relatively new school that began operation in 1960 as an all-white school in the suburbs of the city, in a community then predominantly white. Since that time the racial composition of the population of Brainerd High School had changed, as well as in the surrounding community. Brainerd High enrolled 1,344 students and 62 faculty members with the student population's being 13 percent black and the faculty's being 17 percent black. Most of the students who were attending Brainerd lived in the immediate community surrounding the school even though the school system had a freedom-of-choice plan of student assignment. Brainerd's racial mix had shifted until it was the most mixed by race of any of the high schools in the Chattanooga School System.

Some of the specific changes in the Brainerd High School during the sixties are shown in table 12-1. The racial mix in both the faculty and the student body had been changing until the school's population mix by race was about the same as the racial mix of the general population in the immediate community surrounding the school.

However, when the distribution of families by race in the Brainerd community was shown on a map, the resulting picture was one in which the black families were not evenly distributed throughout the total area of the community. In fact, the center of the Brainerd community was composed of mostly white families encircled by black families.

Table 12–1
Changes in Brainerd "Racial Mix," 1960 to 1971

	Students				Faculty			
Year	White	Percent	Black	Percent	White	Percent	Black	Percent
1960–1961	1,050	100	0	0	44	100	0	0
1966–1967	1,085	97.7	26	2.3	45	100	0	0
1969–1970	1,224	88.0	170	12.0	50	89.3	6	10.7
1970–1971	1,160	86.3	184	13.7	51	82.3	11	17.7

Source: Data obtained from Chattanooga school records.

Brainerd High School, as well as its immediate community, was part of much social change during the latter part of the sixties. It may be well to think of Brainerd High as only one strand woven into the social fabric of this total Chattanooga area. The effects of social forces acting on the Brainerd strand or any other strand in the complex social webbing of the metropolitan area could not be isolated and studied apart from their relationships with the total social fabric of the Chattanooga community.

Tensions in the Brainerd School mounted during the 1969–1970 school year. They reached such a high degree of intensity that the school closed in April 1970 for 7.5 days and, even prior to this time, because of its tense atmosphere the entire city was placed under a curfew for five days until tensions were reduced to a less explosive level. The causes and effects of the closing of Brainerd High School were not insulated from the rest of the Brainerd community nor from the larger Chattanooga area, but rather the events at Brainerd High spilled over into the community, and the community's feelings and behavior flowed back into the school. The closing of the school, according to one school official, was not just a school problem but a social upheaval in the total community.

It is not the purpose in this section to document in detail all the historical activities of the school and other social institutions and groups in the community prior to and during the closing of Brainerd High, interrelated as they are, but a few of our pertinent observations will be reported.

The closing of Brainerd came on April 13, 1970, but the school had experienced a near closing situation in October 1969. On October 3, 1969, police had to intervene at a football game between Brainerd and another area high school when disorders grew out of the crowd having become polarized over the use of "Dixie" as Brainerd's fight song and the Confederate flag as its symbol. Five days later, about 400 students walked out of the Brainerd school building to protest the suggestion of the school's human-relations committee, composed of black and white members, that a vote be taken on whether or not to change the school's symbols. Most of the students who walked out of the school building returned to class that day. However, a small number of students (about 40 to 60) left school, and during the day some cars paraded around the city displaying Confederate flags.

During the period of time between October 1969 and the closing of Brainerd High in April 1970, the school's tense and explosive atmosphere, which had emerged from a conflict of basic social values, was not defused, although the situation did receive much discussion, often heated, between individuals and groups throughout the city. During this time, the school superintendent expressed very well the general situation that existed in the Chattanooga schools and especially at Brainerd High. In a speech on December 15, 1969, at the annual school-community relations meeting, he stated:

> Many of you have said things are calming down, leave them alone. Don't fool yourself; on the surface things may be calm, but underneath among the students and the teachers there is a tenseness and a seething that is not wholly in the power of the schools to cope with. [3]

The superintendent then noted that in one elementary school the principal had told him:

> More fights, spats, arguments, and other indicators of tenseness have been noticed this year, and even in the last month, than for any other equivalent period in that principal's knowledge. [4]

He commented further about some of the major difficulties the school system faced because of changing social values, poverty, and so on. He stated:

> Put all these factors into a pot and turn on the heat of racial suspicion, opportunism and friction. Stir this concoction with the three TV stations, with camera equipment, who monitor all police calls and are filming an incident before the police car even arrives, and you have a pressure cooker. [5]

The Chattanooga Education Association in October 1969 expressed its concern to the Chattanooga School Board about the level of disorders in the schools. The president of the Chattanooga Education Association stated that "school disorders threaten the health, safety and well-being of both students and teachers in many schools."[6]

Several important changes were made in the administration of the total school system during the school year prior to the closing of Brainerd High School. The school system's policy on corporal punishment was revised in January 1970 to give the school staff more freedom in paddling students.

This change was passed by the school board without total support of its members and amid mixed reactions from the school system's professional staff. The school board in October 1969 established administrative procedures that individuals were required to follow in appearing before it. These procedures restricted individuals and groups from appearing before the board without prior appointment and further required that the individual or group spokesman present, in writing, two copies of the presentation to the board at the time he appeared. Also in January 1970 several assistant superintendents were shifted into different assignments, and one new assistant superintendent from outside the school system was hired.

The "pressure cooker" exploded on April 13, 1970, at Brainerd High School when fighting among students erupted midmorning. School operation was not resumed on an uninterrupted basis until April 30 and then only on a limited basis with many of the usual extracurricular activities being cancelled until the school's atmosphere cooled to a more normal level. Between the initial closing of Brainerd on April 13 and the beginning of uninterrupted school operation on April 30, a total of 7.5 days of school were lost, plus smaller amounts of time lost to interruptions and false reopenings and closings of the school during this period of time.

The news media in words and pictures vividly documented many of the events at Brainerd. For the purposes of this discussion, it is sufficient to report only that during the initial disruptions at Brainerd, the Chattanooga Police Department dispatched "all on-duty police, including detectives, to the school."[7] Also, 23 off-duty policemen who were available were sent to the school.[8] Pictures that appeared in the two major Chattanooga newspapers[9] during this time showed a very tense situation: groups of students jeering at each other; policemen and attack dogs standing by the school; and an empty school building with some broken glass. Despite the vast polarization of students and citizens over basic social issues and the "appropriate" procedures necessary to get the school back into operation, one overriding fact, on which most agreed, was that the school had to be reopened with a minimum of delay. Thus a program of planned change was initiated as described in the following section.

A Program of Planned Change

Brainerd High School's program of planned change was implemented by the school system's administrative subsystem in a very tense social atmosphere in order to correct the dysfunctions in the school's operation that we discussed in the previous section. It may be characterized as a planned reaction of the school organization to forces of unplanned change that impinged on it; an attempt toward innovation that emerged from dissent with tradition. Knowing whether or not such a program of planned change would be capable of bringing the school back to a dynamic equilibrium depended on the availability of valid knowledge about the school organization.

In chapter 11 we presented a model of a program of planned change that also served as a framework for the analysis of the proposed planned change. The change model of the proposed intervention took into consideration the total change program and approximately all the changes that occurred in totality. The primary objective of the program of planned change was to reduce tensions among students, teachers, administrators and the community in order to move the school toward "System 4," as denoted on the "Likert School Profile Questionnaire (LSPQ)," (System 4 will be explained in more detail in chapter 13). Therefore, it was the purpose of this program of planned change to improve the attitudes of all individuals in the school and community whereby better behavior and improved interactive relationships would be the observable result. Not only improved behaviors were expected but also the program was proposed as a means of improving performance levels of teachers, students, and administrators. Changes that were expected at Brainerd were not conceptualized as being a direct result of one specific cause or change effort but rather a change was perceived as having many causes that occurred through a chain of intervening events.

The major strategy for inducing change involved the use of "survey-feedback techniques." Consultants from outside the organization were employed by the Chattanooga School System's administration as they were needed to facilitate change in specific areas of the school's operation. Consultants were utilized mainly to conduct short workshops for specific purposes. In addition to outside resource persons, Brainerd added three special resource personnel to its staff as permanent members.

Survey-feedback techniques were employed to assist the school organization in analyzing its operation and planning for needed change. Inherent in the survey-feedback techniques was the requirement that the process extend over a period of time. Also this technique required that the data that were fed back to the school be analyzed by individuals and groups in the organization through time-consuming meetings in which group interaction was possible. Further, the technique required that persons from outside the organization who were experts in survey-feedback techniques consult and guide the organization in its use of the data to implement needed change. The authors, along with Dr. Rensis Likert and Associates, worked from this perspective.

The major focus of the change efforts was directed at changing the behavior of all the school members, especially students as they interacted in the organizational setting. These efforts were expressed through several specific tactics. The power used to accomplish changes was largely normative in the sense that the process involved the collaboration of individuals of the school in establishing the program's objectives and in attempting to achieve them.

Since survey-feedback techniques were used, many group meetings were held to discuss the survey data, to diagnose organization problems, and to plan means to achieve needed changes. In addition to this transactive planning approach, several short workshops for school personnel were conducted by "experts" from outside the organization throughout the school year. Also it should be noted that some changes in organizational structure, as well as changes in organizational rules and regulations, were made, especially as they related to the student personnel of the school.

Although the behavior of all individuals in the school was affected by the many unplanned events prior to the program of planned change, the quality of the students' behavior in the organization was of special concern to the school. Therefore, the improvement of the teacher-student managerial relationship was a prime concern of the change program. Also the huge difference in the perceptions of the school's actual operation by black and white students was an inequity at which major change efforts were directed. These desired changes in student attitudes and behavior were sought by efforts focused directly at the students, as well as through more indirect efforts focused at changing the behavior of other school personnel and modifying some school regulations and structure. All the efforts of the program of change are not described, but some examples are presented in the following paragraphs.

An additional assistant principal (black) was appointed to the Brainerd administrative staff to work with students as well as staff members. He became part of the school's administrative team, which had previously comprised a white principal and a white assistant principal. His duties were a direct extension of those performed by the principal and assistant principal. The rationale for creating this new position was simply an attempt to make the total administrative staff more effective, especially in its managerial relationship with students in all school activities.

Two directors of student activities were added to the school staff with a major responsibility of promoting positive student involvement in the total school program. It was the design in selecting these two new staff members to appoint persons with qualifications to which students from a wide spectrum could relate. A woman and man, black and white, were selected.

In addition to personnel changes, several school policies and regulations pertaining to student behavior were written, and others were changed or dropped. Some of these changes were directed at making the students more aware of their responsibilities and the school's responsibilities in the school's total operation. However, the major thrust of these changes was toward creating a situation in which more participation in school functions would be ensured for students from a broad spectrum of the student population. Some specific examples of changes of this type are listed:

1. The student council's constitution was revised to ensure the participation of more students from a wide cross-section of the student population.
2. Regulations governing the election of students to clubs and other school groups were revised to ensure that students from a broad section of the school actually participated, especially black students.
3. The use of the Confederate flag and "Dixie" was discontinued as Brainerd's emblem and fight song.
4. Written school regulations and a code of student conduct were developed.

The directors of student activities kept a weekly log of activities conducted during the year. This log reflected a wide pattern of student involvement planned by the school personnel during the year. Biracial student committees were utilized often to plan and conduct specific student activities as well as being utilized for seeking solutions to school problems as they developed. The activities included in the log reflected the school staff's awareness of the need to relax racial tensions between students and to get more black students actually involved in school functions. A selected sample of these activities are reported below:

1. Several meetings involving students, staff, and parents were held for the purpose of orienting them to new and modified school policies, rules, and regulations.
2. A biracial group made pep signs, and the school purchased 500 blue and white shakers to substitute for the discontinued "old symbols" at the first football game.
3. Students participated in study groups to revise the student council.
4. A student committee was organized to help operate the school's intramural sports program.
5. A biracial student group planned a school dance.
6. Brainerd students were utilized as aides in a neighboring elementary school's gymnastics program.
7. A contest was held to write a new school fight song to replace "Dixie."
8. A committee of students was formed to create a new school seal.
9. A biracial committee planned homecoming activities.
10. Two workshops for student leaders were held to teach them parliamentary procedure (seventy students attended each).

Several workshops for students, parents, and school staff members were held as part of the program of planned change. The workshops were conducted by consultants from outside the organization and were usually half a day in length. The workshops were designed to focus on specific areas in which change was needed. The experience of members in a workshop was designed to serve as a catalyst for further study and follow-up discussions within the group after the initial workshop experience had ended. The workshops are briefly outlined below:

1. May 1970. Workshop 1: For Brainerd teachers. The major objective was to help the teachers explore ways in which they could get more students involved in school activities especially related to educational program planning, development, and implementation of programs for the benefit of students.

2. September 1970. Workshop 2: For Brainerd parents. The major objective was to help parents gain a broader understanding of the wide range of student differences represented in the student body.

3. December 1970. Workshop 3: For Brainerd High student representatives. Seventy students attended the two, three-hour sessions in which the group learned about parliamentary procedure and its use in solving problems.

4. January 1971. Workshop 4: A three-hour session for Brainerd teachers. The major objective of the workshop was to help teachers explore a variety of teaching techniques that they could use in working more effectively with students in the classroom.

Also it should be noted that workshops were held with teachers prior to the program of planned change under study and just prior to the closing of Brainerd school. The major objective was to help the teacher become more effective in work with students in a racially tense atmosphere. These workshops are not described since they fell outside the period of time in which the program of planned change under study was conducted, but it should be noted that their impact was probably felt more during the program of planned change than before.

It should be noted that monies for the additional personnel and some teaching equipment used at Brainerd in the change program were obtained through Title III, Elementary and Secondary Education Act (ESEA).

Summary

In the first section of this chapter we presented some selected characteristics of Brainerd High School as they existed in the early 1970s. Since desegregation of this urban high school was being initiated, the major emphasis of the planning activities was on how to achieve change in a complex educational organization. Thus a program of planned change was designed.

The program of change involved essentially three approaches to inducing change, which are: (1) survey-feedback techniques; (2) change in some personnel and organizational personnel and rules and regulations; and (3) several short workshops directed at a specific element of the school's personnel and for a specific objective. The program was implemented as a planned reaction to the dysfunctions that had developed in the school's operation resulting in the closing of the school just prior to the change program. Specifically, the school was viewed as an interdependent part of the Chattanooga society, and, consequently, the program was described in this context and the results should also be viewed in this framework. Some of the more obvious social forces impinging on the school were related to racial attitudes, mobility of population, and a changing attitude among young people that they ought to have more to say about their school's operation.

Notes

1. Daniel Katz and Robert Kahn, *The Social Psychology of Organization* (New York: Wiley, 1966), p. 27.

2. Jack Lawrie, Speech to the Third Annual Chattanooga School-Community Relations Dinner, December 15, 1969. Quoted in *Chattanooga News-Free Press,* December 16, 1969, p. 10. Reprinted with permission.

3. Ibid.

4. Ibid.

5. Ibid.

6. *Chattanooga News-Free Press,* October 18, 1969, p. 11. Reprinted with permission.

7. *Chattanooga News-Free Press,* April 16, 1970, p. 1. Reprinted with permission.

8. Ibid.

9. *The Chattanooga Times* and *Chattanooga News-Free Press.*

13

Measuring Program Effectiveness: A Continuation of the Case Study in Chapter 12

It was important for the authors serving as external planners and researchers and the school officials to know whether or not the program of planned change described in chapter 12 was of any value. Thus another source was solicited. Because of his outstanding record of accomplishments in studies of organizations, it was decided to seek the assistance of Dr. Rensis Likert and Associates to provide guidance in measuring the outcomes of the proposed program of planned change at Brainerd High School. This contact with Likert and Associates was made in the spring of 1970, and at that time we proceeded to design procedures for data collection to gain knowledge of the climate at Brainerd.

Valid knowledge of the school's operation was obtained from a pretest of Brainerd personnel on the *Likert School Profile Questionnaire* (LSPQ)[1] administered in May 1970. In addition to the data from the LSPQ, quantitative data from other sources such as school records and study groups were provided.

The LSPQ was used for pretest and posttest measurements of certain causal and intervening organizational variables interacting in the operation of the Brainerd High School as a social system. One of the major aims of the change program was to improve the school's operation on the variables measured on the LSPQ. Another major objective was the improvement of the organization's end-result variables (organization output) as measured on selected performance indicators.

The LSPQ was adapted from an earlier instrument that Rensis Likert developed during his continuous research concerning the operation and performance of organizations.[2] The LSPQ measures a school as it functions on 27 variables. The measurement of each variable is expressed along a continuum or scale divided into four major intervals referred to as "organization systems."

The System 4 type of organization is fully explained by Likert,[3] but it may be briefly summarized by listing three key organizational principles underlying it. The principle of supportive relationships in all the organizational processes stresses the personal worth and importance of the individual member as he or she performs in the organization. Further, group decision making and group supervision are encouraged in the work groups. This

163

means that the organization encourages individuals to contribute their talents and ideas in the decision-making process. Supervision thus is directed toward achieving high work-group cohesion, group loyalty, and a climate in which individuals are encouraged to cooperate rather than compete. A third principle encourages all individuals to hold high performance aspirations. In a System 4 organization the leadership attempts to cultivate a high level of individual motivation toward achieving high organizational goals rather than management unilaterally setting and enforcing high standards through only close supervision. The more nearly like System 4 an organization is scored for a variable, the higher it is considered to be functioning on that variable. For example, a score of 4.2 on a variable is considered higher than a 3.4. Simply stated, the higher the numerical value of an organization's score on a variable, the better the organization's performance.

In figure 13–1, a simple item from the teacher's form of the LSPQ illustrates how each respondent marks his or her response on the scale for each item in the instrument along a continuum from 1.0 to 5.0. Where the response is placed depends on how the respondent perceives his or her school's operating on that particular variable relative to the descriptive statement under each major interval on the scale. The X in figure 13–1 shows that the respondent perceived his or her school's operating on a System 4 level or, more precisely, at 4.6 on the continuum for the variable "upward receptivity of academic ideas"[4] as this variable relates to the teacher-principal relationship in the school. This response represents a relatively high level of school performance as defined by the LSPQ.

A few features of the LSPQ should be pointed out since understanding these features will aid the reader in interpreting the data that are presented and analyzed later. The response to each item on the LSPQ is considered interval data. Also different forms of the LSPQ are used with respondents in different roles in the school. Although the same organizational variables

ITEM 72

UPWARD RECEPTIVITY:

How often are your
ideas sought and
used by the principal
about:
a. Academic Matters?

See appendix for the complete LSPQ. Used by permission of Rensis Likert Associates, Inc.

Figure 13–1. Sample Item from Likert School Profile Questionnaire, ISR Form 2/3, Teacher

are measured by each form of the LSPQ, these variables may not be measured at the same level of the organization on each LSPQ form. For example, the variable "upward receptivity" is measured as it occurs in several different role relationships in the school. Therefore, in analyzing scores on the LSPQ, one approach is to examine the variables in a role relationship. Further, the numbering of items on the LSPQ varies from one form to another. For example, the measurement of variable A in the student-teacher relationship appears on the student's form as question 19, on the teacher's form as question 24; the same variable in the teacher-principal relationship appears as item 20 on the principal's form and item 72 on the teacher's form. The number of items on each form varies, also. (See appendix for the complete LSPQ.)

Organizational Variables Measured on the LSPQ

The LSPQ measures a wide range of organizational processes based on the school's operating characteristics. These processes are grouped into two major classes of variables—causal and intervening. The variables are further grouped by areas such as communication and decision making.

The variables, listed below under ten major areas, have been identified first by a phrase or word, followed by a sample question used in this descriptive list for the purpose of clarification. However, the sample question used in this list to illustrate each variable may or may not be stated in exactly the same words as the item that is used in any one of the LSPQ forms to measure that variable. This procedure was used because different LSPQ forms (student, teacher, principal) often varied the wording of a question for a given variable depending on the role group being surveyed and at what relationship level the organizational variable was being measured.

   I. Causal variables
     A. Upward receptivity
       1. Seeks and uses ideas—academic. How often does immediate superior seek and use your ideas about academic matters?
       2. Seeks and uses ideas—nonacademic. How often does your immediate superior seek and use your ideas concerning nonacademic matters?
     B. Decision making
       3. Decision levels—school problems. At what levels in the school system are decisions made concerning your school problems?
       4. Involvement—major decisions. How much are you involved in the making of major decisions that affect you?

   5. Should have say—academic. How much say should you have
      about academic matters?
   6. Should have say—nonacademic. How much say should you
      have about nonacademic matters?
C. Supervisory leadership
   7. Supportiveness—tries. How often do superiors try to be sup-
      portive?
   8. Supportiveness—actual. How often are superiors actually
      friendly and supportive?
   9. Trust by leaders. How much trust do your superiors have in
      you?
  10. Interest in subordinate's success. How much interest does your
      superior have in your success?
  11. Help with subordinate's problems. How much support does
      your superior give you?
D. Supervisory interaction
  12. Supervisory interaction. What is the character of the interac-
      tion between members in your school?
  13. Who holds high performance goals?
  14. High performance responsibility. Who feels responsible to
      achieve high performance goals in your school?

II. Intervening variables
 A. Trust in leaders
  15. Trust in leaders. How much trust do you have in your leaders
      in your school?
 B. Communication
  16. Problem awareness. How aware is your immediate superior of
      problems you face?
  17. Talk free to you—academic. How free do you feel to talk to
      your immediate superior about your school work?
  18. Talk free to you—nonacademic. How free do you feel to talk
      to your immediate superior about nonacademic school mat-
      ters?
  19. Direction information flows—academic. What direction(s)
      does information about academic matters flow in your school?
  20. Direction information flows—nonacademic. What direction(s)
      does information about nonacademic matters flow in your
      school?
  21. Accuracy of upward-flowing information. How accurate is the
      information that is passed up the organization?
  22. Extent of trust in information. To what extent do you trust
      information you receive from superiors? Subordinates?

C. Peer interaction
   23. Peer interaction. What is the character and amount of interaction among teachers in your school?
D. Teamwork
   24. Amount of teamwork. In your school, does everyone work as a team, or is it "every man for himself"?
E. Motivation
   25. Attitude toward school. How do you feel toward your school as a place to work?
   26. Decision/influence versus motivation. To what extent does the decision-making process contribute to the individual's desire to do a good job?
   27. Goal resistance. How much resistance is there in your school to achieving high performance goals?[5]

III. End-result variables[6]

Change in the organization's level of performance on the end-result variables is determined by measuring its performance on selected performance indicators. In this study the performance indicators were restricted to those for which there were sufficient data available for a two-year period of time. The school's level of performance on the indicators during the time of the change program, period A, was compared to its performance on the same indicators during an equal length of time just prior to the change program, period B. The end-result variables were as follows:

1. Pupil attendance
2. Teacher attendance
3. Students on honor roll
4. Dropout rate of students
5. Number of days school closed because of student disorders
6. Student suspensions
7. Students referred to social worker

Selected LSPQ Pretest Data

The pretest data indicated that the school was functioning generally on a System 3 level of operation. This is a reasonably high level of operation. However, the organization's absolute-score level was a less significant factor than the *differences* in scores between various respondent groups on the same variable or the relative differences in scores between variables for one respondent group.

The pretest data revealed some clear differences in scores between respondent groups. The lower the respondent group's position in the organization's hierarchy, the lower the group generally rated the school's performance. Also when the student respondent group's scores were separated by race, black students rated the school's performance lower than white students on 35 of the 41 LSPQ items. Further, teachers rated the school's performance at the time of the pretest lower than they remembered its performance a year earlier on 48 out of 55 LSPQ items.

The greatest change in teachers' scores from May 1969 to May 1970 at the time of the pretest, was in *teacher attitude* toward the school. The greatest difference in black and white students' scores occurred in *trust in principal* for which black students scored the school a full 1.25 points lower than did the white students. Also, the black students' mean score on school attitude was 1.21 points lower than the mean score of white students. These findings on the LSPQ pretest were not surprising in view of the report of the Brainerd Parents Advisory Committee and the history of the school's difficulties during the school year immediately prior to the pretest.

The Brainerd Parents Advisory Committee, comprising six whites and three black parents of Brainerd students and appointed by the Chattanooga School Board, conducted a study to find the major causes of the closing of the school. A report was written after over 200 interviews were held with parents, school personnel, students, and others, as well as after much study of written records. The report to the Chattanooga School Board, signed by all nine members, identified seven major factors that they found had contributed to the closing of Brainerd High School.

The seven factors identified by the committee were: (1) lack of appropriate administration-school board rules and regulations relative to student behavior; (2) deterioration of student discipline at home and at school; (3) frustration of black students; (4) overcrowding of the school; (5) racism; (6) lack of student involvement in school activities—especially black students; and (7) symbolism. Some excerpts from the committee's report are presented below:

Perhaps the most deep-seated initiating cause of the tension and unrest is the frustration of the black students. It arises from many sources. Various groups point to and document its existence.

The investigation established an abundant evidence of racism. While there may have been some outside activity of this nature encouraging the development of the intense feelings that resulted in violence, very little positive evidence of such activity has been found. Once violence erupted, however, outside and internal racism became operative upon the part of students, faculty, parents and groups, both black and white, connected and not connected in any way with the school.

It is clear from an examination of the ratio of white and black students to ratio of white and black club membership that the black students are only nominally involved in the activities program of Brainerd High School. Every group interviewed agreed that the club system has long been a problem.

The focal point and the single factor most discussed was the problem of symbols; i.e., (a) the name "Rebel"; (b) the song "Dixie"; (c) the Confederate flag.[7]

In summary, this section has provided an introduction to the LSPQ and selected performance indicators. The LSPQ was first developed for use with organizations in an industrial setting and later adapted for use in an educational organization. In the next section we shall investigate the program of planned change through utilization of the LSPQ.

Analysis of Planned Change

This section contains the presentation and analysis of data obtained from the *Likert School Profile Questionnaire* (appendix) and selected performance indicators relative to the effectiveness of the program of planned change conducted in the Brainerd High School in Chattanooga, Tennessee, which we have described earlier. These analyses were built around the perceptions of teachers, students, and principals obtained on a premeasurement of the school's operation in May 1970 and a postmeasurement in May 1971.

The changes that occurred in mean scores for students, teachers, and principals on the LSPQ provided the major source for data analysis. Two types of comparisons of mean scores for members of Brainerd High School were investigated. First, the mean scores obtained on the premeasurement and the postmeasurement were compared for students and teachers, and the changes in the absolute-score level were analyzed. Second, mean discrepancy scores on the postmeasurement between black and white students, between teachers and principals, and between students and teachers on the LSPQ were analyzed. Also measurements of the students' and teachers' performances on selected performance indicators during the program of planned change were compared to their performance on the same indicators during an equal period of time just prior to the program of planned change.

As described previously, the need for Brainerd to improve its functioning as a social system was manifested dramatically in student disorders that resulted in the closing of the school for 7.5 days. It was believed that the downward spiral of the school's operations as a social system could be arrested and eventually improved through the planned change efforts.

The declining performance of the school was viewed as having several causes. However, the major causal forces stemmed from changed attitudes and beliefs of its members that the school needed to handle more effectively, especially the dissident racial attitudes and behaviors that resulted in friction between students. Obviously, many of these attitudes were generated outside the school, but it was believed that the school, through reexamining and changing some of its own practices, could produce positive effects in the relationships of blacks and whites.

The program of planned change had four major objectives. If it were successful, the achievement of the four objectives probably would not occur simultaneously, but at varying rates. Thus in judging the success of the program, *time* was a factor that needed to be considered. The four objectives, listed in the order in which they were most likely to be achieved, were: (1) to reduce racial tension and hostility in the school; (2) to reduce disagreement among various role groups concerning the school's operation; (3) to increase the absolute-score level of the school as measured on the LSPQ; and (4) to increase the school's final output (student achievement, attendance, honor roll members, and so on).

The success of the program was examined by testing the following four hypotheses:

Hypothesis I

> As a result of the program of planned change, the Brainerd high school's operating characteristics will move toward System 4 on each variable as perceived by the Brainerd teachers and students and as measured on the LSPQ.

Teachers. Data for teachers relative to hypothesis I are presented and analyzed first. This hypothesis was rejected for 54 of the 55 items measured for teachers on the LSPQ, form 2/3. (Statistical significance for the first three hypotheses was set at the .05 level of confidence.) Twenty-six LSPQ items did make a positive change, while 2 showed no change, and 27 revealed a negative change. Of the 27 LSPQ items that showed a negative change, 5 were statistically significant beyond the .05 level.

Teachers' scores remained rather stable during the change program. The LSPQ items for which significant change did occur are shown in table 13-1. Teachers' attitudes regarding whether or not students should have a voice in academic matters were represented by a mean increase of .24 points, which was significant beyond the .05 level of confidence. However, teachers perceived that *upward communication* in the school was less accurate in 1971 than at the time of the premeasurement. Further, they reported that fewer individuals held high performance goals; and that increased resistance to high performance goals existed in the school. In 1971, teachers

Table 13-1
Teachers' Scores That Changed Significantly During the Period of the Change Program

LSPO Number and Item		1971 Mean	1970 Mean	Difference	t
T-30	Students should have say about academic matters.	3.18	2.94	+ .24	2.36†
T-58	Teachers see principal as friendly and supportive.	3.89	4.24	− .35	− 2.92*
T-92	How accurate is upward communication.	3.96	4.17	− .21	− 2.17†
T-98	Character and amount of interaction between teachers and principals.	3.53	3.90	− .37	− 3.23*
T-114	Who holds high performance goals.	3.56	3.88	− .32	− 2.80*
T-116	Level of resistance to achieving high performance goals.	3.55	3.80	− .25	− 2.37†

†$p < .05$
*$p < .01$

saw the principal as being less friendly and supportive and a decrease in the quality of teacher-principal interaction than at the beginning of the change program.

Teachers' Scores at the Teacher-Principal Relationship Level in the School. Changes in teachers' mean scores at the teacher-principal level are shown in figure 13-2. The configuration of the 1970 and 1971 scores are quite similar; however, 18 LSPQ items were scored lower on the postmeasure than a year earlier. Variables 1 and 2 (upward receptivity) were scored lower than any other LSPQ items in 1970, and both showed a decline on the postmeasurement. Variable 8 (principal's support) and variable 22 (accuracy of upward communication) were among the highest scores in 1970, but both showed a significant decline in 1971.

Teachers' Scores at the Student-Teacher Relationship Level in the School. Teachers' mean scores at the student-teacher level, as shown in figure 13-3, remained very stable during the year with only three items showing a significant change. The teachers' belief that students should have a voice in academic matters (variable 5) increased significantly. On the other hand, teachers saw significantly greater resistance to high performance (variable 14) and fewer individuals who held high performance goals (variable 13) at the end of the change program than they did at the program's inception a year earlier.

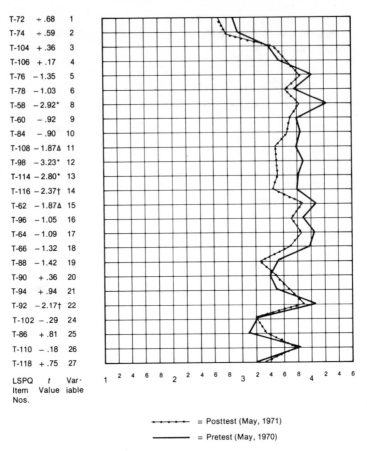

LSPQ Item Nos.	t Value	Variable
T-72	+.68	1
T-74	+.59	2
T-104	+.36	3
T-106	+.17	4
T-76	−1.35	5
T-78	−1.03	6
T-58	−2.92*	8
T-60	−.92	9
T-84	−.90	10
T-108	−1.87Δ	11
T-98	−3.23*	12
T-114	−2.80*	13
T-116	−2.37†	14
T-62	−1.87Δ	15
T-96	−1.05	16
T-64	−1.09	17
T-66	−1.32	18
T-88	−1.42	19
T-90	+.36	20
T-94	+.94	21
T-92	−2.17†	22
T-102	−.29	24
T-86	+.81	25
T-110	−.18	26
T-118	+.75	27

······ = Posttest (May, 1971)

——— = Pretest (May, 1970)

Note: $\Delta p < .10$, $\dagger p < .05$, $*p < .01$

Figure 13-2. Change in Mean Scores of Teachers' Perceptions of the School's Performance on Variables at the Teacher-Principal Relationship Level as Measured on the LSPQ, Teacher Form 2/3

Students. Students' scores changed during the period of the change program to a far greater extent than those reported by teachers. Of the 41 items measured for students on the LSPQ, 39 showed a negative change. Hypothesis I was rejected for students on all 41 LSPQ items.

The prediction that students would perceive the school operating at a significantly higher level at the end of the change program than at its inception was not supported for any of the items. For 31 of the 41 items, a significant change occurred beyond the .001 level, but opposite to the direction hypothesized.

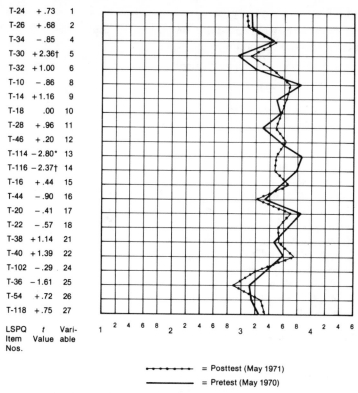

LSPQ Item Nos.	*t* Value	Variable
T-24	+ .73	1
T-26	+ .68	2
T-34	− .85	4
T-30	+2.36†	5
T-32	+1.00	6
T-10	− .86	8
T-14	+1.16	9
T-18	.00	10
T-28	+ .96	11
T-46	+ .20	12
T-114	−2.80*	13
T-116	−2.37†	14
T-16	+ .44	15
T-44	− .90	16
T-20	− .41	17
T-22	− .57	18
T-38	+1.14	21
T-40	+1.39	22
T-102	− .29	24
T-36	−1.61	25
T-54	+ .72	26
T-118	+ .75	27

•••••• = Posttest (May 1971)
——— = Pretest (May 1970)

Note: †$p < .05$, *$p < .01$

Figure 13–3. Change in Mean Scores of Teachers' Perceptions of the School's Performance on Variables at the Student-Teacher Relationship Level as Measured on the LSPQ

The 10 LSPQ items showing the greatest mean drop—more than .40 points—are presented in table 13–2 in the order in that the greatest negative mean change occurred. All the ten students' scores showing the greatest negative change, except one, related to the students' attitude concerning the student-principal relationship. All these changes were great enough to be statistically significant beyond the .001 level. It is important to note, however, that all other students' scores also declined sharply, but the distinction is that those related to the principalship showed the greatest drop by far. Why did all the students' scores drop so sharply during the change program? In particular, why were the most severe negative changes related to the student-principal relationship? These questions could not be answered from the LSPQ scores alone, but a few reflections of past events at Brainerd provided some clues.

Table 13–2
Students' Scores Showing Greatest Change (−.40 Points or More)
During the Change Program

LSPQ	Number and Item	1971 Mean	1970 Mean	Difference	t
S–34	Students' confidence and trust in principal	2.72	3.59	−.87	−13.60°
S–46	Student attitude toward school	2.69	3.48	−.79	−12.21°
S–26	Principal's view of student on nonacademic matters	2.36	3.00	−.64	−11.28°
S–39	Students' acceptance of communication from principal	2.66	3.24	−.58	−9.63°
S–13	Student effort to support principal	2.98	3.54	−.56	−7.99°
S–16	Principal's interest in student success	2.64	3.19	−.55	−9.05°
S–32	Students' view of the principal's confidence and trust in them	2.60	3.08	−.48	−8.59°
S–18	Students' view of the principal's awareness of student problems	1.92	2.39	−.47	−8.50°
S–24	Principal's use of student ideas about nonacademic matters	1.69	2.11	−.42	−7.75°
S–25	Principal's view of student influence on academic matters	2.25	2.65	−.40	−7.22°

°$p < .001$

Brainerd received a new principal in January 1970 to "head" the school's principalship, and a new assistant joined the school in August 1970. Also, as the reader will recall, Brainerd was closed for 7.5 days in April 1970 because of student disorders with racial overtones and accompanying shock waves that were felt far beyond the school.

The organizational changes and the rapid social changes, especially those related to achieving racial equality and the emerging belief in the inherent right of all individuals (students too) to participate in making decisions affecting their daily existence, no doubt increased social strains and psychological tensions in the Brainerd School. It is quite likely, as the preceding discussion suggests, that those social forces continued to forcefully operate on the school after the student disorders ended, pushing the students' scores further downward despite whatever counterforces the program of planned change may have provided.

It could be further argued that the reason for the largest drop of student scores being focused at the principalship role occurred because it was the most likely target for alienated students to project their hostility since the principalship represented "the school" by virtue of its being the "head" or chief figure of authority in the school.

The fact that student scores did not decline more in the face of these negative forces may be an indication of high organizational efforts expended to combat the many forces impinging on the school during this period of time. Such reasoning is not contrary to the theoretical underpinnings presented in chapters 3 and 4. Research shows that the length of time that is required for an organization to realize the full impact of planned change or other forces acting on its members' attitudes, role interactions, and general behavior may be up to five years.

However, many factors other than those just given may have been related to the actual changes that occurred in the Brainerd School. The strategy of the change program may have been relatively weak, or it may have moved too fast in its early stages without enough student involvement and thus obtained less than full student commitment to its goals. There may have been an actual change in the principalship's performance and style of operation that did not gain wide support and trust of the students.

In analyzing the students' scores relative to hypothesis I, it is quite apparent that the LSPQ registered a downward trend in the students' perceptions of the school's performance. The causes were, however, not so apparent.

Students' Scores for the Student-Teacher Relationship Level of the School. These scores are presented in figure 13–4. A decline in the school's functioning during the year occurred for 21 of the 22 variables measured at this level. Of these changes, 15 were great enough to be significant at the .001 level, and two at the .01 level.

The configuration of the premeasurement scores and the postmeasurement scores are almost identical. However, the postmeasurement scores consistently appeared lower on the LSPQ scale.

As shown in figure 13–4, nine of the variables were scored in the System 2 level of performance on the postmeasurement. These variables represented key areas of the school that had great impact on student behavior. Upward receptivity (variables 1 and 2) was scored low on the premeasure but even lower on the postmeasure. This was a vital area of the organization since the students' perception of their influence and acceptance as a viable part of the school, as opposed to being alienated, depended greatly on how they saw their ideas being sought and used in the school.

Other variables scored in System 2 in 1971 indicated that students did not see themselves being involved in major decisions and only being consulted occasionally. Students rated teachers low in understanding their problems. They saw teachers trying to help them only somewhat; and they described the school as a place where they felt only slightly free to talk to their teachers about academic matters; and they reported that only relatively little cooperative teamwork occurred in the school.

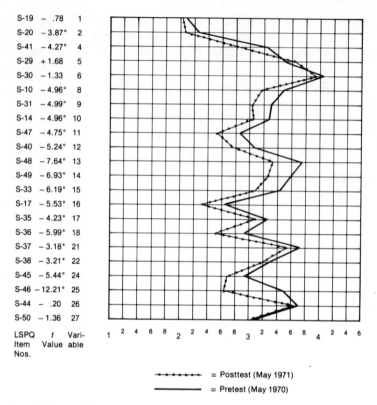

LSPQ Item Nos.	t Value	Vari- able
S-19	− .78	1
S-20	− 3.87°	2
S-41	− 4.27°	4
S-29	+ 1.68	5
S-30	− 1.33	6
S-10	− 4.96°	8
S-31	− 4.99°	9
S-14	− 4.96°	10
S-47	− 4.75°	11
S-40	− 5.24°	12
S-48	− 7.64°	13
S-49	− 6.93°	14
S-33	− 6.19°	15
S-17	− 5.53°	16
S-35	− 4.23°	17
S-36	− 5.99°	18
S-37	− 3.18*	21
S-38	− 3.21*	22
S-45	− 5.44°	24
S-46	− 12.21°	25
S-44	− .20	26
S-50	− 1.36	27

•••••••• = Posttest (May 1971)

———— = Pretest (May 1970)

Note: *p < .01, °p < .001

Figure 13–4. Change in Mean Scores of Students' Perceptions of the School's Performance on Variables at the Student-Teacher Relationship Level as Measured on the LSPQ

The postmeasurement on variable 6 showed that students continued to believe that they should have a high degree of voice in the school, but variables 1 and 2 showed that students still did not believe that their ideas were sought or used. The discrepancy between what students perceived as the "ideal" and what they believed the "actual" situation to be was 1.88 points.

A major objective of the program of planned change was to increase the consensus among various role groups in the school as to how the school was operating. The many encounters between groups and individuals before and during the student disorders resulted in a highly charged emotional atmosphere and increased polarization in the school and the community. According to the Brainerd principal, there was very little middle ground among individuals in the school and the community on any continuum one might have used to measure their feelings about the school. This observation was abundantly supported by the letters, stories, and news about the Brainerd situation carried in the two local newspapers during this period of time. The degree to which this objective was accomplished was evaluated by testing hypothesis II.

Hypothesis II

At the end of the one year of planned change, there will be no significant differences between the perceptions of students and teachers; between students and principals; and between teachers and principals on how the school is operating based on the variables that are measured on the LSPQ.

Teacher-Principal Relationships. The data relative to the teacher-principal discrepancy scores are presented in table 13-3. These data reflected the way teachers and principals viewed their mutual working relationships. As the data indicated, hypothesis II was rejected for 5 of the 26 variables.

The teachers and principals were in substantial agreement at the end of the program of planned changed on their mutual working relationships for 21 of the variables. However, on 5 variables there were significant differences.

Changes from Premeasure to Postmeasure. During the year, the teachers' scores generally remained stable with a slight downward trend shown for the variables. The principals' scores, on the other hand, shifted downward considerably. Also a wider variance existed for the principals' scores in 1971 than in 1970, indicating more disagreement within the principals' group on how the school was performing. In 1970 principals scored 21 of the variables higher than teachers, but in 1971 they scored only 7 variables higher than teachers. The net effect of these changes in group scores resulted in 5 variables' having significant discrepancy scores in 1971 as compared to 9 in 1970.

Upward Receptivity (Variables 1 and 2). The discrepancy scores increased during the year on the two variables so that the discrepancy scores for both were significant in 1971. However, for this variable, unlike so many of the others in the 1971 measurement, the principals continued to rate the teacher-principal relationships higher than did the teachers.

Teacher Influence (Variable 5). This was a value item in that teachers and principals were asked to report the amount of influence, ideally, that they believed teachers should have. In 1970 the two groups were in close agree-

Table 13-3

Mean Discrepancy Scores Between Teachers-Principals on How They Perceived the School's Operating at the Teacher-Principal Relationship Level on Variables Measured on the LSPQ

Causal Variable		LSPQ Item	Premeasure (May 1970)				Postmeasure (May 1971)			
			No.	Mean	Standard Deviation	t	No.	Mean	Standard Deviation	t
Upward recetivity	(1)	T-72 P-20	46 2	2.86 3.60	.97 .57	-1.73Δ	55 3	2.74 3.53	.94 .50	-2.51†
	(2)	T-74 P-21	46 2	2.92 3.60	1.04 .57	-1.58	55 3	2.80 3.53	.99 .50	-2.30†
Decision making	(3)	T-104 P-66	46 2	3.41 3.70	.77 .14	-1.93Δ	55 3	3.46 3.00	.58 .40	1.89Δ
	(4)	T-106 P-41	46 2	3.59 4.00	.95 .28	-1.69Δ	55 3	3.62 3.73	.82 .31	-.52
	(5)	T-76 P-24	46 2	4.03 4.10	.62 .14	-0.52	55 3	3.87 3.53	.56 .23	2.23†
	(6)	T-78 P-25	46 2	3.77 4.10	.67 .14	-2.36†	55 3	3.64 3.67	.58 .23	-.20
Supervisory leadership	(8)	T-58 P-10	46 2	4.24 3.50	.49 .71	1.46	55 3	3.89 3.27	.71 .90	1.17
	(9)	T-60 P-14	46 2	3.82 4.10	.54 .42	-.91	55 3	3.72 2.87	.55 1.00	1.46
	(10)	T-84 P-35	46 2	3.86 4.10	.72 .14	-1.65	55 3	3.73 2.53	.72 1.36	1.52
	(11)	T-108 P-44	46 2	3.80 4.00	.70 .28	-.90	55 3	3.51 3.27	.86 .50	.77
Supervisory interaction	(12)	T-98 P-37	46 2	3.90 3.60	.54 .28	1.41	55 3	3.53 3.20	.61 .87	.65
Goal emphasis	(13)	T-114 P-45	46 2	3.88 4.40	.52 .57	-1.27	55 3	3.56 4.00	.63 .53	-1.39

		N	Mean	SD	t	N	Mean	SD	t
Trust in leader									
(14)	T-116	46	3.80	.49	-1.47	55	3.55	.57	.51
	P-46	2	4.40	.57		3	3.13	1.42	
(15)	T-62	46	4.18	.54	3.78°	55	3.96	.64	1.78Δ
	P-15	2	3.70	.14		3	2.93	.99	
Communication									
(16)	T-96	592	3.86	.64	-1.76Δ	55	3.73	.59	.00
	P-33	2	4.10	.14		3	3.73	.12	
(17)	T-64	46	4.05	.70	-3.15*	55	3.88	.87	.39
	P-16	2	4.50	.14		3	3.73	.64	
(18)	T-66	46	4.00	.78	-.58	55	3.70	.90	-1.95Δ
	P-17	2	4.30	.71		3	4.13	.23	
(19)	T-88	46	3.49	.87	-3.98°	55	3.26	.73	-.39
	P-29	2	4.00	.00		3	3.07	.83	
(20)	T-90	46	3.41	.89	-4.20°	55	3.47	.76	-.57
	P-30	2	4.10	.14		3	3.60	.35	
(21)	T-94	46	3.53	.53	-3.46*	55	3.62	.42	2.42†
	P-32	2	3.80	.00		3	3.27	.23	
(22)	T-92	46	4.17	.51	2.69*	55	3.96	.45	1.76Δ
		2	3.60	.28		3	3.13	.81	
Peer interaction									
(23)	T-100	46	3.00	.68	0.50	55	3.21	.69	0.80
	P-38	2	2.60	1.13		3	2.80	.87	
(24)	T-102	46	3.26	.69	-0.13	55	3.22	.67	1.14
	P-39	2	3.30	.42		3	2.47	1.13	
Motivation									
(25)	T-86	46	3.19	.81	-3.29*	55	3.31	.64	0.51
	P-28	2	3.70	.14		3	3.07	.81	
(26)	T-110	46	3.86	.56	-170Δ	55	3.84	.55	2.01†
	P-42	2	4.00	.00		3	3.33	.42	
(27)	T-118	46	3.21	.80	-4.48°	55	3.32	.65	.63
	P-47	2	3.90	.14		3	3.13	.50	

Δ $p < .10$
† $p < .05$
* $p < .01$
° $p < .001$

ment, but in 1971 there was significant disagreement. Scores for both groups declined on this variable, but the principals' mean score dropped more. Therefore the principals, instead of assigning a higher value than teachers for this variable, assigned .34 points lower value to the need for teachers to have influence in academic matters than teachers thought they ought to have.

Communication (Variable 21). The accuracy of communication upward was viewed significantly different on the 1970 measurement, principals seeing the process occurring at a higher level than teachers. In 1971 it was still significantly different, but the discrepancy was reduced. The teachers' mean score increased while the principals' mean score decreased so that in 1971 the principals saw the process occurring at a lower level than did the teachers.

Motivation (Variable 26). In 1970 the perceptions of teachers and principals on who felt responsible for achieving high performance in the school were in substantial agreement, principals rating the variable higher than teachers. However, in 1971 there was significant disagreement, with the principals viewing the situation at a lower level than the teachers.

Supervisory Leadership (Variable 10). While there was not a significant difference between the groups for the 1970 or 1971 scores on this item, some changes that occurred need pointing out. In 1970 principals reported that teachers felt that principals were interested in their success at 4.10, which was higher than teachers reported. However, in 1971 the principals' mean score dropped to a low of 2.53, or 1.20 points lower than teachers reported. The standard deviation score for principals showed a wide variance in the principals' group as to how they saw this variable in 1971.

Trust in Leader (Variable 15). This variable registered a significant difference between the groups in 1970, but no significant difference existed in 1971. Both groups dropped in score on this variable, but the principals' score dropped more—1.03 points lower than the teachers scored it. However, there was a .99 standard deviation in the principals' scoring, indicating wide differences within the principals' group.

Other variables not discussed in detail may be examined by the reader in table 13-3 where both the 1970 and 1971 scores have been recorded. Also a summary of changes that occurred from 1970 to 1971 is presented in table 13-4 for concise reference.

Student-Principal Relationships. All the data relative to the student-principal discrepancy scores are presented in table 13-5. There were only 11 vari-

Table 13-4
Summary of Change from Premeasurement to Postmeasurement in
t **Values of Discrepancy Scores Between Teacher-Principal Relationships**

		Change in t Value	
Variable	*Number*	*Increase*	*Decrease*
Upward receptivity	1*	X	
	2*	X	
Decision making	3		X
	4		X
	5*	X	
	6†		X
Supervisory leadership	8		X
	9	X	
	10		X
	11		X
Supervisory interaction	12		X
Goal emphasis	13	X	
	14		X
Trust in leader	15†		X
Communication	16		X
	17†		X
	18	X	
	19†		X
	20†		X
	21*†		X
	22†		X
Peer interaction	23	X	
Teamwork	24	X	
Motivation	25†		X
	26*	X	
	27†		X

*Significant difference existed in discrepancy scores on the postmeasurement.

†Significant difference existed in discrepancy scores on the premeasurement.

ables measured for this relationship level since the student and principal forms of the LSPQ have only 11 matched questions at this organizational level. On the postmeasurement, there were 6 variables with significant discrepancy scores; therefore, hypothesis II was rejected for 6 of the 11 variables.

Change in Scores from 1970 to 1971. On the 1970 scores, all 11 variables were scored higher by the principals than by the students; however, on the 1971 scores, the principals scored only 6 variables higher than the students. Both groups generally scored the variables lower in 1971 than in 1970, but

Table 13-5
Mean Discrepancy Scores Between Students and Principals on How They Perceived the School's Operating on Eleven Variables Measured at the Student-Principal Relationship Level

Causal Variable	LSPQ Item	Premeasure (May 1970)				No.	Postmeasure (May 1971)			
		No.	Mean	Standard Deviation	t		No.	Mean	Standard Deviation	t
Upward receptivity (1)	S-23	592	1.83	.90		-3.32°	601	1.53	.71	-6.55°
	P-22	2	3.50	.71			3	3.13	.42	
(2)	S-24	592	2.11	1.03		-7.30°	601	1.69	.83	-7.27°
	P-23	2	4.30	.42			3	3.47	.42	
Decision making (5)	S-29	592	3.56	.84		-.20	601	3.64	.80	.80
	P-26	2	3.60	.28			3	3.53	.23	
(6)	S-30	592	4.03	.77		-.85	601	3.97	.79	3.23*
	P-27	2	4.20	.28			3	3.53	.23	
Supervisory leadership (10)	S-16	592	3.19	1.03		-3.70°	601	2.64	1.07	-1.43
	P-36	2	4.30	.42			3	3.33	.83	
Goal emphasis (13)	S-48	592	3.71	.79		-1.71Δ	601	3.34	.88	-2.14†
	P-45	2	4.40	.57			3	4.00	.53	
(14)	S-49	592	3.60	.78		-1.98†	601	3.26	.91	.16
	P-46	2	4.40	.57			3	3.13	1.42	
Communication (16)	S-18	592	2.39	1.04		-8.94°	601	1.92	.86	-11.38°
	P-34	2	4.20	.28			3	3.80	.20	
Teamwork (24)	S-45	592	2.99	.94		-1.04	601	2.70	.90	.35
	P-39	2	3.30	.42			3	2.47	1.13	
Motivation (26)	S-44	592	3.65	.90		-2.36†	601	3.64	.85	2.64*
	P-34	2	3.90	.14			3	2.87	.50	
(27)	S-50	592	3.13	.92		-7.28°	601	3.06	.85	-.24
	P-47	2	3.90	.14			3	3.13	.50	

Δ $p < .10$
† $p < .05$
* $p < .01$
° $p < .001$

the principals' scores showed the sharper drop. Not much change occurred in the number of variables with significant differences between the groups— 7 variables in 1970 and 6 in 1971. Several of these variables merit further individual discussion.

Upward Receptivity (Variables 1 and 2). Significant differences existed in 1970 between the groups as to the degree students' ideas were sought and used by the principals. These differences continued to exist at a significant level in 1971. The students' mean scores dropped to a low of 1.53 for variable 1 and 1.69 for variable 2, indicating that they believed their ideas were rarely sought by principals. The principals, on the other hand, reported that they often sought and used student ideas on both academic and nonacademic matters. No doubt, how the students saw the organizational leaders dealing with them on this variable had profound effects on whether or not they felt a part of the school. The discrepancy during that time was quite serious, especially with the student scores being the lower of the two. It was suggested that this discrepancy must be resolved if the students were not to feel alienated—just a face in the crowd with no control over their daily lives.

Decision Making (Variable 6). The two groups were in close agreement in 1970 on this variable, but significant disagreement existed in 1971. The students' scores did not change as the principals' scores did. The principals believed that students should have less voice in nonacademic matters than they believed in 1970. This represented a shift downward in the principals' ideals and values concerning the place of student influence. This shift may have had some bearing on the discrepancy scores for variables 1 and 2.

Motivation (Variable 26). The principals' view of the degree that organizational decisions motivated students to work declined from 3.90 to 2.87 during the year. The discrepancy scores were significant for both years, but the difference to note is that in 1970 the principals scored this variable higher than the students while in 1971 they scored it lower. The students' scores were essentially the same for both measurements. Thus the principals in 1971 saw this variable having "relatively little" motivational power, whereas students considered it to contribute "a considerable amount" to their desire to do quality work.

Communication (Variable 16). According to the principals' scores, they believed that they knew the problems students faced far better than the students scored this process. The discrepancy score for this variable had a t value of 8.94 in 1970, the highest of any other variable, and in 1971 it still remained the higest t value (11.38) for the variables.

Goal Emphasis (Variable 13). The principals were more optimistic concerning who held high goals than were the students. This was true in 1970, but the discrepancy was higher in 1971. These data clearly show that some important changes occurred in the student-principal relationships during the year that were not encouraging as far as reflecting a climate in which student participation in the school would be fostered. A brief summary of the data reflecting change during the year is presented in table 13-6.

Student-Teacher Relationships. Data relative to the 22 variables measured for the mutual working relationships of students and teachers are presented in table 13-7. The data showed that in 1971, disagreement between the students and the teachers occurred at a significant level for 20 of the 22 variables.

Hypothesis II Was Rejected for 20 of the Variables. The lack of consensus among teachers and students on how they perceived their working relationships existed for 20 of the 22 variables in 1970. Thus from 1970 to 1971 the number of variables in which the groups were in disagreement had remained the same. There were, of course, shifts in the degree of disagreement for variables.

The *t* value for the discrepancy scores of 5 variables on the postmeasurement exceeded − 8.00. In all cases these large *t* values increased over

Table 13-6

Summary of Change from Premeasurement to Postmeasurement in *t* Values of Discrepancy Scores Between Student-Principal Relationship

		Change in *t* Value	
Variable	*Number*	*Increase*	*Decrease*
Upward receptivity	1*†	X	
	2*†		X
Decision making	5	X	
	6*	X	
Supervisory leadership	10†		X
Goal emphasis	13*	X	
	14†		X
Communication	16*†	X	
Teamwork	24		X
Motivation	26*†	X	
	27†		X

*Significant difference existed in discrepancy scores on postmeasurement.
†Significant difference existed in discrepancy scores on premeasurement.

Table 13-7
Mean Discrepancy Scores Between Students-Teachers on How They Perceived the School's Operating at the Student-Teacher Relationship Level on Variables Measured on the LSPQ

Causal Variable		LSPQ Item	Premeasure (May 1970)				Postmeasure (May 1971)			
			No.	Mean	Standard Deviation	t	No.	Mean	Standard Deviation	t
Upward receptivity	(1)	S-19 T-24	592 46	2.11 3.07	.90 .72	-8.54°	601 55	2.07 3.18	.87 .79	-9.89°
	(2)	S-20 T-26	592 46	2.25 3.09	.98 .81	-6.67°	601 55	2.04 3.19	.89 .65	-12.13°
Decision making	(4)	S-41 T-34	592 46	3.24 3.55	1.01 .45	-3.96°	601 55	2.98 3.47	1.09 .50	-6.07°
	(5)	S-29 T-30	592 46	3.56 2.94	.84 .49	7.74°	601 55	3.64 3.18	.80 .53	5.86°
	(6)	S-30 T-32	592 46	4.03 3.35	.77 .54	7.94	601 55	3.97 3.47	.79 .67	5.21°
Supervisory leadership	(8)	S-10 T-10	592 46	3.43 3.85	.83 .59	-4.50°	601 55	3.19 3.75	.84 .57	-6.66°
	(9)	S-31 T-14	592 46	3.32 3.53	.86 .54	-2.41†	601 55	3.07 3.65	.87 .49	-7.73°
	(10)	S-14 T-18	592 46	3.28 3.59	.87 .58	-3.34°	601 55	3.04 3.59	.80 .57	-6.59°
	(11)	S-47 T-28	592 46	2.83 3.34	.98 .58	-5.40°	601 55	2.57 3.45	.91 .57	-10.31°
Supervisory interaction	(12)	S-40 T-46	592 46	3.05 3.60	.88 .53	-6.39°	601 55	2.78 3.62	.90 .44	-12.04°
Goal emphasis	(13)	S-48 T-114	592 46	3.71 3.88	.79 .52	-2.04†	601 55	3.34 3.56	.88 .63	-2.39†

Table 13-7 continued

Causal Variable		LSPQ Item	Premeasure (May 1970)				Postmeasure (May 1971)			
			No.	Mean	Standard Deviation	t	No.	Mean	Standard Deviation	t
Goal emphasis continued	(14)	S–49	592	3.60	.78	-2.53†	601	3.26	.91	-3.40°
		T–116	46	3.80	.49		55	3.55	.57	
Trust in leader	(15)	S–33	592	3.43	.93	-1.45	601	3.10	.91	-6.55°
			46	3.57	.60		55	3.62	.52	
Communication	(16)	S–17	592	2.66	.95	-5.68°	601	2.37	.86	-11.14°
		T–44	46	3.35	.78		55	3.23	.51	
	(17)	S–35	592	3.25	.95	-4.61°	601	3.01	1.01	-7.45°
		T–20	46	3.81	.78		55	3.75	.67	
	(18)	S–36	592	2.95	1.10	-5.83°	601	2.57	1.09	-8.85°
		T–22	46	3.67	.78		55	3.58	.78	
	(21)	S–37	592	3.71	.69	4.04°	601	3.58	.72	.57
		T–38	46	3.44	.41		55	3.54	.47	
	(22)	S–38	592	3.36	.84	-2.60*	601	3.21	.77	-7.38°
		T–40	46	3.60	.58		55	3.75	.49	
Teamwork	(24)	S–45	592	2.99	.94	-2.48†	601	2.70	.90	-5.34°
		T–102	46	3.26	.69		55	3.22	.67	
Motivation	(25)	S–46	592	3.48	1.18	3.63°	601	2.69	1.05	-2.27†
		T–36	46	3.10	.63		55	2.90	.61	
	(26)	S–44	592	3.65	.90	4.70°	601	3.64	.85	4.09°
		T–54	46	3.18	.63		55	3.27	.62	
	(27)	S–50	46	3.13	.92	$-.65$	601	3.06	.85	-2.76*
		T–118	46	3.21	.80		55	3.32	.65	

†$p < .05$
*$p < .1$
°$p < .001$

those for the same variables in 1970. These variables will be analyzed separately because of the increased differences that occurred during the year between teachers and students.

Upward Receptivity (Variables 1 and 2). In 1971 the difference between students and teachers on both variables was greater than the 1970 difference. This occurred as a result of students' perceiving the variables at a lower level and the teachers' scores increasing. This was a serious change because of its potential negative influence on the students' motivation. The students in 1971 saw their ideas being sought and used less than in 1970, while the teachers reported it was occurring more.

Supervisory Leadership (Variable 11). A wide gap existed in 1970 between the students and the teachers concerning the level at which they saw students being helped with problems by teachers. The gap was wider in 1971 with a lower students' mean score and a higher teachers' mean score. The important point is not which represented the actual situation (probably neither), but rather how the students saw the situation since their perceptions of the situation were key motivating factors in their behavior. As the gap increased, with the teachers perceiving an improved situation, it may have been more difficult for them to be sympathetic with any student behavior evolving from what the students believed to be a deteriorated situation.

Supervisory Interaction (Variable 12). The spreading gap between students' and teachers' views of the quality of the classroom interaction between them was indicated by a drop in the students' mean score and an increase in the teachers' mean score. This condition was probably closely tied in with the major changes noted in variable 11. Under such circumstances, the students were less likely to expend as much effort in reaching high instructional objectives as they would have been if the gap between the groups had been bridged by an improved view of the situation by the students.

Problem Awareness (Variable 16). An important ingredient in a classroom situation is the feeling of students that the teacher is sensitive to their problems. In 1970 the difference in the way students and teachers saw this occurring was significant, but it increased during the year. In 1971 students believed that the teachers were aware of the problems they faced only "somewhat" while the teachers believed they knew about the students' problems "quite well."

In table 13-8, a summary of changes that occurred in the perceived student-teacher mutual working relationships is presented. Significant differences existed between these groups in both 1970 and 1971 with a tendency for the gap to become wider.

Table 13–8

Summary of Change from Premeasurement to Postmeasurement in _t_ Values of Discrepancy Scores Between Student-Teacher Relationship

		Change in t Value	
Variable	Number	Increase	Decrease
Upward receptivity	1*†	X	
	2*†	X	
Decision making	4*†	X	
	5*†		X
	6*†		X
Supervisory leadership	8*†	X	
	9*†	X	
	10*†	X	
	11*†	X	
Supervisory interaction	12*†	X	
Goal emphasis	13*†	X	
	14*†	X	
Trust in leader	15*†	X	
Communication	16*†	X	
	17*†	X	
	18*†	X	
	21		X
	22*†	X	
Teamwork	24*†	X	
Motivation	25*†		X
	26*†		X
	27*	X	

*Significant difference existed in discrepancy scores on the postmeasurement.
†Significant difference existed in discrepancy scores on the premeasurement.

Hypothesis III

At the end of one year of planned change, there will be no significant differences between the perceptions of black students and white students on how the school is operating based on the variables that are measured on the LSPQ.

A third major objective of the program of planned change was to reduce the differences between black and white students' perceptions relative to the school's performance. The rationale for this objective was closely related to the one discussed for hypothesis II. However, this objective rated the highest priority in the program because it was believed that improvement had to occur in the racial relationships of the Brainerd School members before an improvement could occur for the other objectives of the program. The progress made in accomplishing objective 3 was checked by testing hypothesis III. Eight of the 41 LSPQ items on the postmeasurement showed significant discrepancy scores, and hypothesis III was rejected. These will be discussed in the following paragraphs.

Between 1970 and 1971 several changes occurred in the black-white discrepancy scores. In 1970, 20 of the 41 LSPQ items had significant discrepancy scores, but in 1971 only 8 were significant. Figure 13-5 visually presents changes that occurred during the year on all the LSPQ items. It is not difficult to see immediately that the 1971 discrepancy scores tended to be lower than those for 1970 and that fewer areas of extreme disagreement existed in 1971. Thus a higher consensus between black and white was present in 1971 than was the case in 1970. The reduced discrepancy between groups occurred for LSPQ items dealing with all role groups so apparently all groups contributed to this change.

In 1970 the black students' scores were lower than white students' scores on 35 of the 41, or 85 percent, of the LSPQ items. However, in 1971 they were lower than the white students' scores on only 21, or 50 percent, of the items. Thus the white students' scores tended to decline far more than did the scores for the black students.

The greatest disparity in scores in 1970 occurred for trust in principal (LSPQ item 34). The discrepancy score for this item was -1.25 with the white students reporting a much higher level of trust than the blacks. However, in 1971 the discrepancy score has been reduced to a nonsignificant level with the black students scoring this item higher than the white students. Further, the black students' mean score was higher in 1971 than it was in 1970.

The second greatest disparity in scores in 1970 occurred in student attitude toward the school (LSPQ item 46). The discrepancy score for this item was -1.21 in 1970. However, for 1971 it was only $-.01$. This very important overall assessment of the students' general picture of the school reflected an absolute mean score increase for the black students of $+.30$, while the white students' mean score declined $-.92$. In other areas, the black students went against the general downward trend registered by the white students. The black students reported that a change from 2.58 to 3.04 in the resistance to achieving high performance goals (LSPQ item 50) had occurred during the year while the white students reported that resistance had actually increased.

Several other items in figure 13-5 also reflect where a marked decrease in the black-white differences occurred during the year. Again in most cases where these decreased in the discrepancy scores occurred, the white students' mean scores usually dropped sharply with the black students' mean scores, showing less or no downward change—often an increase.

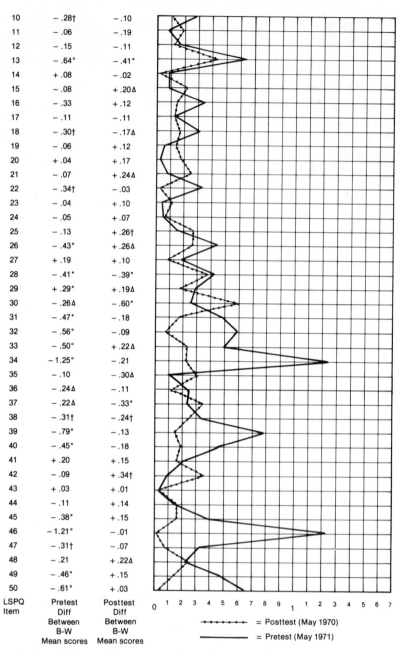

LSPQ Item	Pretest Diff Between B-W Mean scores	Posttest Diff Between B-W Mean scores
10	− .28†	− .10
11	− .06	− .19
12	− .15	− .11
13	− .64°	− .41*
14	+ .08	− .02
15	− .08	+ .20Δ
16	− .33	+ .12
17	− .11	− .11
18	− .30†	− .17Δ
19	− .06	+ .12
20	+ .04	+ .17
21	− .07	+ .24Δ
22	− .34†	− .03
23	− .04	+ .10
24	− .05	+ .07
25	− .13	+ .26†
26	− .43*	+ .26Δ
27	+ .19	+ .10
28	− .41*	− .39*
29	+ .29*	+ .19Δ
30	− .26Δ	− .60*
31	− .47*	− .18
32	− .56°	− .09
33	− .50°	+ .22Δ
34	− 1.25°	− .21
35	− .10	− .30Δ
36	− .24Δ	− .11
37	− .22Δ	− .33*
38	− .31†	− .24†
39	− .79°	− .13
40	− .45°	− .18
41	+ .20	+ .15
42	− .09	+ .34†
43	+ .03	+ .01
44	− .11	+ .14
45	− .38*	+ .15
46	− 1.21°	− .01
47	− .31†	− .07
48	− .21	+ .22Δ
49	− .46*	+ .15
50	− .61°	+ .03

 = Posttest (May 1970)
 = Pretest (May 1971)

Note: A minus difference indicates that white students scored higher than black students; a plus shows blacks scored higher. Δ p < .10, †p <.05, * p < .01, ° p <.001

Figure 13-5. Change in Mean Discrepancy Scores Between Black and White Students on How They Perceived the School's Operating on the Variables Measured on the Student Form of the LSPQ

The decrease in the discrepancy between the black and white students occurred in most cases at the expense of the white students' assessment of the school. The white students may have been expressing some hostility over the increased attention the school showed toward the black students by trying to serve more equitably their needs. It is possible that the white students (in the majority, 83 percent) felt that they had lost power and influence in the school at the expense of the black students. The white students' scores showing the greatest decline were related to the role of the principalship that may have occurred because it was the most visible target of authority for alienated students to register discontent.

Hypothesis IV

> The performance levels of both teachers and students will be higher as measured by selected performance indicators during the period of planned change than during a similar period of equal time just prior to the program of planned change.

The fourth major objective of the change program was to increase the performance of the teachers and students. The achievement of this objective obviously was contingent in large degree on the changes that occurred in the other objectives. It was expected therefore that the forces operating on the school (change program, racial attitudes, and others) would not produce an immediate effect on this objective. Hence, because of the time lag just referred, little change was expected during the first year. However, it was predicted that change would occur as stated in hypothesis IV.

During the 1970 school year, little change occurred in professional staff members' attendance compared to the 1969–1970 school year. As shown in table 13–9, a slight drop in the percentage of attendance was recorded, but it was not great enough to represent significant change for this variable.

Student attendance for the two years being compared remained essentially the same as shown by the data in table 13–10. (During the student dis-

Table 13–9
Comparison of Attendance Record of Brainerd's Professional Staff During the Program of Planned Change and During an Equal Time Period Just Prior to the Program of Planned Change

Time Period	Number of Professional Staff Work Days	Work Days Lost	Percent of Work Days Lost
Sept. 1, 1969–May 12, 1970	12,060	451.5	3.74
Sept. 1, 1970–May 12, 1971	12,780	498.0	3.90

Table 13-10
Comparison of Average Student Attendance During the Program of Planned Change and During an Equal Period of Time Just Prior to the Change Program

Time Period	Average Student Attendance	Average Daily Attendance	Percent Daily Attendance
Sept. 1, 1969–May 14, 1970	1,328	1,232	92.77
Sept. 1, 1970–May 14, 1971	1,297	1,204	92.83

Table 13-11
Comparison of Student Dropout Rate During the Program of Planned Change and During an Equal Period of Time Just Prior to the Program of Planned Change

Time Period	Average Student Enrollment	Number of Dropouts	Percent
Sept. 1, 1969–May 14, 1970	1,328	20	1.51
Sept. 1, 1970–May 14, 1971	1,297	18	1.39

orders in 1969–1970 some of the time lost because of student absenteeism of short duration may not be reflected in these official figures.)

The dropout rate for the students during the two periods of time, as shown in table 13-11, remained at about the same rate, with a slight percentage decline occurring during the 1970–1971 school year.

The percentage of the student body achieving honor roll status for the first semester of the 1969–70 school year occurred at a slightly higher rate than for the first semester of the 1970–1971 school year, as shown in table 13-12. The change did not appear to be large enough to represent any true differences in the student performance. There did appear to have been a higher level of organizational performance during the 1970–1971 school year than in 1969–1970 in providing more help to students in the form of social assistance. Probably all the students who needed social assistance during either period did not receive it. Therefore any change upward in the percentages of students assisted in 1970–1971 represented an improvement in the school's functioning. In table 13-13, it can be seen that the percentage of the student body referred to social workers increase by 1.77 points during the 1970–1971 school year.

Table 13-12
Comparison of Students Achieving the Honor Role During the Program of Planned Change and During an Equal Period of Time Just Prior to the Program of Planned Change

Time Period	Average Student Enrollment	Number of Students Achieving Honor Roll	Percent of Students on Honor Roll
Sept. 1, 1969–Jan. 14, 1970	1,328	313	25.57
Sept. 1, 1970–Jan. 14, 1971	1,297	305	23.52

Table 13-13
Comparison of Number of Students Referred to Social Workers During the Program of Planned Change and During an Equal Period of Time Just Prior to the Change Program

Time Period	Average Student Enrollment	Number Referred to Social Worker	Percent
Sept. 1, 1969–May 14, 1970	1,328	60	4.52
Sept. 1, 1970–May 14, 1971	1,328	81	6.25

Table 13-14
Comparison of Number of Days the School was Closed Because of Disorders During the Program of Planned Change and During an Equal Period of Time Just Prior to the Change Program

Time Period	Number of School Days	Days School Closed	Percent
Sept. 1, 1969–May 14, 1970	175	7.5	4.29
Sept. 1, 1970–May 14, 1971	175	0.0	0.00

The last indicator used to assess change in performance was the number of days the school was closed because of student disorders. Obviously, the school year of 1970–1971 showed a great improvement on that indicator, as shown by the data in table 13–14. In 1969–1970, the school was closed for 7.5 days, plus many unrecorded shorter periods of time were lost to normal school functioning because of class interruptions, school interruptions, and similar acts.

The 7.5 days during which the school was closed amounted to a total of 9,960 student days that were lost. This does not reflect the extra hours of time required of many people because of the disorders. Financially, the student disorders were costly (no accurate figures available) to the whole city—police, fire department, school system. Perhaps the most costly factor was the impact the disorders had on the school's operation in terms of decreased performance of the "human element" of the school. Unfortunately, after the disorders ended, their causal forces and others generated by them continued to operate on the school, so that even a year later their effects still continued to sap the functioning of the school.

Summary

This study was concerned with the general problem of student unrest in a senior high school located in a metropolitan area in which much social change with racial overtones had been and was occurring. Specifically, it dealt with evaluating the program of planned change conducted by the school system for the purpose of correcting and preventing further organizational dysfunctions that had been manifested in student disorders.

As noted in the preceding sections, the basic elements of this study included a conceptual framework from which a description of the school and its environment was made, a description of the program of planned change, and an evaluation of the relative success of the program in accomplishing the desired changes.

Student disorders were viewed as having no single cause but rather as being caused by many interacting forces coming from both within and without the school. Obviously, under such circumstances the school could not even identify all the forces causing the disorders much less help to completely control, influence, or change them.

It was believed, however, that a major influence over organizational members' perceptions and attitudes and consequently their behavior in the school was the school itself. Thus it was predicted that through planned change within the school, racial tensions could be reduced, thereby improving the school's operation.

These proposed planned changes did not involve just changing the attitudes and behaviors of individuals. They were more complex because they dealt with an attempt to change the attitudes and behaviors of organizational members during their performance of a task in a role relationship in the school. Changing the behavior of an individual was seen as being intricately interwoven with the perceptions, attitudes, and behaviors of many other school members as they worked in a role relationship in the school. Therefore for student behavior in the school to be changed, it was also necessary for the attitudes and behavior of teachers and principals to change.

A central conception underlying the program of planned change was that the school had to change in order to be effective in its rapidly changing environment. It was seen as a social organization that not only had to continually adapt in order to deal realistically with the changing needs and characteristics of its students but also had to intelligently interpret its external environment and act through planned means—not just react to its total situation. Organization posture ideally would not be rigid but rather strong and courageous enough to facilitate changes when needed, flexible enough not to break apart under the pressures of changing forces, and wise enough to adapt its functioning as justified by its external and internal environments.

The specific organization and the program of planned change that was evaluated fit, to a degree, some of the characteristics previously outlined. The program of planned change is a good example of one that came about as a result of organizational reaction to strong forces tearing at its very existence. The genesis of the program was not a planned act but rather represented organizational reaction to circumstances created by unplanned change threatening to the school. However, its development and execution were planned through the use of social-science knowledge, albeit with many shortcomings and limitations that were imposed by pragmatic considerations generated by the very politically and socially tense atmosphere in which the program had to gain its roots and survive.

General procedures used in the execution of the change program being evaluated in this study were: (1) to gain valid knowledge about the school through a premeasurement of its operation on the *Likert School Profile Questionnaire* (LSPQ); (2) to make valid information available to the school through several survey-feedback techniques; (3) to develop and execute an appropriate strategy of change as indicated by the knowledge gained from the premeasurement and other sources; and (4) to evaluate the program's effects relative to the school's performances as gauged by the postmeasurement data after one year of operation.

The primary purpose of this study was to evaluate the effects of the change program. However, as pointed out earlier, the other basic elements of planned change (change agent, client system, goals, strategy, and tactics) could not be separated or ignored from the evaluation element of the study. Indeed, in addition to having some understanding of the other elements involved in planned change, unplanned forces and the fragmented environmental preconditions setting the stage on which the program of change performed had to be related to the elements of the change program in order to make any sense out of the evaluation data.

Thus throughout this study other elements of the change program were related to the evaluative process. Further, the reader will find the results of the change program (evaluation) more meaningful when interpreted in light of the special situation and circumstances in which the program was conducted.

General Change

The general change in school attitude of various groups during the school year is perhaps one of the best indicators for gauging the general overall view of how the school members saw their school changing during the year. As shown in table 13–15, the greatest change (negative) occurred for white students, while the black students, contrary to the general feeling of their white peers, actually showed an increase in their perceptions of the school as a place to be.

One possible trend the school officials could expect was the apparently growing discontent of the white students. Their scores revealed large losses during the year. It was difficult to assign reasons for this change, but it may be that the white students as a majority group were reacting to a *perceived* loss of power and influence in the school to the black minority group.

General Conclusions

The program of planned change fell short of its stated objectives, which admittedly were very high goals to hope to accomplish in its first year of operation in view of the disorders and negative forces affecting the school. However, it can be argued that the program had positive influence on the school's operation but that it was not strong enough during such a short period of time to overcome the negative forces impinging on the school. Some major conclusions drawn from this study are:

1. *Planned change in a school occurs in a highly sociopolitical framework.* Any change affecting basic attitudes and behaviors of school members occurs in a highly sociopolitical framework in which many individuals, both inside and outside the school, may bring great pressures to bear on the school to function in a certain way. The planned change of attitudes and behaviors in a public school is a very visible and vulnerable process in which strong feelings and high emotions may be baffled about before a workable consensus is reached.

2. *Unplanned change and environmental preconditions are vital factors that also must be considered in planned change.* Planned change in a school that is defined as a deliberate, conscious, and collaborative effort to

Table 13-15
General School Attitude of Various School Groups in 1971 Compared to 1970

Group	LSPQ Item Number	1971 Mean	1970 Mean	Mean Difference
Principals	P-65	4.00	4.10	− .10
Teachers	T-84	3.73	3.86	− .13
Students (white)	S-46	2.69	3.61	− .92
Students (black)	S-46	2.74	2.40	+ .34

plan change in advance through the use of social science and planning theories is possible. However, in this case study we noted many forces that were generated from the problems of the larger society and tearing at the school's very social fabric. These forces acted on the school during the planned change program and were major causal factors along with the planned change forces in determining the school's total performance. A school is an open social system in which forces and conditions in its external environment must be integrally related to its very being. Therefore it must be emphasized that planned change efforts are affected by external environmental forces and preconditions that set the stage, may even dictate the rules of the game, on which the planned changes must function. Thus in conducting planned organizational change, more attention must be given to preconditions and the forces of unplanned change than has been the case in the past.

3. *Planned change techniques are often first used by an organization as a reaction to unplanned change.* The use of planned change techniques are often used first by an organization to extricate itself from a threatening situation it has allowed to occur through "drift" with unplanned events. It is a case of using social-science techniques and planning methodologies to bail itself out of a critical situation in which it has drifted to the point where its very life is in danger. Ideally planned change techniques should be a set of organizational tools constantly employed to keep the organization in healthy internal repair and in a viable position in its external environment.

4. *The effects of planned change in a school are difficult to attribute definitely to specific components of the program or to other causes.* In evaluating broad change programs in a school, it is possible and practical to measure changes in certain organizational functioning. It is much more difficult in a school under actual working field conditions to fix the specific causes of change because of the nature of the extremely "open system" in which the change is occurring. Therefore in the evaluation of planned

change in an organization, the experimental design is often less suited than other types of research designs that deviate from the experimental research design.

5. *To change a school's functioning in which the intricate social relationships of many people are involved required a long period of time.* It is not possible to make a decision at the top of the organization to shift organizational course and expect an immediate change in the school since many individuals must also shift. Each person has individual control to a degree over his or her role performance, though obviously those actions are related to the general system in the school, so that he or she has tremendous power to sabotage a change program in which he or she does not agree or feel a part.

Many forces other than planned change were operating in this study. Lewin has forcefully pointed to the importance of many forces interacting in the situation to produce change—the change program being only one.[8] In the Brainerd case, we originally underestimated the influence of many social forces from the society at large that were to shape organizational events and performance. Thus we tended to overestimate the impact of the change program on the school during the first year of its operation.

The above observations seem even more plausible in view of the wide polarization of individuals and groups present in both the school and the community at the beginning and during the change program. The very unsettled and emotionally tense atmosphere in the whole metropolitan area, which had been kindled and rekindled by the changing ideas about what was appropriate racial accommodation in the society's basic social institutions, reflected the vast differences that existed in basic values and beliefs of many citizens. The behaviors that the program of planned change hoped to produce often ran counter to many beliefs, values, and attitudes of a large number and consequently involved proposed changes in basic social attitudes that were bound to be slow to be accepted.

Likert's research supports the concept of planned change occurring slowly in an organization and often requiring up to five years before its full impact is realized.[9] Such a time requirement does not seem unreasonable when it is realized that in the case of the school, the change involved modifying and changing intricate role relationships among members functioning in a complex, interrelated social setting. In the Brainerd case, it also involved resolving highly charged emotional attitudes related to ingrained race relations that had long permeated the total social fabric of the school and community but that were considered by many as inadequate and unacceptable.

Several basic school changes were made at Brainerd prior to the actual beginning of the 1970–1971 school year. For example, the school board's policy decision in the summer of 1970 to change the school's song and emblem were made with little student participation because of the specific circumstances. While these changes were reasonable, sensible, and definitely needed to cool some burning social problems, many students, especially white students, may have viewed the actions of the school authorities as a "sell out" or "give in" to pressures from prevailing currents of social pressure. Further, white students (majority group) may have viewed the early changes as a loss of power and influence the black students (minority group). Full commitment and trust of the students in the change program thus may have been slowed by early events.

In the 1980–1981 school year, we can report that the school was operating normally. To quote an educator in the Chattanooga area, "You should just see how well things are going now."

Notes

1. See appendix for a copy of the LSPQ. For further information, contact Rensis Likert Associates, Inc., 630 City Center Bldg., Ann Arbor, MI 48103.

2. For a detailed discussion of Likert's original profile, see Rensis Likert, *The Human Organization* (New York: McGraw-Hill, 1967); Rensis Likert, *New Patterns of Management* (New York: McGraw-Hill, 1961); and Rensis Likert, *New Ways of Managing Conflict* (New York: McGraw-Hill, 1976).

3. For example, see: Rensis Likert, *The Human Organization* (New York: McGraw-Hill, 1967), pp. 4–10, 14–24, 47–49, 75–77, 120–121, 136–140.

4. From the Likert School Profile Questionnaire, ISR Form 2/3, Teacher.

5. Likert School Profile Questionnaire (LSPQ). Rensis Likert Associates, Inc., 630 City Center Bldg., Ann Arbor, MI 48103: Profile of a School Form 1 (High School Student), Combined Forms 2 and 3 (Teacher), and Form 4 (Principal).

6. Rensis Likert, *The Human Organization,* p. 29.

7. As printed in *Chattanooga News-Free Press,* July 5, 1970, p. F5. Reprinted with permission.

8. Kurt Lewin, "Frontiers in Group Dynamics," *Human Relations* (June 1947):34.

9. Likert, *The Human Organization.*

Appendix: Likert School Profile Questionnaire (LSPQ)

Profile of a School

Form 1
(High School Student)

This questionnaire is part of a study designed in cooperation with your school to learn more about how students, teachers, school principals, and others can best work together. The aim is to use the information to make your education more satisfying and productive.

If this study is to be helpful, it is important that you answer each question as thoughtfully and frankly as possible. This is not a test and there are no right or wrong answers.

The answers on the questionnaires are processed by computers which summarize the responses in statistical form so that individuals cannot be identified. To ensure COMPLETE CONFIDENTIALITY please do not write your name anywhere on the questionnaire.

Instructions: On the lines below each item, place an *N* at the point which, *in your experience,* describes your school at the present time (*N* = now). Treat each horizontal line as continuous from the extreme at one end to the extreme at the other; i.e., do not think of the vertical lines as barriers.

Since each teacher and student differs one from the other, answer the questions as describing the average situation or reaction.

Prepared by Jane Gibson Likert and Rensis Likert. Adapted from Rensis Likert, *The Human Organization: Its Management and Value* (New York: McGraw-Hill, 1967). Copyright © 1967 by McGraw-Hill, Inc. By permission of McGraw-Hill Book Company, Inc. No further reproduction or distribution authorized without permission of McGraw-Hill. Used by permission of Rensis Likert Associates, Inc. The new edition of this series is available from Rensis Likert Associates, Inc., Ann Arbor, Michigan.

Item No.	Question	1.	2.	3.	4.	5.	Column No.
10	How often is the behavior of your teachers friendly and supportive?	Rarely	Sometimes	Often	Almost always		1:21–22
	How often do you try to be friendly and supportive to:	Rarely	Sometimes	Often	Almost always		
11	a. other students?						1:23–24
12	b. your teachers?						1:25–26
13	c. your principal?						1:27–28
14	On the average, how much do you feel that your teachers are interested in your success as a student?	Not interested	Slightly interested	Quite interested	Very interested		1:29–30
15	On the average, how much do you feel that other students are interested in your success as a student?	Not interested	Slightly interested	Quite interested	Very interested		1:31–32
16	How much do you feel that the principal is interested in your success as a student?	Not interested	Slightly interested	Quite interested	Very interested		1:33–34
17	How well do your teachers know the problems you face in your school work?	Not well	Somewhat	Quite well	Very well		1:35–36
18	How well does your principal know the problems you face in your school work?	Not well	Somewhat	Quite well	Very well		1:37–38

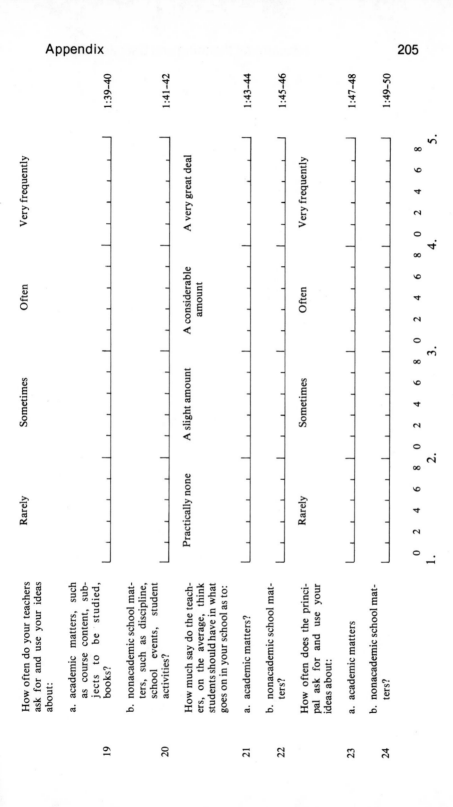

	Rarely	Sometimes	Often	Very frequently	

How often do your teachers ask for and use your ideas about:

19 a. academic matters, such as course content, subjects to be studied, books? — 1:39–40

20 b. nonacademic school matters, such as discipline, school events, student activities? — 1:41–42

	Practically none	A slight amount	A considerable amount	A very great deal	

How much say do the teachers, on the average, think students should have in what goes on in your school as to:

21 a. academic matters? — 1:43–44

22 b. nonacademic school matters? — 1:45–46

	Rarely	Sometimes	Often	Very frequently	

How often does the principal ask for and use your ideas about:

23 a. academic matters — 1:47–48

24 b. nonacademic school matters? — 1:49–50

```
1.  0 2 4 6 8 0 2 4 6 8 0 2 4 6 8 0 2 4 6 8 0 2 4 6 8
         2.          3.          4.          5.
```

Item No.		1. 0 2 4 6 8 Practically none	2. 0 2 4 6 8 A slight amount	3. 0 2 4 6 8 A considerable amount	4. 0 2 4 6 8 A very great deal	5.	Column No.
	How much say does the principal think students should have in what goes on in your school as to:						
25	a. academic matters?						1:51–52
26	b. nonacademic school matters?						1:53–54
	How much say do students, on the average, think they should have in what goes on in your school as to:						
27	a. academic matters?						1:55–56
28	b. nonacademic school matters?						1:57–58
	How much say do *you* think students should have in what goes on in your school as to:						
29	a. academic matters?						1:59–60
30	b. nonacademic school matters?						1:61–62
31	In general, how much confidence and trust do your teachers have in you?						1:63–64

No.		Practically none	A slight amount	A considerable amount	A very great deal	Column
32	How much confidence and trust does your principal have in you?	Practically none	A slight amount	A considerable amount	A very great deal	1:65–66
33	How much confidence and trust do you have in your teachers?	Practically none	A slight amount	A considerable amount	A very great deal	1:67–68
34	How much confidence and trust do you have in your principal?	Practically none	A slight amount	A considerable amount	A very great deal	1:69–70

How free do you feel to talk to your teachers about:

No.		Not free	Slightly free	Quite free	Very free	Column
35	a. problems associated with your work?					1:71–72
36	b. nonacademic school matters?					1:73–74

No.		Usually inaccurate	Often inaccurate	Fairly accurate	Almost always accurate	Column
37	How accurate is the information you give to your teachers concerning class or school matters?					1:75–76

How do you view communications from:

No.		Communications viewed with great suspicion	Some accepted; some viewed with suspicion	Usually accepted; sometimes cautiously	Almost always accepted. If not, openly and candidly questioned	Column
38	a. your teachers?					1:77–78
39	b. your principal?					1:79–80

```
0  2  4  6  8  0  2  4  6  8  0  2  4  6  8  0  2  4  6  8  0  2  4  6  8
1.             2.             3.             4.             5.
```

Item No.		1. (0 2 4 6 8)	2. (0 2 4 6 8)	3. (0 2 4 6 8)	4. (0 2 4 6 8)	5. (0 2 4 6 8)	Column No.
40	How much discussion do have with your teachers about school and other matters?	Very little discussion; usually with fear and distrust	Little discussion; teacher usually maintains distance from students	Moderate discussion; often with fair amount of confidence and trust	Extensive friendly discussion with high degree of confidence and trust		2:21–22
41	To what extent are you involved in major decisions affecting you?	Not at all	Never involved in decisions affecting me; occasionally consulted	Usually consulted, but ordinarily not involved in decisions affecting me	Fully involved in decisions affecting me		2:23–24
42	How much influence do you have in decisions concerning the subjects you study?	Practically none	Some	A considerable amount	A very great deal		2:25–26
43	How much influence do you think students should have in decisions concerning the subjects they study?	Practically none	Some	A considerable amount	A very great deal		2:27–28
44	To what extent does having influence on decisions concerning the subjects you study make you want to work harder? (If you have now say, put a check mark here_____.)	Practically none	A slight amount	A considerable amount	A very great		2:29–30

#	Question					Col.
45	In your school work, is it "every man for himself" or do students, teachers, and principal work cooperatively as a team?	"Every man for himself"	Relatively little cooperative teamwork	A moderate amount of cooperative teamwork	A very substantial amount of cooperative teamwork	2:31–32
46	How do you feel toward your school?	Dislike it	Sometimes dislike it) sometimes like it	Usually like it	Like it very much	2:33–34
47	How much do your teachers try to help you with your problems?	Very little	Somewhat	Quite a bit	Very much	2:35–36
48	*Who holds high performance goals for your school?	Principal only	Prinicipal and some teachers	Principal, most teachers, some students	Principal, teachers, students, parents	2:37–38
49	Who feels responsible for achieving high performance goals?	Principal only	Principal and some teachers	Principal, most teachers, some students	Principal, teachers students	2:39–40
50	How much resistance is there to achieving high performance goals?	Strong resistance	Moderate resistance	Some resistance and some cooperation	Little or no resistance and much cooperation	2:41–42

Scale:

1. 0 2 4 6 8 2. 0 2 4 6 8 3. 0 2 4 6 8 4. 0 2 4 6 8 5. 0 2 4 6 8

*If no one expects a high level of performance, place a check mark here _____ and skip items 48, 49 and 50.

Profile of a School

Combined Forms 2 and 3
(Teacher)

This questionnaire is part of a study designed in cooperation with your school to learn more about how students, teachers, school principals, and others can best work together. The aim is to use the information to make your teaching more satisfying and productive.

If this study is to be helpful, it is important that you answer each question as thoughtfully and frankly as possible. This is not a test and there are no right or wrong answers.

The answers on the questionnaires are processed by computers which summarize the responses in statistical form so that individuals cannot be identified. To ensure COMPLETE CONFIDENTIALITY please do not write your name anywhere on the questionnaire.

Instructions: On the lines below each item, please place an *N* at the point which, *in your experience,* describes your school at the present time (*N* = now). Treat each horizontal line as a continuum from the extreme at one end to the extreme at the other; i.e., do not think of the vertical lines as barriers.

Since each teacher and student differs one from the other, answer the questions as describing the average situation or reaction.

Prepared by Jane Gibson Likert and Rensis Likert. Adapted from Rensis Likert, *The Human Organization: Its Management and Value* (New York: McGraw-Hill, 1967). Copyright © 1967 by McGraw-Hill, Inc. By permission of McGraw-Hill Book Company, Inc. No further reproduction or distribution authorized without permission of McGraw-Hill. Used by permission of Rensis Likert Associates, Inc. The new addition of this series is available from Rensis Likert Associates, Inc., Ann Arbor, Michigan.

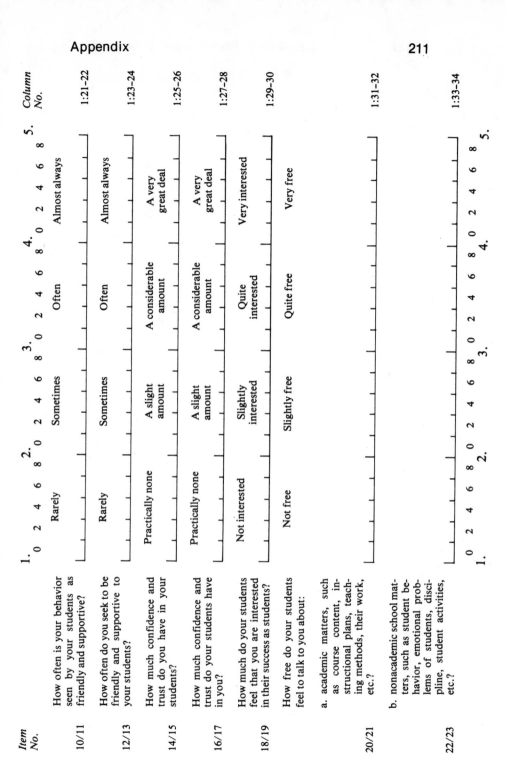

Item No.		1.		2.		3.		4.		5.	Column No.

How often is your behavior seen by your students as friendly and supportive?
(10/11) — Rarely — Sometimes — Often — Almost always — 1:21–22

How often do you seek to be friendly and supportive to your students?
(12/13) — Rarely — Sometimes — Often — Almost always — 1:23–24

How much confidence and trust do you have in your students?
(14/15) — Practically none — A slight amount — A considerable amount — A very great deal — 1:25–26

How much confidence and trust do your students have in you?
(16/17) — Practically none — A slight amount — A considerable amount — A very great deal — 1:27–28

How much do your students feel that you are interested in their success as students?
(18/19) — Not interested — Slightly interested — Quite interested — Very interested — 1:29–30

How free do your students feel to talk to you about:
— Not free — Slightly free — Quite free — Very free

a. academic matters, such as course content, instructional plans, teaching methods, their work, etc.?
(20/21) — 1:31–32

b. nonacademic school matters, such as student behavior, emotional problems, discipline of students, student activities, etc.?
(22/23) — 1:33–34

		1. Rarely	2. Sometimes	3. Often	4. Very frequently	5.	Column No.
Item No.		0 2 4 6 8	0 2 4 6 8	0 2 4 6 8	0 2 4 6 8	0 2 4 6 8	

How often do you seek and use your students' ideas about:

Item No.	Question						Column No.
24/25	a. academic matters?						1:35–36
26/27	b. nonacademic school matters?						1:37–38

		Very little	Somewhat	Quite a bit	Very much		
28/29	How much do your students feel that your are really trying to help them with their problems?						1:39–40

How much say do you think students should have about:

		Practically none	A slight amount	A considerable amount	A very great deal		
30/31	a. academic matters?						1:41–42
32/33	b. nonacademic school matters?						1:43–44

		Not at all	Never involved in decisions affecting them; occasionally consulted	Usually consulted, but ordinarily not involved in decisions affecting them	Fully involved in decisions affecting them		
34/35	To what extent are students involved in major decisions affecting them?						1:45–46

		Dislike it	Sometimes dislike it, sometimes like it	Usually like it	Like it very much		
36/37	What is the general attitude of students toward your school?						1:47–48

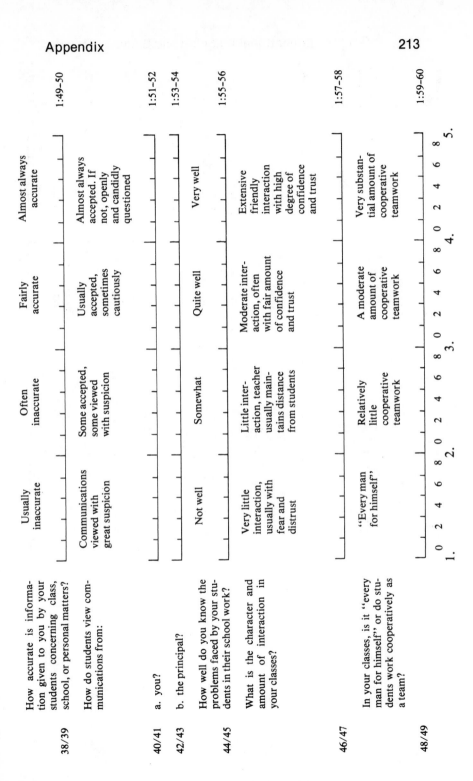

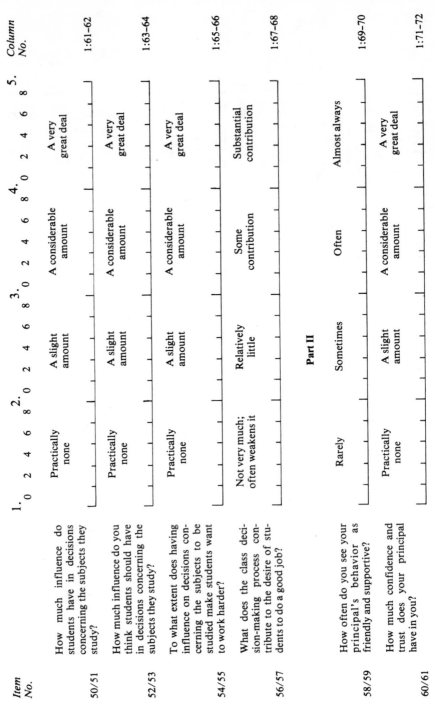

Scale: 1. (0 2 4 6 8)   2. (0 2 4 6 8)   3. (0 2 4 6 8)   4. (0 2 4 6 8)   5.

Item No.	Question	1	2	3	4	5	Column No.
50/51	How much influence do students have in decisions concerning the subjects they study?	Practically none	A slight amount	A considerable amount	A very great deal		1:61–62
52/53	How much influence do you think students should have in decisions concerning the subjects they study?	Practically none	A slight amount	A considerable amount	A very great deal		1:63–64
54/55	To what extent does having influence on decisions concerning the subjects to be studied make students want to work harder?	Practically none	A slight amount	A considerable amount	A very great deal		1:65–66
56/57	What does the class decision-making process contribute to the desire of students to do a good job?	Not very much; often weakens it	Relatively little	Some contribution	Substantial contribution		1:67–68

Part II

Item No.	Question	1	2	3	4	5	Column No.
58/59	How often do you see your principal's behavior as friendly and supportive?	Rarely	Sometimes	Often	Almost always		1:69–70
60/61	How much confidence and trust does your principal have in you?	Practically none	A slight amount	A considerable amount	A very great deal		1:71–72

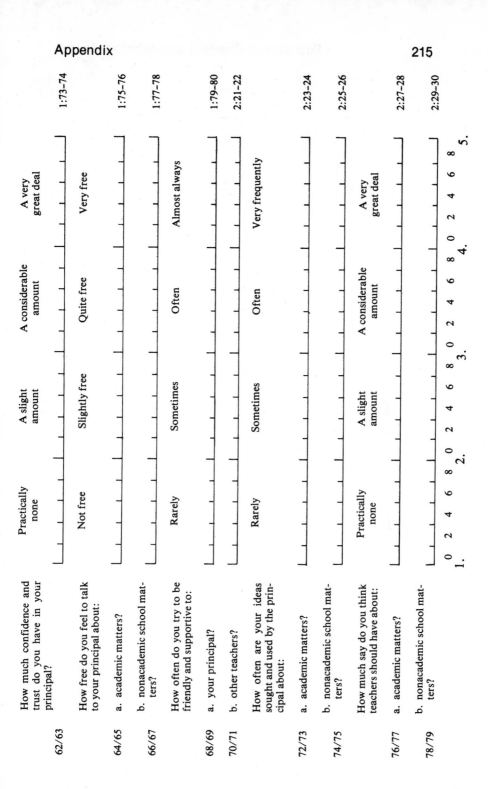

62/63   How much confidence and trust do you have in your principal?   1:73–74

64/65   How free do you feel to talk to your principal about:
a. academic matters?   1:75–76
66/67   b. nonacademic school matters?   1:77–78

How often do you try to be friendly and supportive to:
68/69   a. your principal?   1:79–80
70/71   b. other teachers?   2:21–22

How often are your ideas sought and used by the principal about:
72/73   a. academic matters?   2:23–24
74/75   b. nonacademic school matters?   2:25–26

76/77   How much say do you think teachers should have about:
a. academic matters?   2:27–28
78/79   b. nonacademic school matters?   2:29–30

Scale labels:

Practically none — A slight amount — A considerable amount — A very great deal

Not free — Slightly free — Quite free — Very free

Rarely — Sometimes — Often — Almost always

Rarely — Sometimes — Often — Very frequently

Practically none — A slight amount — A considerable amount — A very great deal

Item No.		1. 0 2 4 6 8	2. 0 2 4 6 8	3. 0 2 4 6 8	4. 0 2 4 6 8	5.	Column No.
	How often are students' ideas sought and used by the principal about:	Rarely	Sometimes	Often	Very frequently		
80/81	a. academic matters?						2:31–32
82/83	b. nonacademic school matters?						2:33–34
84/85	How much do you feel that your principal is interested in your success?	Not interested	Slightly interested	Quite interested	Very interested		2:35–36
86/87	What is the general attitude of teachers toward your school as a place to work?	Dislike it	Sometimes dislike it, sometimes like it	Usually like it	Like it very much		2:37–38
	What is the direction of the flow of information about:	Downward from principal to teacher to student	Mostly downward	Down and up	Down, up, and between teachers and between students		
88/89	a. academic matters?						2:39–40
90/91	b. nonacademic school matters?						2:41–42

How do you view communications from your principal? (92/93) — 2:43–44

Communications viewed with great suspicion	Some accepted, some viewed with suspicion	Usually accepted, sometimes cautiously	Almost always accepted. If not, openly and candidly questioned

How accurate is upward communication? (94/95) — 2:45–46

Usually inaccurate	Often inaccurate	Fairly accurate	Almost always accurate

How well does your principal know the problems faced by teachers? (96/97) — 2:47–48

Not well	Somewhat	Quite well	Very well

What is the character and amount of interaction in your school between principal and teachers? (98/99) — 2:49–50

Very little interaction, usually with fear and distrust	Little interaction: principal and teachers usually maintain distance from one another	Moderate interaction, often with fair amount of confidence and trust	Extensive friendly interaction with high degree of confidence and trust

What is the character and amount of interaction in your school among teachers? (100/101) — 2:51–52

Very little interaction, usually with fear and distrust	Little interaction, teachers usually maintain distance from one another	Moderate interaction, often with fair amount of confidence and trust	Extensive friendly interaction with high degree of confidence and trust

0 2 4 6 8 0 2 4 6 8 0 2 4 6 8 0 2 4 6 8 0 2 4 6 8
1.   2.   3.   4.   5.

Item No.	1.	2.	3.	4.	5.	Column No.
In your school, is it "every man for himself" or do principal, teachers and students work as a team? 102/103	"Every man for himself"	Relatively little cooperative teamwork	A moderate amount of cooperative teamwork		A very substantial amount of cooperative teamwork	2:53–54
At what level are decisions made about school matters, such as course content, instructional plans, teaching methods, student behavior, student activities, etc.? 104/105	All or almost all decisions made by board, superintendent and staff	Largely by board, superintendent and staff, some by principals	Broad policy by board, superintendent and staff. More specific decisions made at lower levels		Throughout school system: principal, teachers, and student participating in decisions affecting them	2:55–56
To what extent are you involved in major decisions related to your work? 106/107	Not at all	Never involved in decisions related to my work; occasionally consulted		Usually consulted, but ordinarily not involved in decisions related to my work	Fully involved in decisions related to my work	2:57–58
How much does your principal really try to help you with your problems? 108/109	Very little	Somewhat		Quite a bit	Very much	2:59–60

110/111 In general, how much does the decision-making process contribute to the desire of teachers to do a good job?

Not very much, often weakens it	Relatively little	Some contribution	Substantial contribution

2:61-62

112/113 In general, how much does the decision-making process contribute to the desire of students to do a good job?

Not very much, often weakens it	Relatively little	Some contribution	Substantial contribution

2:63-64

114/115 *Who holds high performance goals for your school?

Principal only	Principal and some teachers	Principal, most teachers, some students	Principal, teachers, students, parents

2:65-66

116/117 Who feels responsible for achieving high performance goals?

Principal only	Principal and some teachers	Principal, most teachers, some students	Principal, teachers, students

2:67-68

118/119 How much resistance is there to achieving high performance goals in your school?

Strong resistance	Moderate resistance	Some resistance and some cooperation	Little or no resistance and much cooperation

2:69-70

```
   0  2  4  6  8  0  2  4  6  8  0  2  4  6  8  0  2  4  6  8  0  2  4  6  8
  1.                2.                3.                4.                5.
```

*If no one expects a high level of performance, place a checkmark here _____ and skip items 114, 115, 116, 117, 118, and 119.

Profile of a School

Form 4
(Principal)

This questionnaire is part of a study designed in cooperation with your school to learn more about how students, teachers, school principals, and others can best work together. The aim is to use the information to make your own work, as well as that of your associates, and the students themselves, more satisfying and productive.

If this study is to be helpful, it is important that you answer each question as thoughtfully and frankly as possible. This is not a test and there are no right or wrong answers.

The answers on the questionnaires are processed by computers which summarize the responses in statistical form so that individuals cannot be identified. To ensure COMPLETE CONFIDENTIALITY please do not write your name anywhere on the questionnaire.

Instructions: On the lines below each item, please place an *N* at the point which, *in your experience,* describe the present situation under which your school operates (*N* = now). Treat each horizontal line as a continuum from the extreme at one and to the extreme at the other; i.e., do not think of the vertical lines as barriers.

Since each teacher and student differs one from the other, answer the questions as describing the average situation or reaction.

Prepared by Jane Gibson Likert and Rensis Likert. Adapted from Rensis Likert, *The Human Organization: Its Management and Value* (New York, McGraw-Hill, 1967). Copyright © 1967 by McGraw-Hill, Inc. By permission of McGraw-Hill Book Company, Inc. No further reproduction or distribution authorized without permission of McGraw-Hill. Used by permission of Rensis Likert Associates, Inc. The new addition of this series is available from Rensis Likert Associates, Inc., Ann Arbor, Michigan.

Item No.		1.	2.	3.	4.	5.	Column No.
		0 2 4 6 8	0 2 4 6 8	0 2 4 6 8	0 2 4 6 8		
	How often is your behavior seen as friendly and supportive by:	Rarely	Sometimes	Often	Almost always		
10	a. teachers?						1:21–22
11	b. students?						1:23–24
	How often do you seek to be friendly and supportive to:	Rarely	Sometimes	Often	Almost always		
12	a. teachers?						1:25–26
13	b. students?						1:27–28
14	How much confidence and trust do you have in your teachers?	Practically none	A slight amount	A considerable amount	A very great deal		1:29–30
15	How much confidence and trust do your teachers have in you?	Practically none	A slight amount	A considerable amount	A very great deal		1:31–32
		1.	2.	3.	4.	5.	
		0 2 4 6 8	0 2 4 6 8	0 2 4 6 8	0 2 4 6 8		

Item No.		1. 0 2 4 6 8 Not free	2. 0 2 4 6 8 Slightly free	3. 0 2 4 6 8 Quite free	4. 0 2 4 6 8 Very free	5. 0 2 4 6 8	Column No.
	How free do your teachers feel to talk to you about:						
16	a. academic matters, such as course content, instructional plans, teaching methods, their work, etc.?						1:33-34
17	b. nonacademic school matters, such as student behavior, motional problems of students, discipline, students activities, etc.?	Not free	Slightly free	Quite free	Very free		1:35-36
	How free do your students feel to talk to you about:						
18	a. academic matters?						1:37-38
19	b. nonacademic school matters?				Very frequently		1:39-40
	How often do you seek and use your teacher's ideas about:	Rarely	Sometimes	Often			
20	a. academic matters?						1:41-42
21	b. nonacademic school matters?						1:43-44

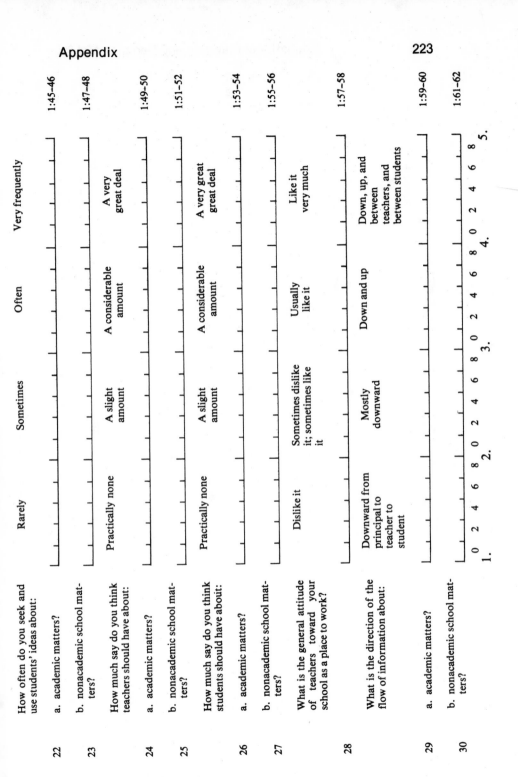

		Rarely	Sometimes	Often	Very frequently	
22	How often do you seek and use students' ideas about:					
	a. academic matters?					1:45–46
	b. nonacademic school matters?					1:47–48
23	How much say do you think teachers should have about:	Practically none	A slight amount	A considerable amount	A very great deal	
	a. academic matters?					1:49–50
	b. nonacademic school matters?					1:51–52
24						
25	How much say do you think students should have about:	Practically none	A slight amount	A considerable amount	A very great deal	
	a. academic matters?					1:53–54
	b. nonacademic school matters?					1:55–56
26						
27	What is the general attitude of teachers toward your school as a place to work?	Dislike it	Sometimes dislike it; sometimes like it	Usually like it	Like it very much	
28	What is the direction of the flow of information about:	Downward from principal to teacher to student	Mostly downward	Down and up	Down, up, and between teachers, and between students	1:57–58
	a. academic matters?					1:59–60
	b. nonacademic school matters?					1:61–62
29						
30						

1. 0 2 4 6 8   2. 0 2 4 6 8   3. 0 2 4 6 8   4. 0 2 4 6 8   5.

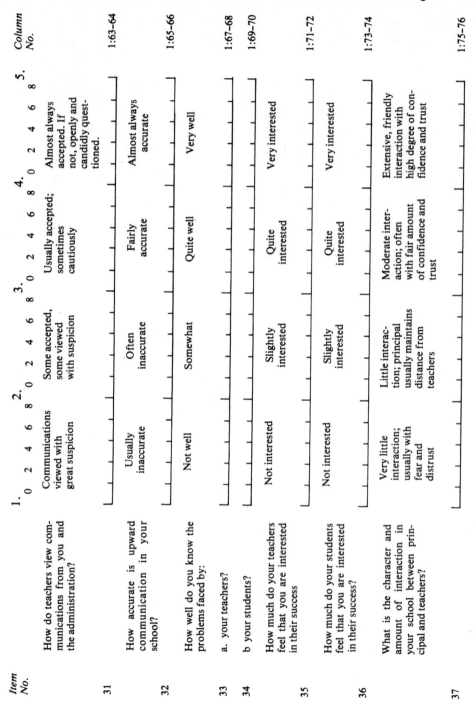

Item No.	Question	1. Communications viewed with great suspicion	2. Some accepted, some viewed with suspicion	3. Usually accepted; sometimes cautiously	4. Almost always accepted. If not, openly and candidly questioned.	Column No.
31	How do teachers view communications from you and the administration?					1:63-64
32	How accurate is upward communication in your school?	Usually inaccurate	Often inaccurate	Fairly accurate	Almost always accurate	1:65-66
33	How well do you know the problems faced by: a. your teachers?	Not well	Somewhat	Quite well	Very well	1:67-68
34	b your students?					1:69-70
35	How much do your teachers feel that you are interested in their success	Not interested	Slightly interested	Quite interested	Very interested	1:71-72
36	How much do your students feel that you are interested in their success?	Not interested	Slightly interested	Quite interested	Very interested	1:73-74
37	What is the character and amount of interaction in your school between principal and teachers?	Very little interaction; usually with fear and distrust	Little interaction; principal usually maintains distance from teachers	Moderate interaction; often with fair amount of confidence and trust	Extensive, friendly interaction with high degree of confidence and trust	1:75-76

	Very little interaction; usually with fear and distrust / "Every man for himself" / All or almost all decisions made by Board, superintendent and staff / Not at all / Not very much, often weakens it	Little interaction; teachers usually maintain distance from one another / Relatively little cooperative teamwork / Largely by Board, superintendent and staff; some by principals / Never involved in decisions related to their work; occasionally consulted / Relatively little	Moderate interaction; often with fair amount of confidence and trust / A moderate amount of cooperative teamwork / Broad policy by Board, superintendent and staff. More specific decisions made at lower levels / Usually consulted but ordinarily not involved in decisions related to their work / Some contribution	Extensive, friendly interaction with high degree of confidence and trust / A very substantial amount of cooperative teamwork / Throughout school system: principal teachers, and students participating in decisions affecting them / Fully involved in decisions related to their work / Substantial contribution	

38. What is the character and amount of interaction in your school among teachers?
— Very little interaction; usually with fear and distrust | Little interaction; teachers usually maintain distance from one another | Moderate interaction; often with fair amount of confidence and trust | Extensive, friendly interaction with high degree of confidence and trust — 1:77–78

39. In your school, is it "every man for himself" or do principal, teachers and students work as a team?
— "Every man for himself" | Relatively little cooperative teamwork | A moderate amount of cooperative teamwork | A very substantial amount of cooperative teamwork — 1:79–80

40. At what level are decisions made about school matters, such as course content, instructional plans, teaching methods, student activities, etc.?
— All or almost all decisions made by Board, superintendent and staff | Largely by Board, superintendent and staff; some by principals | Broad policy by Board, superintendent and staff. More specific decisions made at lower levels | Throughout school system: principal teachers, and students participating in decisions affecting them — 2:21–22

41. To what extent are teachers involved in major decisions related to their work?
— Not at all | Never involved in decisions related to their work; occasionally consulted | Usually consulted but ordinarily not involved in decisions related to their work | Fully involved in decisions related to their work — 2:23–24

42. In general, how much does the decision-making process contribute to the desire of teachers to do a good job?
— Not very much, often weakens it | Relatively little | Some contribution | Substantial contribution — 2:25–26

```
   0  2  4  6  8   0  2  4  6  8   0  2  4  6  8   0  2  4  6  8   0  2  4  6  8
   1.              2.              3.              4.              5.
```

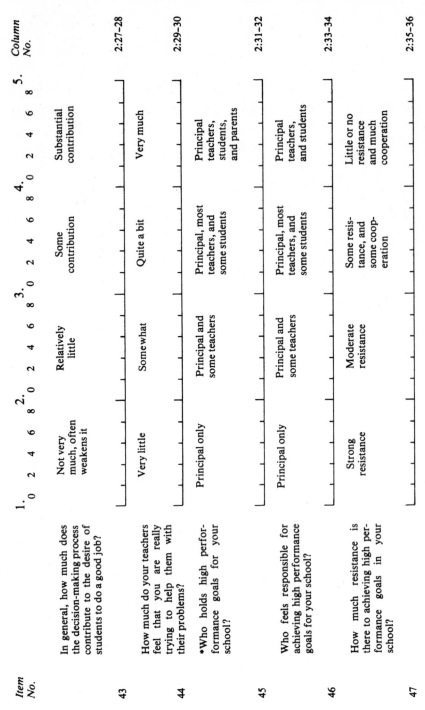

Item No.		1.	2.	3.	4. / 5.	Column No.
		0 2 4 6	8 0 2 4 6	8 0 2 4 6	8 0 2 4 6 8	
43	In general, how much does the decision-making process contribute to the desire of students to do a good job?	Not very much, often weakens it	Relatively little	Some contribution	Substantial contribution	2:27-28
44	How much do your teachers feel that you are really trying to help them with their problems?	Very little	Some what	Quite a bit	Very much	2:29-30
45	*Who holds high performance goals for your school?	Principal only	Principal and some teachers	Principal, most teachers, and some students	Principal, teachers, students, and parents	2:31-32
46	Who feels responsible for achieving high performance goals for your school?	Principal only	Principal and some teachers	Principal, most teachers, and some students	Principal, teachers, and students	2:33-34
47	How much resistance is there to achieving high performance goals in your school?	Strong resistance	Moderate resistance	Some resistance, and some cooperation	Little or no resistance and much cooperation	2:35-36

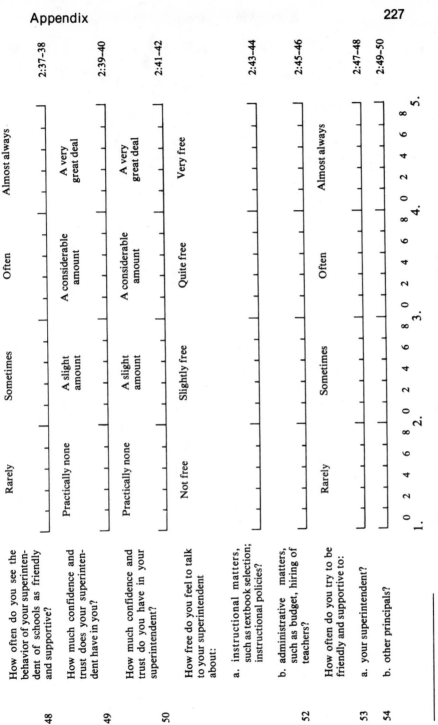

48. How often do you see the behavior of your superintendent of schools as friendly and supportive?
Rarely — Sometimes — Often — Almost always
2:37-38

49. How much confidence and trust does your superintendent have in you?
Practically none — A slight amount — A considerable amount — A very great deal
2:39-40

50. How much confidence and trust do you have in your superintendent?
Practically none — A slight amount — A considerable amount — A very great deal
2:41-42

How free do you feel to talk to your superintendent about:
Not free — Slightly free — Quite free — Very free

a. instructional matters, such as textbook selection; instructional policies?
2:43-44

52. b. administrative matters, such as budget, hiring of teachers?
2:45-46

53. How often do you try to be friendly and supportive to:
a. your superintendent?
Rarely — Sometimes — Often — Almost always
2:47-48

54. b. other principals?
2:49-50

0 2 4 6 8 0 2 4 6 8 0 2 4 6 8 0 2 4 6 8 0 2 4 6 8
1.   2.   3.   4.   5.

*If no one expects a high level of performance, place a checkmark here _____ and skip items 45, 46, 47.

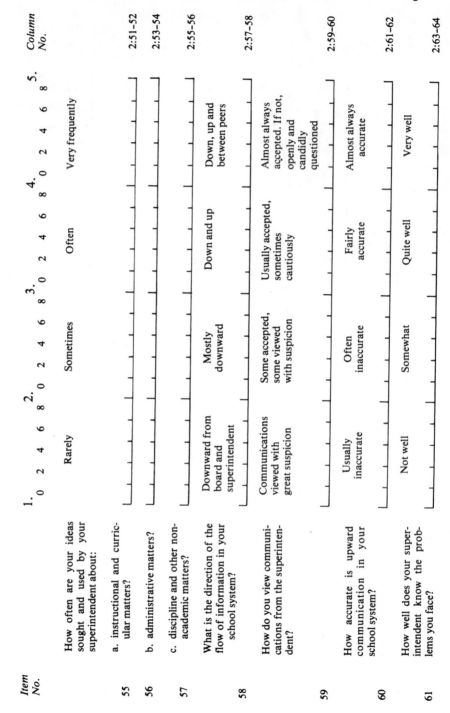

	1. Rarely	2. Sometimes	3. Often	4. Very frequently	5.	Column No.
	0 2 4 6 8	0 2 4 6 8	0 2 4 6 8	0 2 4 6 8	0 2 4 6 8	

Item No.

How often are your ideas sought and used by your superintendent about:

Item	Question	1. Rarely	2. Sometimes	3. Often	4. Very frequently	Column No.
55	a. instructional and curricular matters?					2:51–52
56	b. administrative matters?					2:53–54
57	c. discipline and other non-academic matters?					2:55–56
58	What is the direction of the flow of information in your school system?	Downward from board and superintendent	Mostly downward	Down and up	Down, up and between peers	2:57–58
59	How do you view communications from the superintendent?	Communications viewed with great suspicion	Some accepted, some viewed with suspicion	Usually accepted, sometimes cautiously	Almost always accepted. If not, openly and candidly questioned	2:59–60
60	How accurate is upward communication in your school system?	Usually inaccurate	Often inaccurate	Fairly accurate	Almost always accurate	2:61–62
61	How well does your superintendent know the problems you face?	Not well	Somewhat	Quite well	Very well	2:63–64

	Not interested	Slightly interested	Quite interested	Very interested	
62 How much do you feel that your superintendent is interested in your success?					2:65–66
63 What is the character and amount of interaction in your school system?	Very little interaction; usually with fear and distrust	Little interaction; board, superintendent and principals usually maintain distance from one another	Moderate interaction; often with fair amount of confidence and trust	Extensive, friendly interaction with high degree of confidence and trust	2:67–68
64 In your school system is it "every man for himself," or do the superintendent, principals and teachers work as a team?	"Every man for himself"	Relatively little cooperative teamwork	A moderate amount of cooperative teamwork	A very substantial amount of cooperative teamwork	2:69–70
65 What is your general attitude toward your school system as a place to work?	Dislike it	Sometimes dislike it; sometimes like it	Usually like it	Like it very much	2:71–72
66 How are decisions made in your school system?	Decisions made by school board and superintendent	Decisions made by school board and top administrators with some chance for reactions by lower levels	Decisions made at top after consultation with appropriate lower levels	Lower levels involved in decisions affecting them; decisions usually made through consensus	2:73–74

1. 0 2 4 6 8 2. 0 2 4 6 8 3. 0 2 4 6 8 4. 0 2 4 6 8 5. 0 2 4 6 8

Item No.		1.	2.	3.	4.	5.	Column No.
67	To what extent are you involved in major decisions related to your work?	Not at all	Never involved in decisions related to my work; occasionally consulted	Usually consulted, bur ordinarily not involved in decisions related to my work		Fully involved in decisions related to my work	2:75-76
68	To what extent are decision-makers aware of problems, particularly at lower levels in the organization?	Unaware or only partially aware	Aware of some, unaware of others	Moderately aware		Very aware	2:77-78
69	How much does the superintendent really try to help you with your problems?	Very little	Somwhat	Quite a bit		Very much	2:79-80
70	*Who holds high performance goals for your *school system?*	School board and superintendent of schools	School board, superintendent and some of his staff and principals	School board, superintendent and most of his staff, principals and some teachers		School board, superintendent and his staff principals, teachers, students, and parents	3:21-22
71	Who feels responsible for seeing that high performance goals are achieved in your *school system?*	School board and superintendent of schools	School board, superintendent and some of his staff and principals	School board, superintendent and most of his staff, principals and some teachers		School board, superintendent and his staff, principals, teachers, and students	3:23-24

3:25–26

72

How much resistance is there to achieving high performance goals in your school system?

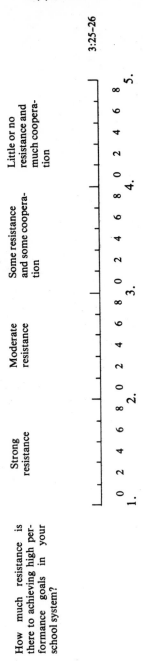

Strong resistance

Moderate resistance

Some resistance and some cooperation

Little or no resistance and much cooperation

1.   0 2 4 6 8
2.   0 2 4 6 8
3.   0 2 4 6 8
4.   0 2 4 6 8
5.   0 2 4 6 8

*If no one expects a high level of performance, place a check mark here _____ and skip items 70, 71, and 72.

Name Index

Subject Index

About the Authors

C. Kenneth Tanner is professor of educational administration, College of Education and the Graduate School, The University of Tennessee. He is the former president of the International Society for Educational Planning, an associate editor for *Educational Administration Abstracts,* and a consultant for government, education, and industry. He has served on the Task Force on Technological Forecasting and as a mathematician, administrator, and public-school teacher in junior high and high school.

Earl J. Williams is an elementary-school principal in the public schools in Anchorage, Alaska. He is a former president of the Cook Inlet Association of School Administrators, Anchorage.

Dr. Williams has been a practicing public-school administrator for the past sixteen years. He has had extensive experience working with various special-help and special-funded programs that interface and extend the regular school program within the total school unit.